IMAGES
of America

TACOMA'S NORTH SLOPE

On the Cover: For their class portrait in 1932, the kindergarten pupils at the Margaret K. Gould School sit in front of the porch. The private school was located in a 12-room, Foursquare-style house, designed in 1890 by Ruehr and Bergfeld. The address was 223 North J Street in the North Slope neighborhood of Tacoma, Washington. (Courtesy of the Northwest Room, Tacoma Public Library.)

IMAGES
of America

Tacoma's North Slope

Karen May

ARCADIA
PUBLISHING

ISBN 978-0-7385-7528-5

Published by Arcadia Publishing
Charleston, South Carolina

Printed in the United States of America

Library of Congress Control Number: 2011920135

For all general information, please contact Arcadia Publishing:
Telephone 843-853-2070
Fax 843-853-0044
E-mail sales@arcadiapublishing.com
For customer service and orders:
Toll-Free 1-888-313-2665

Visit us on the Internet at www.arcadiapublishing.com

To Tobias, Gergana, Kalina, Gyda, and especially Larry—
without whom none of this would have been possible.

Contents

ACKNOWLEDGMENTS

Many thanks go to the staff at the Northwest Room at the Tacoma Public Library, especially Brian Kamens and Bob Schuler, for assistance with research, images, and patient encouragement. Donna Libert and Tiffany Frary were very helpful and have my eternal gratitude for putting this book together in its final form. Also contributing were Jay and Julie Turner, Sherry Munson, Polly Medlock, Marilyn Torgerson, Marshall McClintock, Geoff Corso, and many others. Special thanks go to my daughter, Gyda, whose technical expertise was greatly appreciated. Thank you all.

Unless otherwise noted, all images are courtesy of the Northwest Room at the Tacoma Public Library.

INTRODUCTION

Tacoma's North Slope is located on the gently sloping hill where Job Carr had his homestead claim, called Job Carr's Hill. When he arrived in the area on Commencement Bay that is now called Old Town, he was 51 years old and ready to start a new life. Because he built his cabin near the shore, at the deep part of Commencement Bay, he is well known as the first resident of Tacoma. Around his cabin, Carr planted fruit trees and berries, along with a flower garden. His home served as a post office, and he was the first postmaster, serving the community for about five months. He purchased acreage in a donation, or preemption, claim. But the subject of this book concerns another claim, a homestead of 166 acres on Job Carr's Hill. A homestead, according to the Homestead Act of 1862, was free provided that the applicant resided on and cultivated the public land, usually 160 acres, for five years after the initial claim. Job claimed 160 acres and purchased six more at $1.25 per acre. So, the story of the North Slope begins with Job Carr and his farm. In writing this book, using photographs from archives and local residents, the author needed to limit the scope to a few essential subject areas. The first restriction concerned the time period covered. Considering 80 percent of the houses in the residential area of North Slope were built before 1930, most of the information dates from 1889 to 1930. There were some businesses in the neighborhood, but most business owners who lived here had enterprises in downtown Tacoma.

To begin, there are two organizations that deserve mention, although they were not included in the acknowledgments. First, the Job Carr Cabin Museum graciously loaned Carr family photographs, which were a great help in chapter two. The museum does a great service in telling the story of the Carr family in Old Tacoma, or Old Town, as it is called by Tacomans. However, this book concerns Jacob Carr's second home, which he occupied in his 60s (around 1875) until his death, approximately 10 years later. So, my apologies for spending most of the time on the second home. Also, as with the other people in the book, there was a strong emphasis on the personal life of the family. The reason for that is that the North Slope is primarily a residential area, near to and supporting the business districts. The second organization that should be mentioned is the Tacoma Historical Society. The society has supported all of the historic districts in Tacoma and has provided generous support to us, the Arcadia authors in the city. The group also sponsors the Historic Homes of Tacoma Tour, often in the North Slope district. Especially helpful were the two volumes of *Voices of Tacoma*, published in 1989 and 1990 by the historical society. Most of all, the North Slope Historic District is composed of a wonderful group of people who support all residents in the neighborhood with a webpage; a newsletter, the *Trolley Times*; and many services, including a complete description of all the houses in the North Slope, listed by street and house number.

Herbert Hunt's three-volume *Tacoma, Its History and Its Builders*, published in 1916, was very informative. Written mostly about Old and New Tacoma, the work's general information about the city was helpful. The main focus of the historical images was to showcase the variety of structures in the North Slope and their inhabitants. As stated before, the personal stories were foremost. This means that there are no detailed descriptions of house types and features; these descriptions are, however, available in other sources, such as the Tacoma Public Library, Northwest Room, Buildings Index. Also, the North Slope is very rich in history and culture, and, unfortunately, the second restriction was space, which did not permit the inclusion of every detail. For instance, many distinctive structures and famous inhabitants are not mentioned. The criteria for material in this book included the availability of images, stories, or details of interest to readers—especially if they are not easily found elsewhere.

The first chapter attempts to explore the contrasting perceptions and purposes of the mighty evergreens by the settlers and the First People, or Puyallups. Job Carr's Hill was located in old-growth forestland, and the ways Carr and other new inhabitants utilized the old-growth trees varied greatly from and affected the lives of the Puyallups who had frequented the North Slope and Garfield Gulch for thousands of years. The second chapter observes the history of Job and Rebecca Carr and their life together for over 20 years. This section also explains Job Carr's new life on his orchard on the hill. The book refers to two of Job's ancestors named Caleb. One was the governor of the colony of Rhode Island and Providence Plantations in 1695. The other Caleb Carr was born in New York in 1719.

The third chapter examines the images of different types of sacred buildings and the members who attended services and social events. There have been fascinating accounts of changes in the institutions and their leaders. The Reform temple, as well as the origin of its congregation, has a compelling story, which continued through the 1950s, until the congregation combined with the Orthodox temple in 1960. The new Apostolic church was not included because the date was too recent for the scope of the book. Education was often combined with religion, as in the St. Patrick Parochial School. Other schools also had appealing images, such as the Gould School, which is featured on the cover.

Powerful individuals are featured in the fourth chapter. One figure included is Henry Rhodes, who moved his family away from the North Slope due to personal tragedy—the loss of his only son. Another family misfortune forced one resident, William Nichols, to trade houses with his son after his wife died. The ability of tycoons to rise again after financial disasters, like the panic of 1893, and become even more prosperous is amazing.

In the fifth and final chapter, the North Slope District is examined closely from varied groupings, like row houses, bed-and-breakfasts, and antique apartment buildings, to an iconic ice-cream stand. The history of Garfield Gulch is revealed, and so are the houses on Job Carr's Mountain on I Street, between Seventh and Eighth Streets. Trolleys and streetcars ran on North I Street and on Division Avenue, as well as on North K Street. The roads are examined from bricks to cobblestones, and the street names, which run from I to Q (or Grant), are engraved in the concrete sidewalks. Finally, this chapter acknowledges the trend of residents restoring deteriorating buildings and substandard construction and the subsequent formation of a historic district including diverse residences from grand to modest. Valerie Sivinski is remembered for her timely advice as the preservation officer for the area, and the Memorial Park is highlighted. Overall, there are many exciting images of the North Slope that were discovered as the neighborhood was explored. Tacoma's North Slope is truly a remarkable place.

One

The Mighty Evergreens

Henry Wadsworth Longfellow's words in the poem *Evangeline: A Tale of Acadie*, "This is the forest primeval. The murmuring pines and the hemlocks . . .," could only approximate the view that greeted the explorers who entered Commencement Bay in the early 1800s. Old-growth forests of Douglas fir and cedar overlooked the deep waters of the harbor. Native Americans saw the mighty evergreens in a different way than the European newcomers

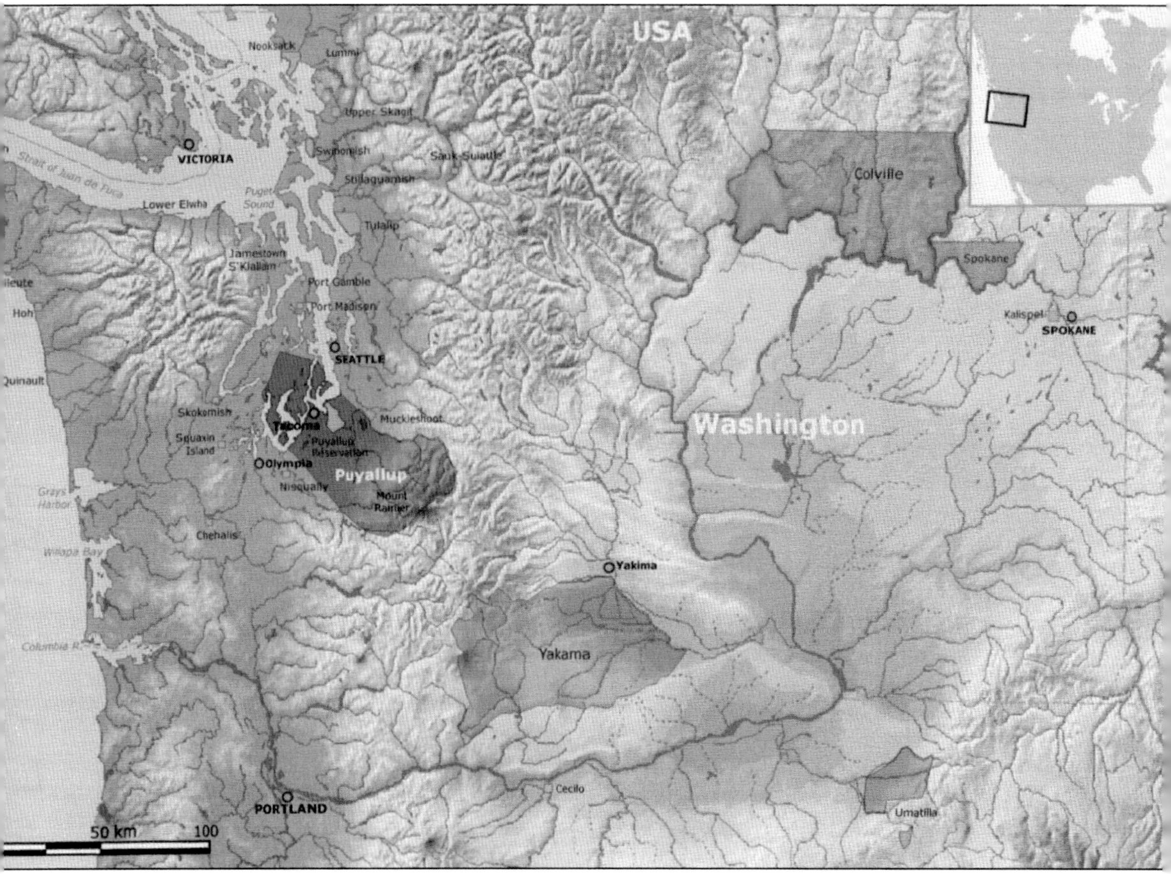

The Puyallup, or S'Puyalupsh, Indian tribe lived in an area surrounding Commencement Bay and South Puget Sound that totaled thousands of acres. They fished in the rivers and gathered clams along the beaches of the bay. The forests, including the North Slope area, were used for timber, hunting, and gathering berries and roots. John Hote (Xot), an elder in the Puyallup tribe in the early 1900s, said the following: "We are part of the Salish-speaking people of the Pacific Northwest. Our particular dialect is called the Lushootseed. Our relatives in the neighboring tribes all spoke the same stock language, but many had different dialects. Many were intimately related by marriage, and we were connected by common religious observances, myths, and traditions. Our people lived in villages from the foothills of Mount Tacoma, along the rivers and creeks, to the shores of Puget Sound. Our villages were scattered throughout the many islands, prairies, and rich valley country of the Pacific Northwest." (Courtesy of Demis website.)

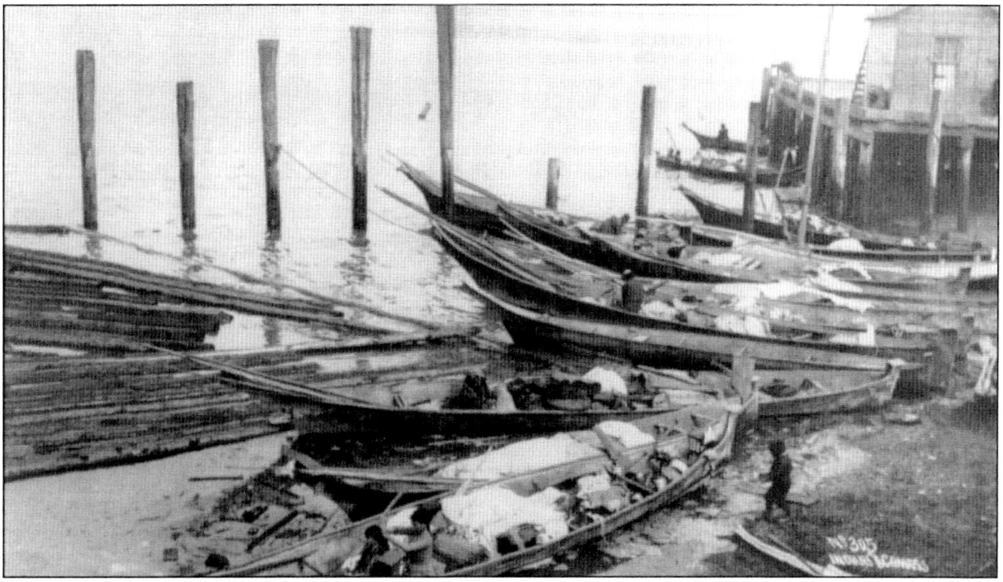

When explorers first came into what is now Commencement Bay, Puyallup tribal canoes were gathered along the base of the cliffs, which rose up to the high, tree-covered hill. The Puyallups and others would often gather in the mouths of the deep gulches, which cut into the hill. The canoes were styled from old-growth timber and were long and narrow, unlike the large seagoing canoes of coastal tribes.

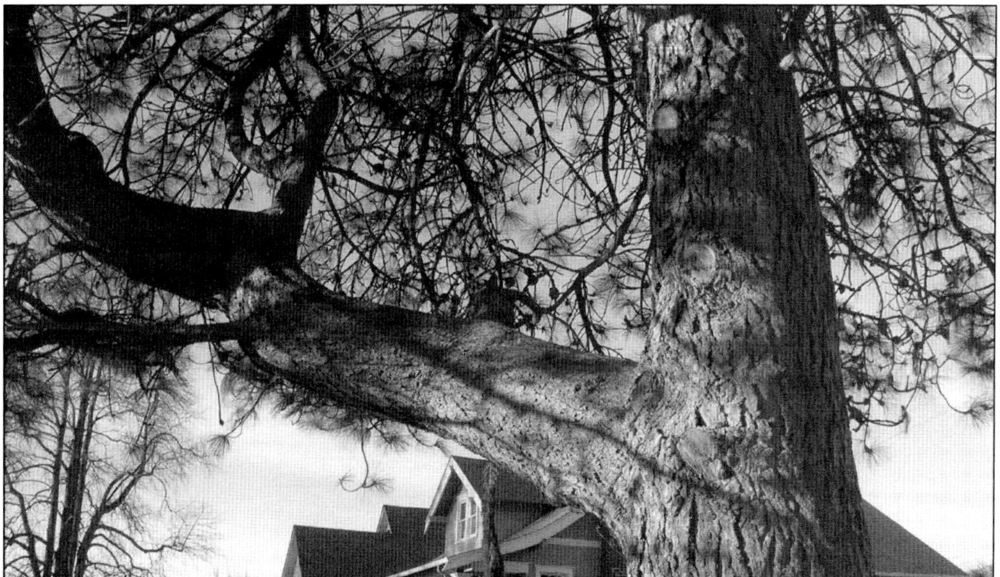

This great evergreen still grows in the North Slope neighborhood, and one use of a tree like this by the Puyallups was for burials. The deceased person was wrapped in cedar bark and attached in the crook of a tree branch. As time went on, the skeleton would be exposed due to weather, animals, and, of course, time. The Indian men would then collect the bones and reverently bury them. (Gyda May photograph.)

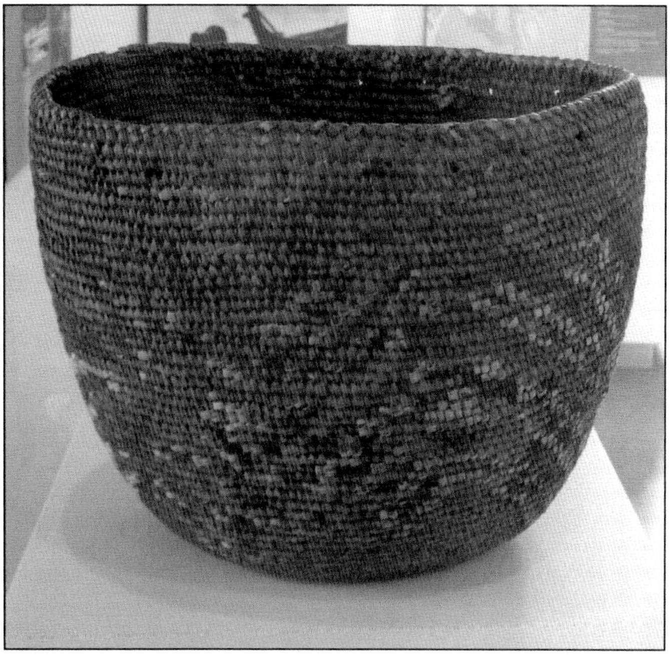

During the salmon runs, or fishing season, life was busy; the rest of the year was considered the off-season. Work was necessary only for housing, clothing, and tools. Leisure time was still left for complex ceremonies, potlatches (gift-giving festivals), a rich oral tradition, elaborate woodcarvings (sacred objects), highly stylized art motifs, and some of the finest basketry in the world. (Courtesy of Joe Mabel.)

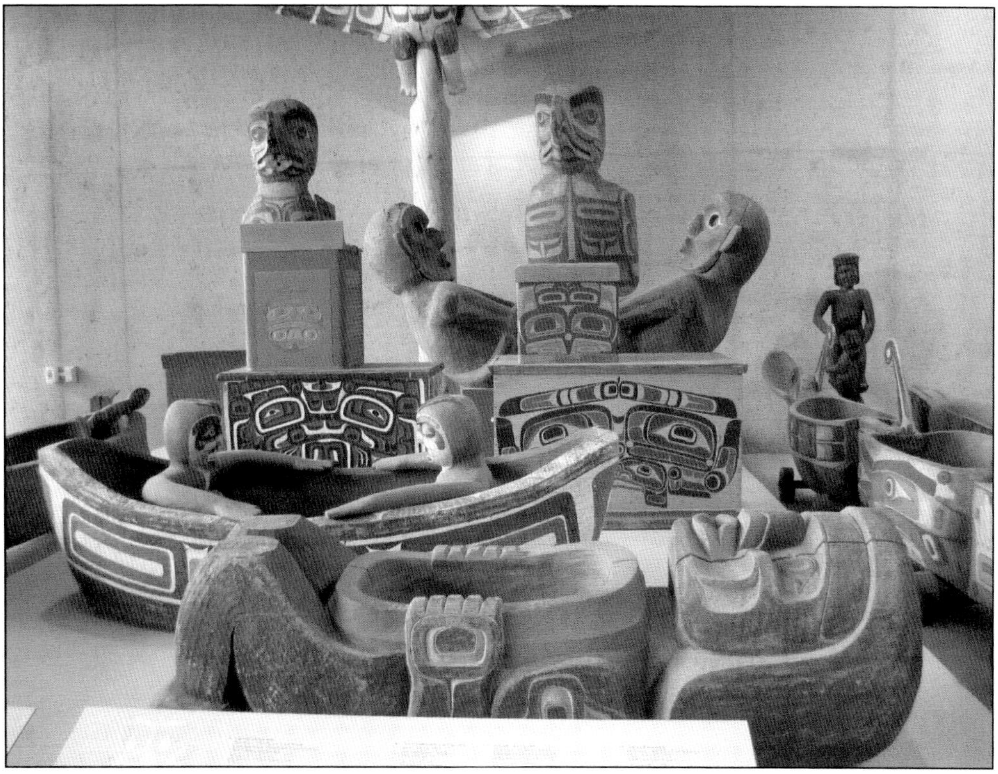

This photograph of art objects made by coastal tribes shows how the creative woodworking was decorative as well as practical. Sacred objects were also carved from cedar, but they were not publicly displayed due to native beliefs that they should be private and used only for worship inside the lodge. The culture can be seen in the display of art. (Courtesy of Leoboudv.)

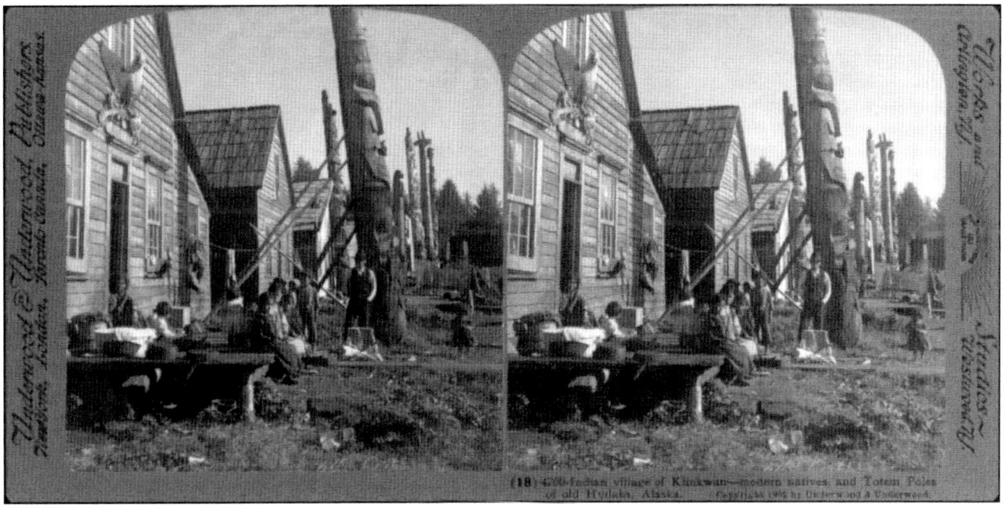

Among the great trees was the huge western red cedar, which can be split easily and in one continuous plane for great lengths. Its wood is lightweight and easy to work yet very tough and lasting. Its bark can be shredded almost into coarse threads. The Puyallups used cedar logs for their river canoes and cedar planks for their longhouses, the gabled communal dwellings. Cedar bark was used for clothing, basketry, hats, plaited mats, and baskets for storage, carrying, and cooking. A mild climate assured food year-round. Located in the forests were deer, elks, and bears, as well as berries and certain roots. Woodlands along the Pacific coast provided shelter for Northwest tribes. These stereoscopic views (above, 1902; below, pre-1920) show Alaskan tribes' communal longhouses that were similar to those found throughout the Pacific Northwest. (Courtesy of New York Public Library.)

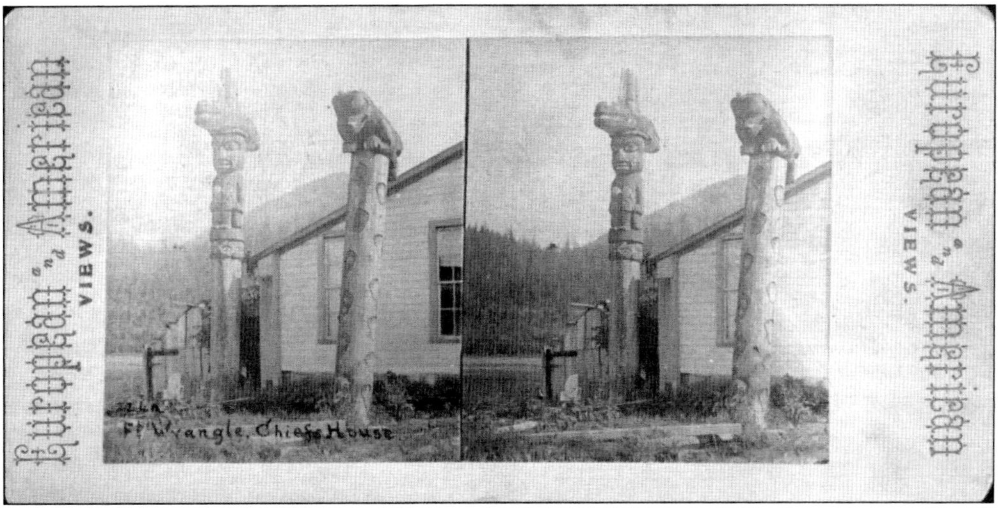

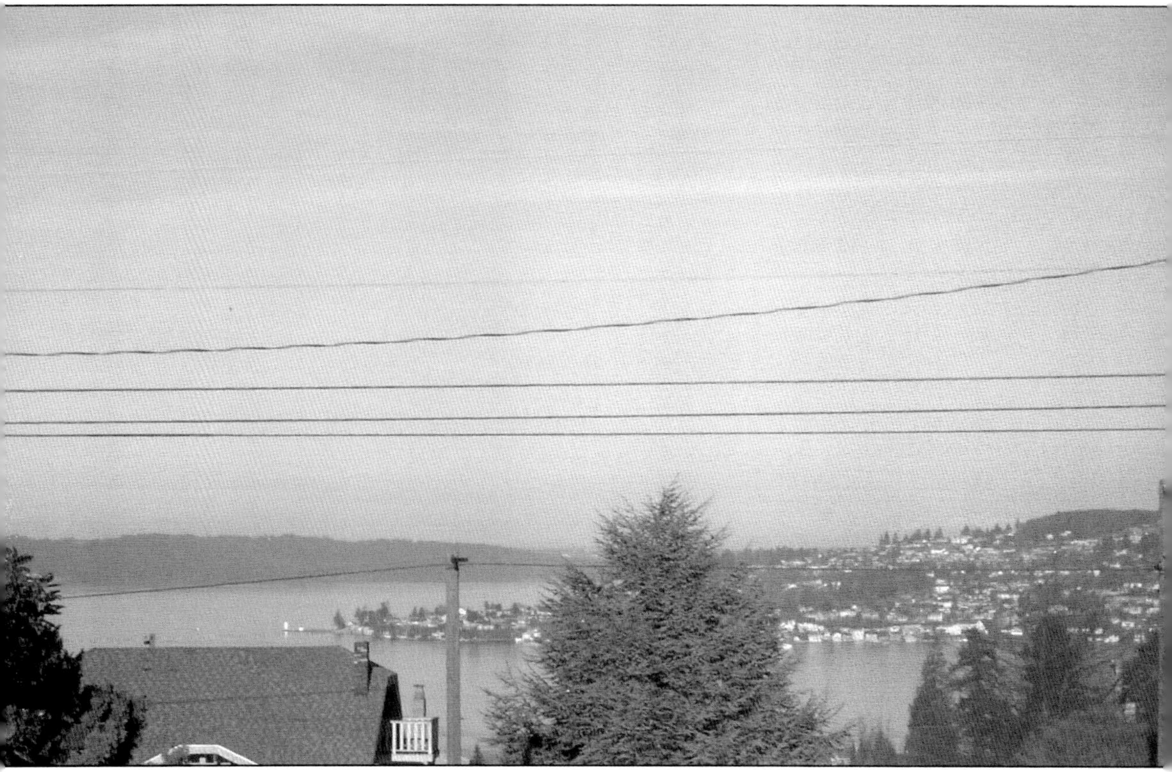

Even today, the view to the north across Commencement Bay from the North Slope is awe-inspiring. Looking over the treetops and across the water to Browns Point, which was where the Puyallups and their guests would gather, and beyond to the Olympic Mountain Range in the west, one can understand the sacred significance of nature to the First People. During the 1855 Indian Treaty Council (documents in National Archives), Stachas, a Cayuse chief, explained the Indian concept of land to Gov. Isaac Stevens as follows: "My friends I wish to show you my mind, interpret right for me. How is it I have been troubled in mind? If your mothers were here in this country who gave you birth, and suckled you, and while you were suckling some person came and took away your mother and left you alone and sold your mother, how would you feel then? This is our mother, this country, as if we drew our living from her." (Gyda May photograph.)

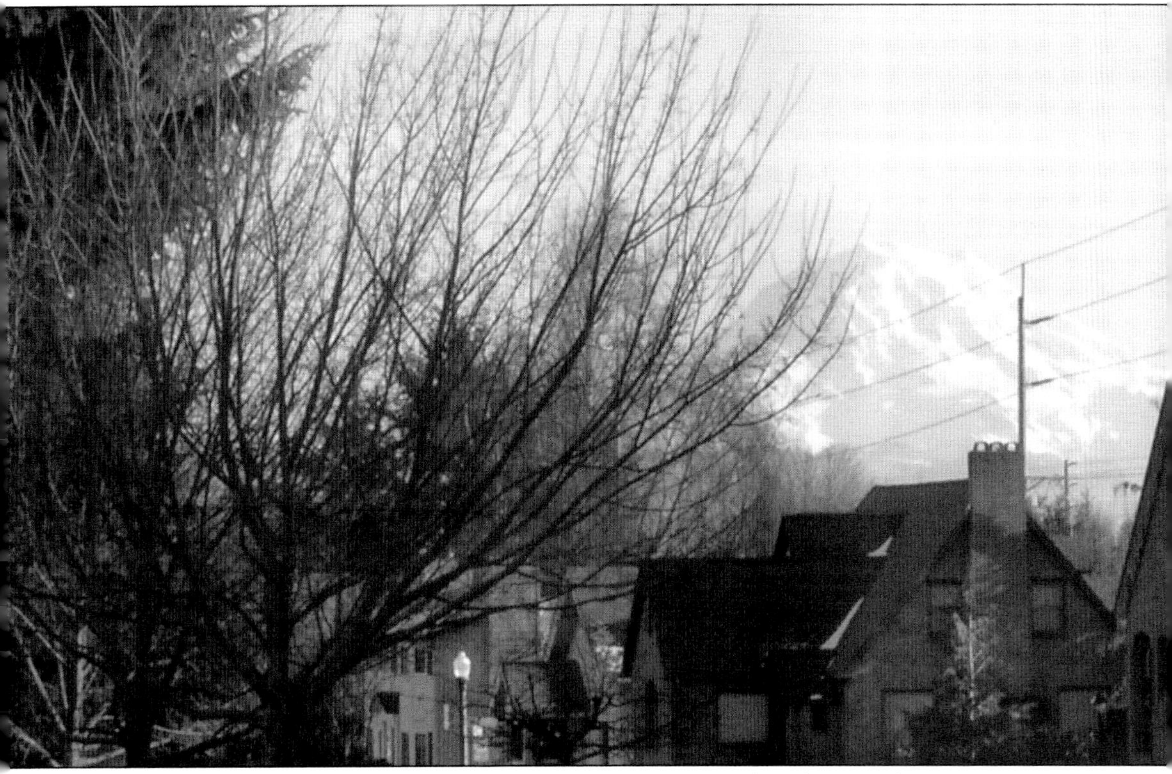

Looking in the opposite direction, to the southeast, one can catch a glimpse of Mount Rainier, or Mount Tahoma to the First People. The mountain was also pronounced Tacobet, or Tacoma. On a clear day, more of the Cascade Range is also in sight. On the rare occasion when it snows, snowcapped Mount Tahoma is transformed into a sleeping giant, a slumbering volcano covered in white. The mountain was revered, as were the forests. The North Slope was in the lands that were inhabited by the Puyallup tribe, and its mighty evergreens were also respected, as was all life. But the red cedar, which provided so much of their daily life, was especially honored. Today, residents of the North Slope can imagine the old growth, which once covered their neighborhood, while enjoying the view of Mount Tahoma, still blanketed in dense forests protected from excessive logging yet open for hikers, skiers, tourists, and lovers of nature. (Gyda May photograph.)

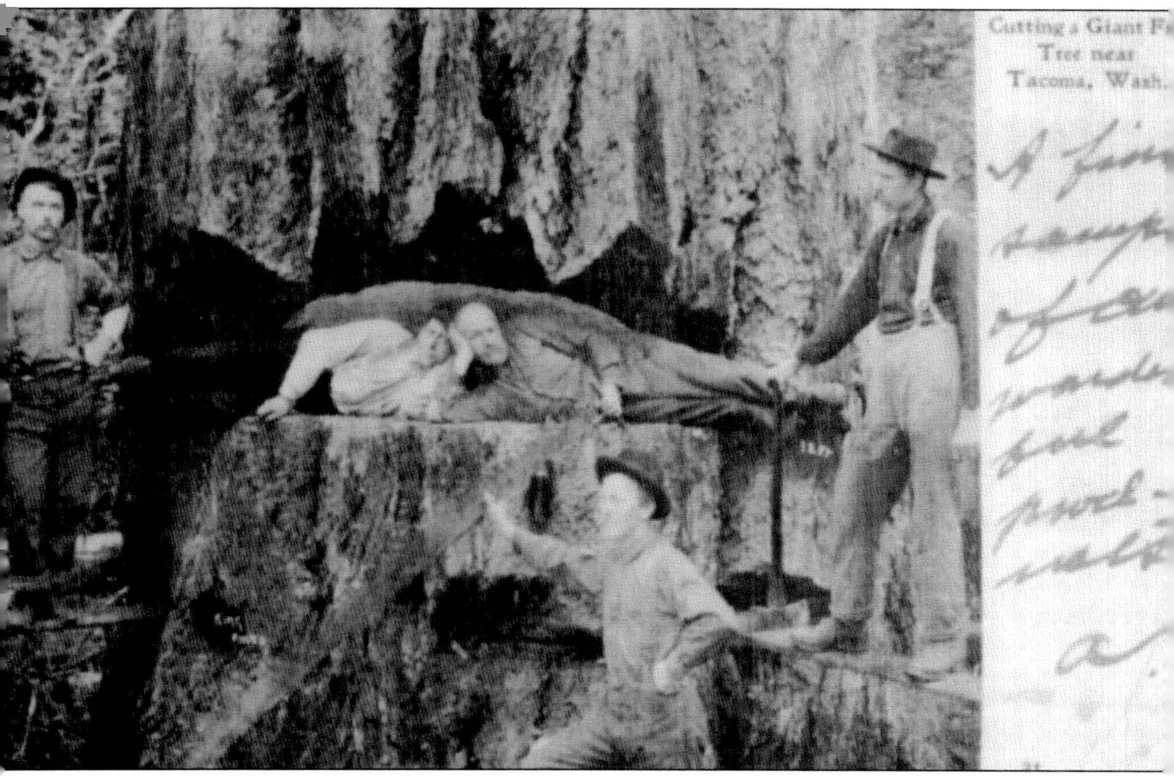

"A fine sample of our wonderful products" is the message on this postcard. These loggers are demonstrating just how large the trees are that they are harvesting. Old-growth forests contained huge evergreen trees, and giant logs were dubbed "Tacoma toothpicks." Some trees were carved out so a car could drive through them. With the timber depleted in Wisconsin and Michigan, all eyes were on the forests in the West. In 1900, the Weyerhaeuser Timber Company made the largest purchase of timberland in history from the Northern Pacific Railway. Weyerhaeuser decided to make Tacoma its headquarters, and the lumber industry was fueling the local economy. The St. Paul and Tacoma Lumber Company had doubled the size of its plant in 1901 and was turning out record amounts of product. Approximately 38 other sawmills, shingle mills, and woodworking plants were operating in or around Tacoma. In 1930, more than 80 mills in Tacoma converted lumber into finished products. A total of 21 local furniture-making factories used Tacoma timber to build tables, chairs, and other wooden products. Tacoma had led the nation in lumber production since 1905.

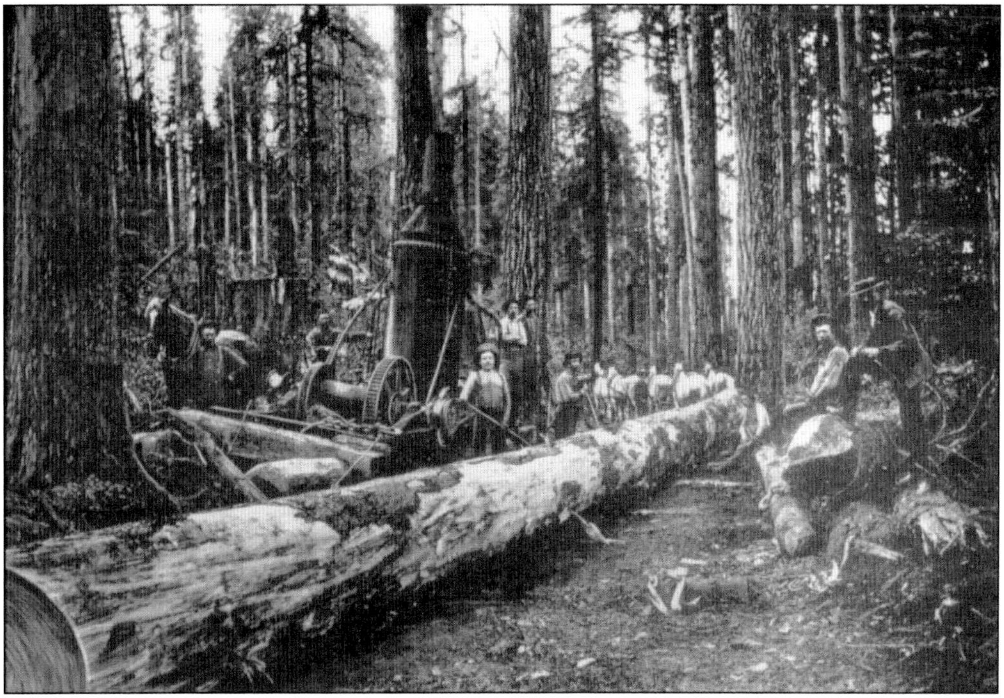

The image above from around 1907 is labeled a "logging scene near Tacoma." Early loggers are shown after felling a large tree, with a steam donkey in the background. The steam donkey was a hoisting machine used to haul logs from the woods. The donkey revolutionized the logging industry and improved productivity when it replaced manpower, oxen, horses, and water flumes. The photograph below from 1929 shows great trains of logs being brought to the sawmills in Tacoma before being sent worldwide.

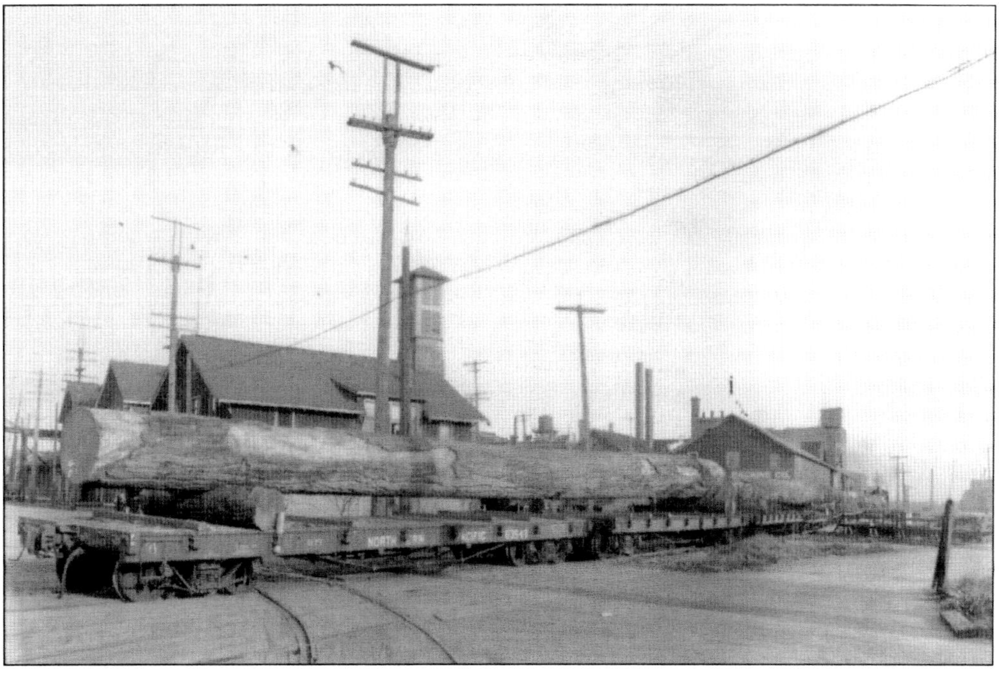

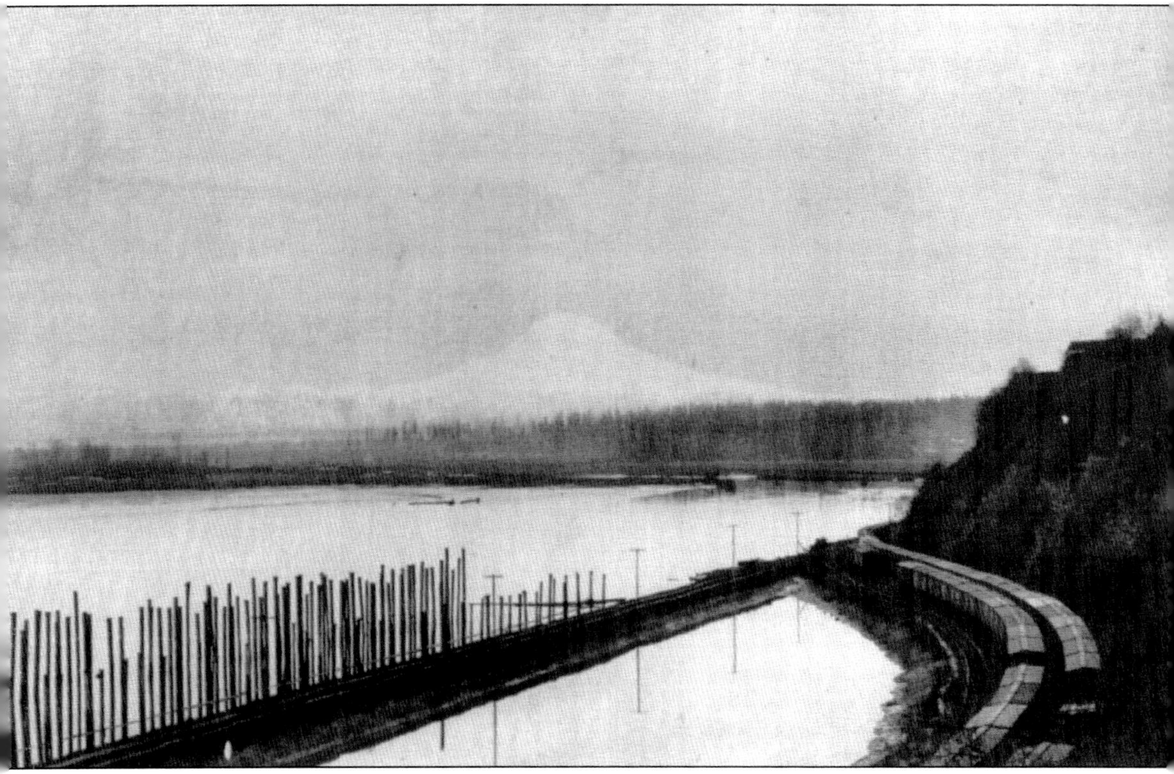

The Puyallups who lived near Mount Rainier held the great white peak in awe, and legends about the origin of the mountain abounded. At the time of historic contact, the Puyallup tribe controlled the lands immediately adjacent to the mountain. In this 1885 photograph, Mount Tacoma (Rainier) looms in the background with woods surrounding the Puyallup River, which flows into Commencement Bay. The tidal flats are at the edge of the bay. The customary dwelling places of the tribe were located near the mouth of the river or along the banks of the bay. Near the lower right of the photograph, train cars are in the storage area at the base of the cliff where the Stadium District is located. The tracks were built on fill dirt. Not yet filled in, the half-moon yard still contains water. The North Slope lies further up the hill. Trees are visible on the bluffs.

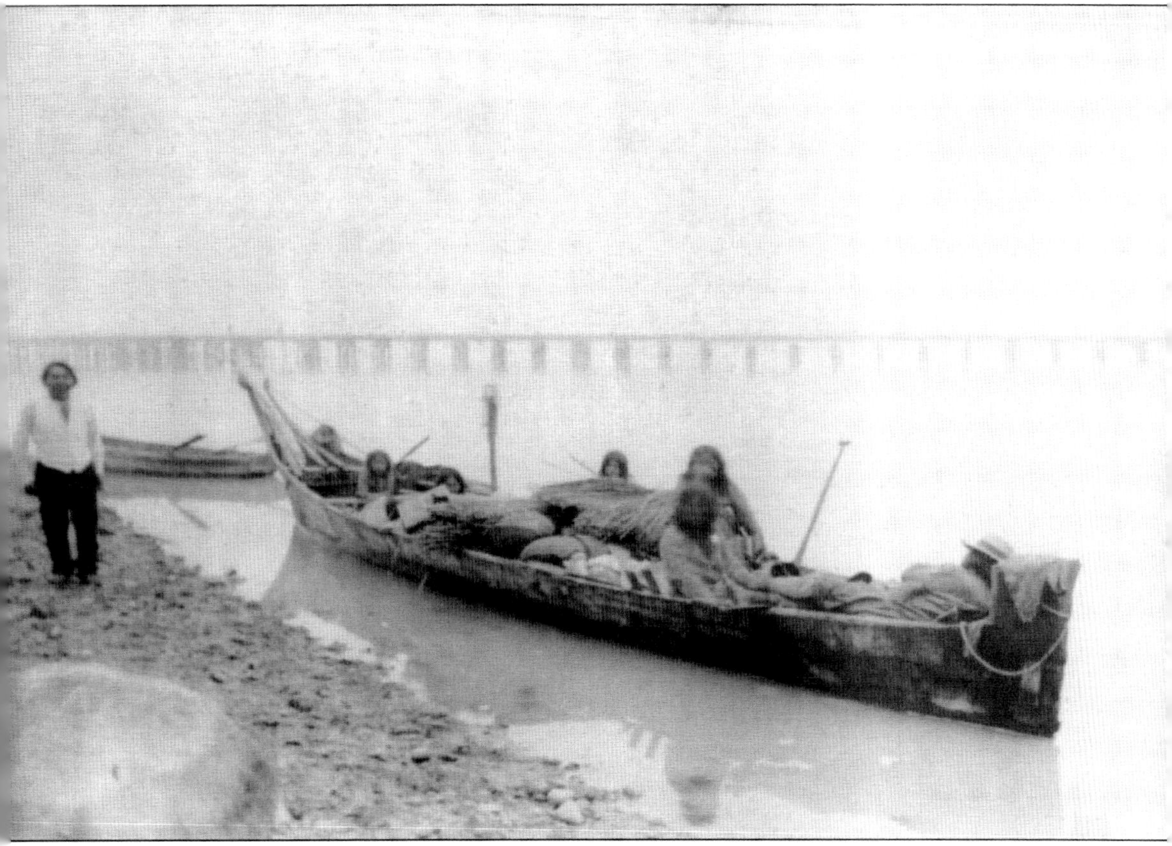

Political leaders thought progress was being delayed by anxiety regarding peace with Indians who lived along proposed railroad routes. They decided to "pacify" the natives. According to Herbert Hunt, Chief Squatahan of the Puyallups was one of the signers of the Medicine Creek Treaty, which was ratified on March 3, 1855. Other Puyallup chiefs at this time were Sinawah (Tyee Dick); Sitwulch (Sitwell), who had great influence; and Za-qua-la-co (Tom Thompson). The Pacific Northwest tribes were not accustomed to practicing war, partly because they lived in small, scattered groups, which made it impractical. Also, it was not typical for the tribes to argue over property, because they all believed the land belonged to everyone. When hostilities later broke out between Indians and settlers, Squatahan moved most of the Puyallups to Henderson Bay, near Gig Harbor, to avoid bloodshed. Chief Chee-chap-witch helped move the Indians. It was said that only about 30 members of the Puyallup tribe took part in the Treaty War of 1855–1856. The Puyallups shown in the 1886 photograph are relaxing, with the Northern Pacific railroad trestle in the background.

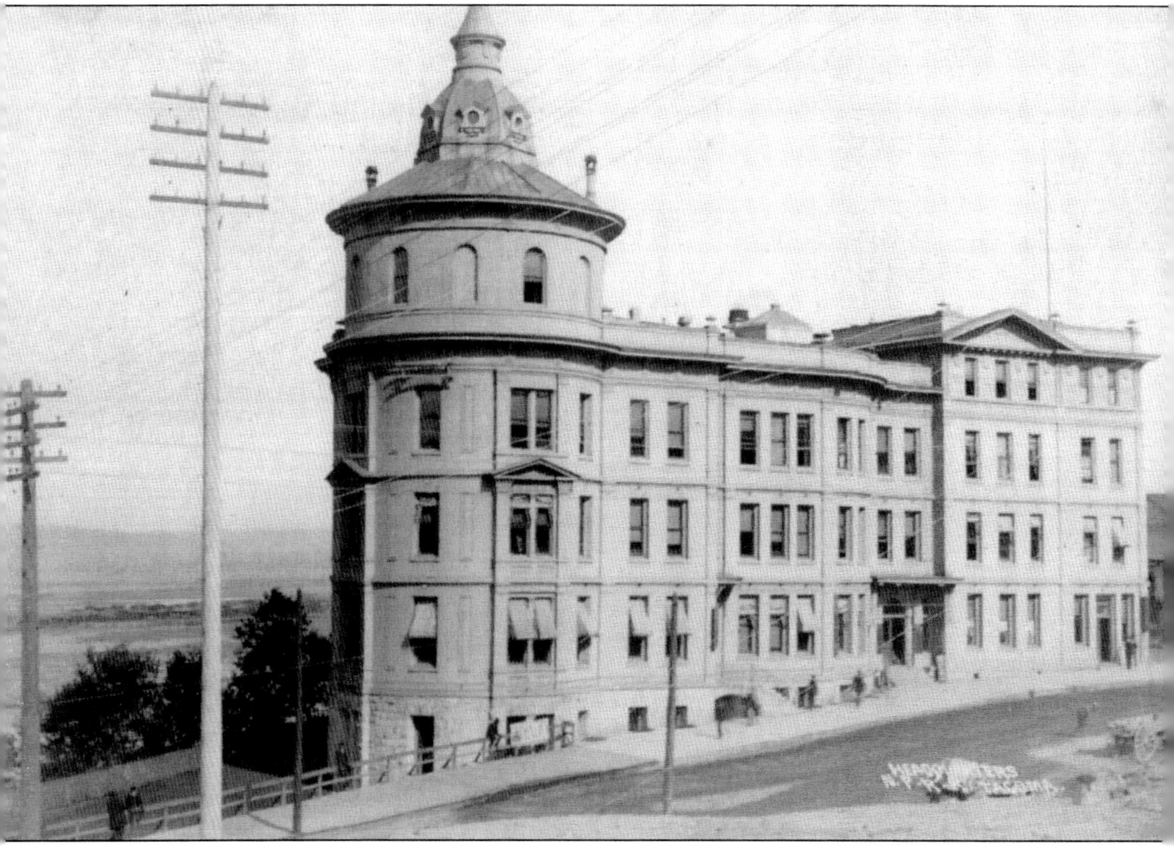

This picture shows the Northern Pacific Railway headquarters at 621 Pacific Avenue around 1889. The railroad had arrived by the time this photograph was taken. In the North Slope, people were rapidly building houses among the stumps of fallen trees for railroad officials and heads of companies dealing with lumber, land, real estate, and financing. With the treaties signed, and the Puyallups on reservations, the forest on the hill was ready to be used. The railroad had chosen Tacoma as its western terminus in 1873, and from that point, the city would grow furiously from a small hamlet to a metropolis of about 30,000 by 1890. Construction of Northern Pacific's stone-and-brick headquarters with its distinctive tower, located on the bluff overlooking the company's half-moon railroad yards, began in the summer of 1887 and was completed the following year. The Tacoma Land Company, Weyerhaeuser Timber Company, and Northern Pacific Railway utilized its 53 offices and storerooms and 19 vaults.

Two

Job Carr's Hill

Job Carr, a direct descendant of Rhode Island colonial governor Caleb Carr, arrived in Tacoma in December 1864. He purchased land in Old Tacoma and also homesteaded property on the crest of what became known as Job Carr's Hill. Carr was a Quaker, a man of peace, yet he was also a patriot who had been wounded defending the Union as well as a master gardener who cleared the forest to plant fruit trees.

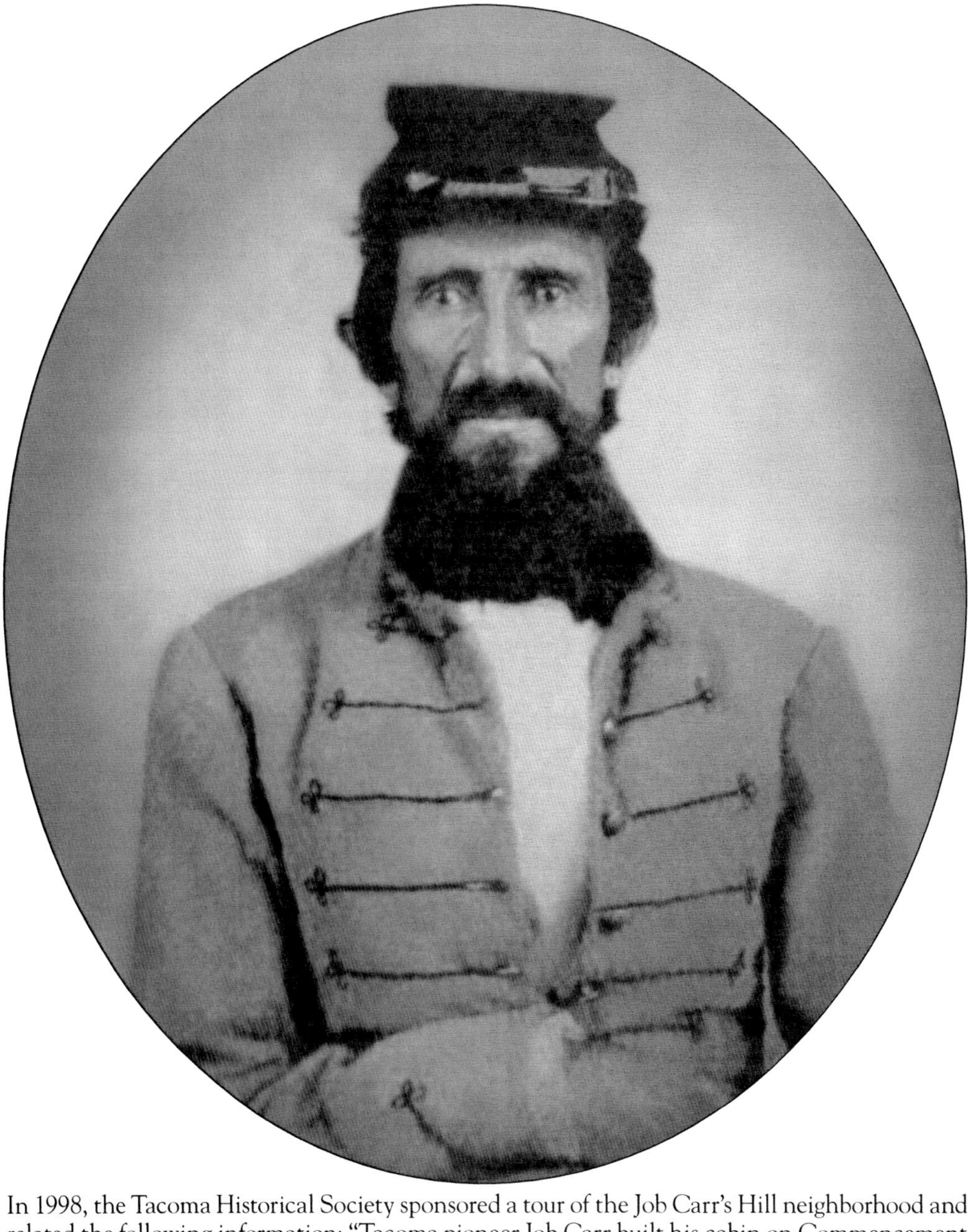

In 1998, the Tacoma Historical Society sponsored a tour of the Job Carr's Hill neighborhood and related the following information: "Tacoma pioneer Job Carr built his cabin on Commencement Bay, in the area known as Old Tacoma, in 1865. He purchased 147 acres of land from the federal government for $1.25 an acre. His westernmost holdings, bounded roughly by North I Street and North Sprague Avenue, Division Avenue, and North Prospect Street, became known as Carr's Hill. The high spot along North I Street, between Seventh and Eighth Streets, was called 'Job Carr's Mountain.' Carr built his own residence at 715 North Sheridan Avenue in the late 1870s. Much of his once heavily forested acreage was already developed by the time of his death in 1887. Many of the early residences built on Carr Hill remain today." The photograph is of Job Carr in his Grand Army of the Republic (GAR) uniform. The GAR was an organization of Union army veterans, and Job Carr was the Custer post commander in 1881. (Courtesy of Job Carr Cabin Museum.)

Rebecca V. Ritman was born in 1822 in St. Clairsville, Ohio. She married Job Carr on January 2, 1840, in Richmond, Indiana, and they had four children. In 1861, Job, Rebecca, and their son Anthony joined the Union army. Rebecca served as the matron of a regimental field hospital. Regarding her service, Steve Martin, a reference librarian in Richmond, Indiana, made the following comments: "Out of the nearly 3,500 men that served from Wayne County, hers is the only female name in the book [*Directory and Soldier's Register of Wayne County*]. She is also, as far as we know, the only woman to have earned a pension for her services rendered." In 1864, Howard, another son of Job and Rebecca, who was not quite 18, enlisted in the army. Job went to Iowa in October 1864, and Anthony bought Rebecca a rooming house in Richmond. (Right, courtesy of Job Carr Cabin Museum.)

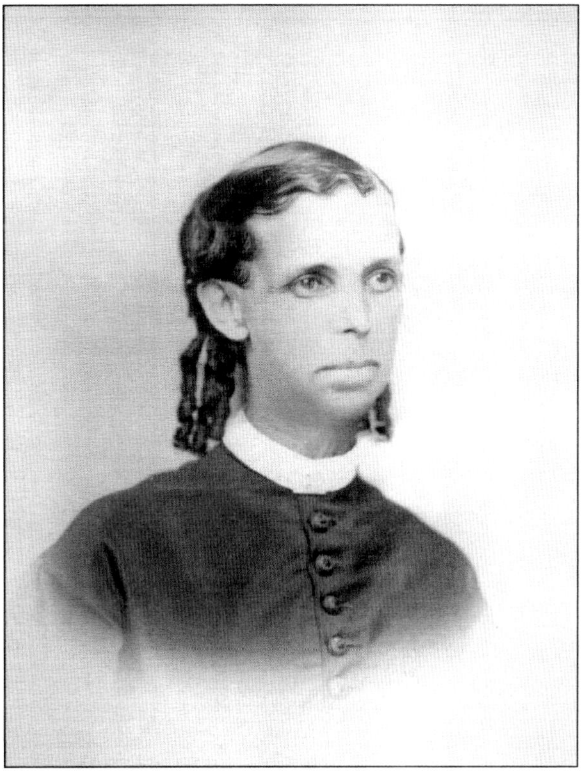

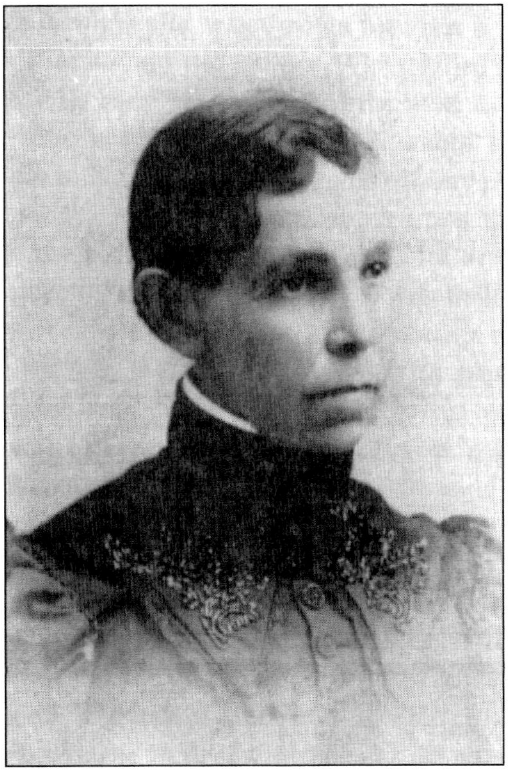

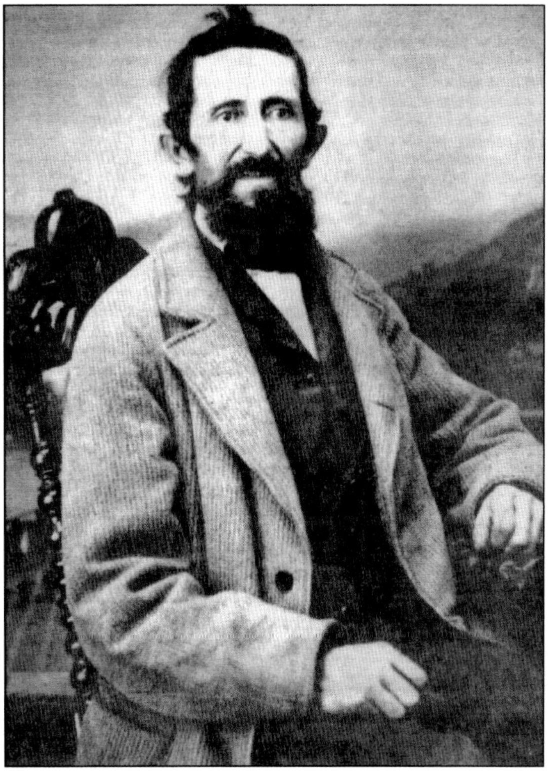

Job Carr was born in Little Egg Harbor, New Jersey, in 1813. His parents were Job and Ruth Mason Carr. His Quaker great-grandfather, Caleb Carr, had been a colonel in the Revolutionary War and part of George Washington's personal staff. As a young man, Job went to Indiana, where he married Rebecca Ritman in 1840. Strongly against slavery, Job joined the Union army. He was wounded in 1862 at the Battle of Corinth, in Mississippi, and again in 1863 at the Battle of Chickamauga, in Georgia. According to historian Herbert Hunt, Rebecca took Job home and nursed him back to health. In the autumn of 1864, Job sold the nursery he had bought in Iowa and looked toward the Oregon Trail, where opportunity beckoned. In December 1864, he arrived in Tacoma. (Both, courtesy of Job Carr Cabin Museum.)

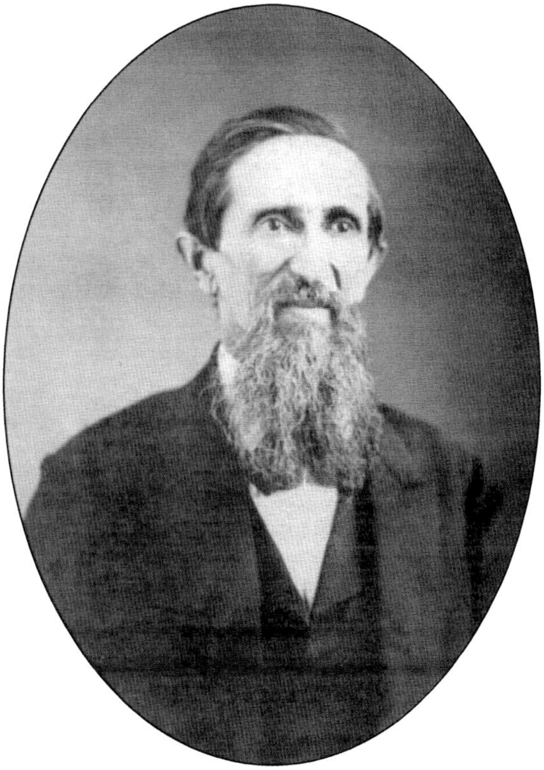

Anthony Pitman "A.P." Carr was the eldest son of Job and Rebecca Carr. In 1865, Anthony came to live with his father in his small cabin on land purchased on Commencement Bay. Anthony was a photographer and went into business with E.A. Light, who furnished camera equipment. During the Civil War, Anthony had delivered photographs and messages to President Lincoln and saw Isaac Stevens, the first governor of the territory of Washington, die at the Battle of Chantilly, in Virginia in 1862. (Courtesy of Job Carr Cabin Museum.)

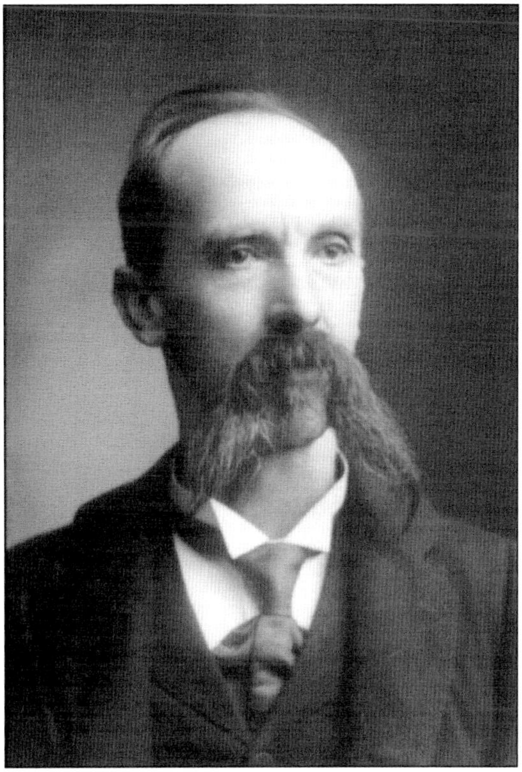

Hunting in an old-growth forest, Edward "Ed" Anthony Carr is shown at left with his father, Anthony, and a dog. Ed was the only son of Anthony and Josephine "Josie" Byrd Carr. He was born in Tacoma on February 16, 1872. On January 26, 1891, not quite 19 years old, he died of overexposure while hunting on the Olympic Peninsula. (Courtesy of Job Carr Cabin Museum.)

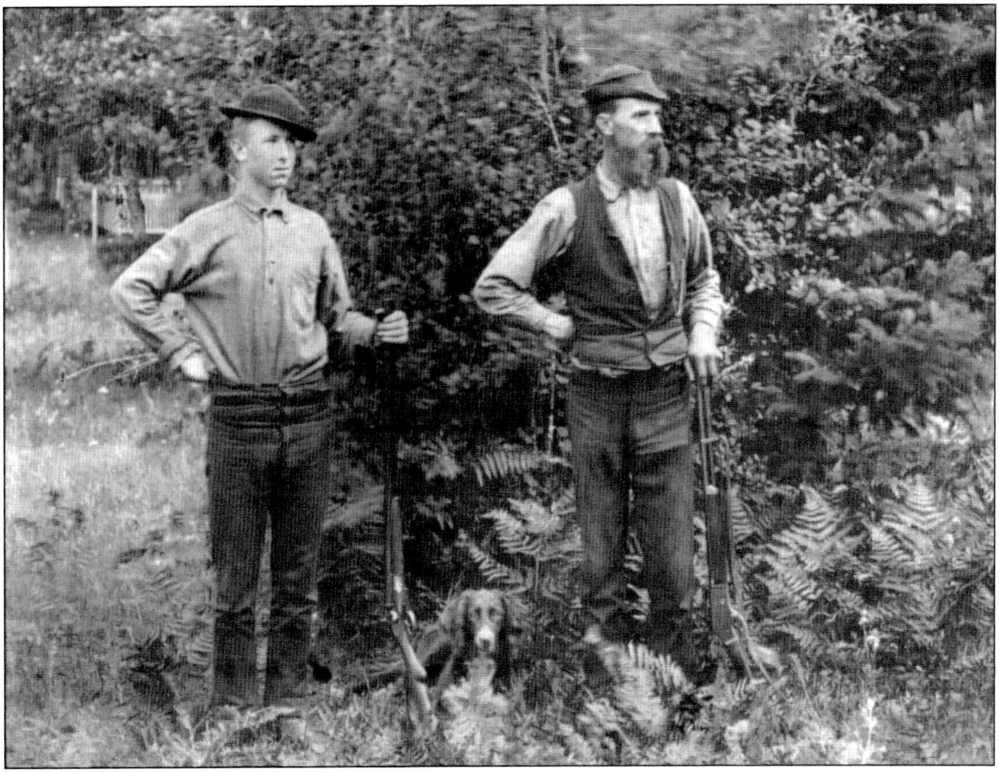

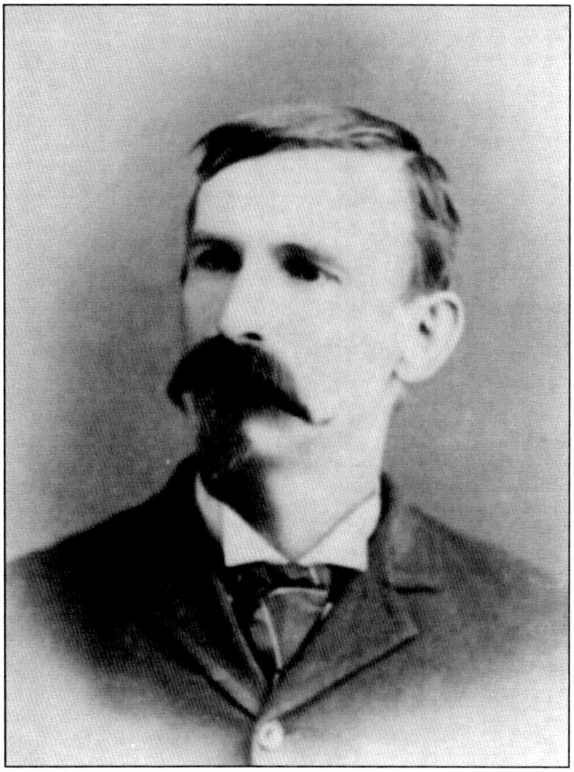

Francis Howard (left), the youngest of the Carrs, had followed Anthony to Tacoma in 1866. Both he and his father played the dulcimer that Howard had brought to Tacoma after the war. Howard was the first marshal of Old Tacoma. Jane Bradley (below), a student, met Howard Carr in 1872 when he visited her Catholic school. They decided to elope, the Old-Tacoma style, and went out on a boat in the harbor and were married by officials. Howard and Jane had two daughters, Ruth and Wynona. Their sons included Francis Eugene; Caleb, who was known as Calvin; Howard Jr., who was in the lumber business; and Anthony, who lived at 1617 Division Avenue. Rebecca obtained a divorce from Job and married Albert Staley. Staley later died, leaving her a widow. In September 1884, Job married a girl from New York, Addie Emery, a "mail-order bride." He was 71 years old. (Both, courtesy of Job Carr Cabin Museum.)

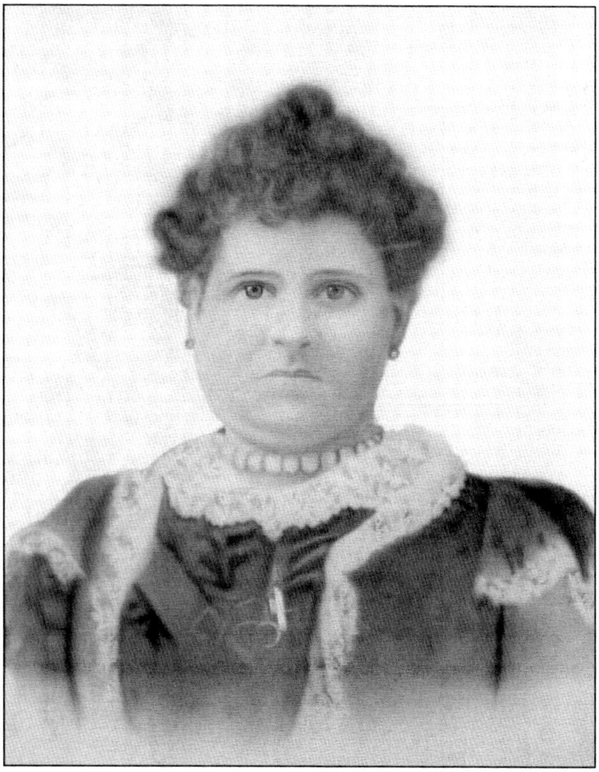

In the photograph at right are, Marietta Carr (left) and her brother-in-law and sister, Al and Margaret Ann Carr Wentworth. Marietta, born around 1842, and Maggie (below), born around 1844, had stayed with their mother in Richmond when Job went west. Rebecca was a seer, or clairvoyant, and welcomed many clients to the home. She was also a suffragette. In 1867, Howard went to fetch Marietta. Rebecca paid the boat passage to Washington. On January 16, 1869, Marietta married William H. Mahon in Tacoma. In 1875, on a ship bound for San Francisco to visit Margaret Ann, Marietta and her small son died when ships collided off Cape Flattery, Washington. In 1885, Rebecca, or "Grandma Staley," came to Tacoma to be with her sons. (Both, courtesy of Job Carr Cabin Museum.)

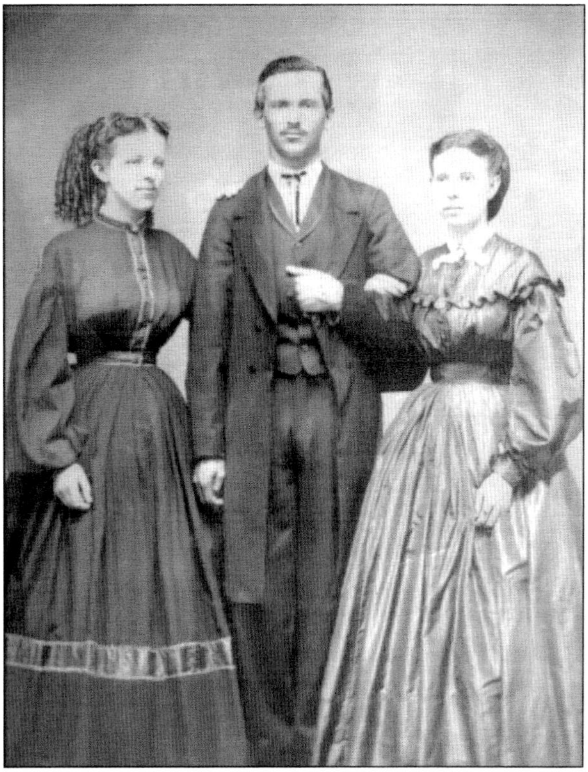

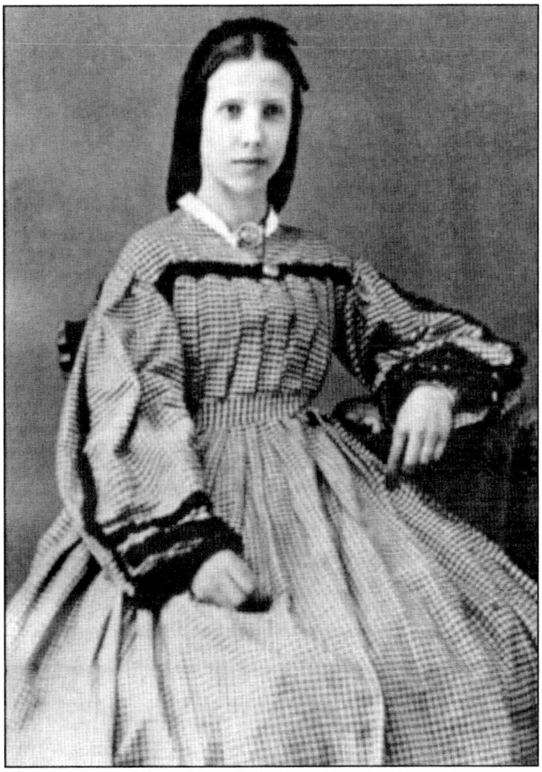

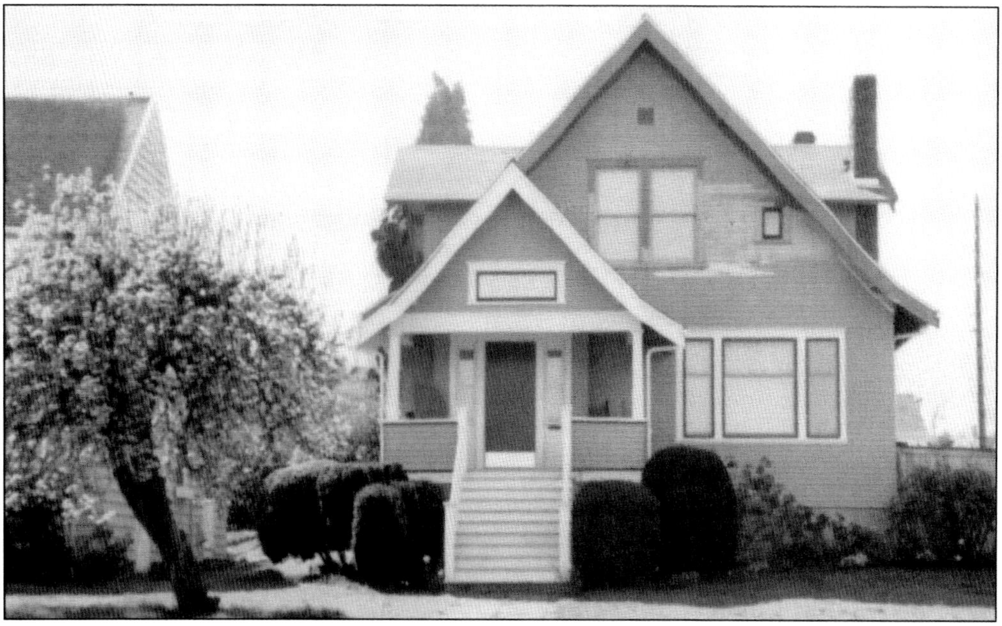

This Tudor Revival house at 624 North M Street was built in 1900 for Dewitt C. Jackson. He was the ticket agent at the Northern Pacific Railway city office. The house was constructed on the former Job Carr farm and orchard. It is spring in the photograph above, and the small pear tree to the left is in bloom. In the wintertime photograph below, neighboring homes are visible through the pear tree's branches. The small tree is said to be one of the original trees in the Carr orchard. That would date it from before 1887. (Below, Gyda May photograph.)

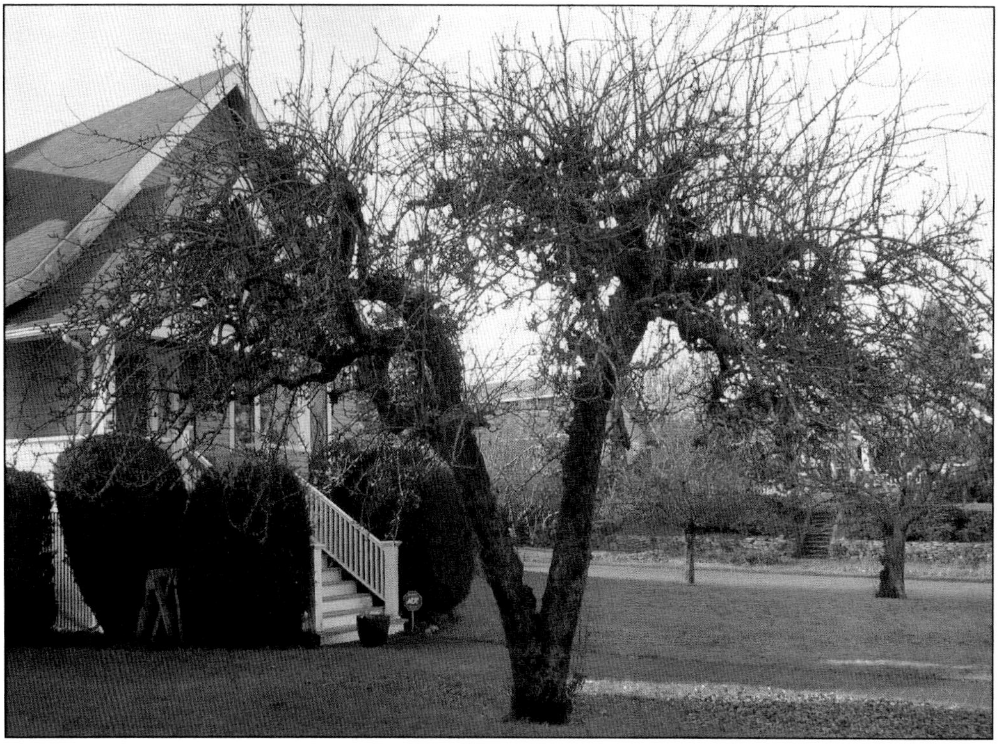

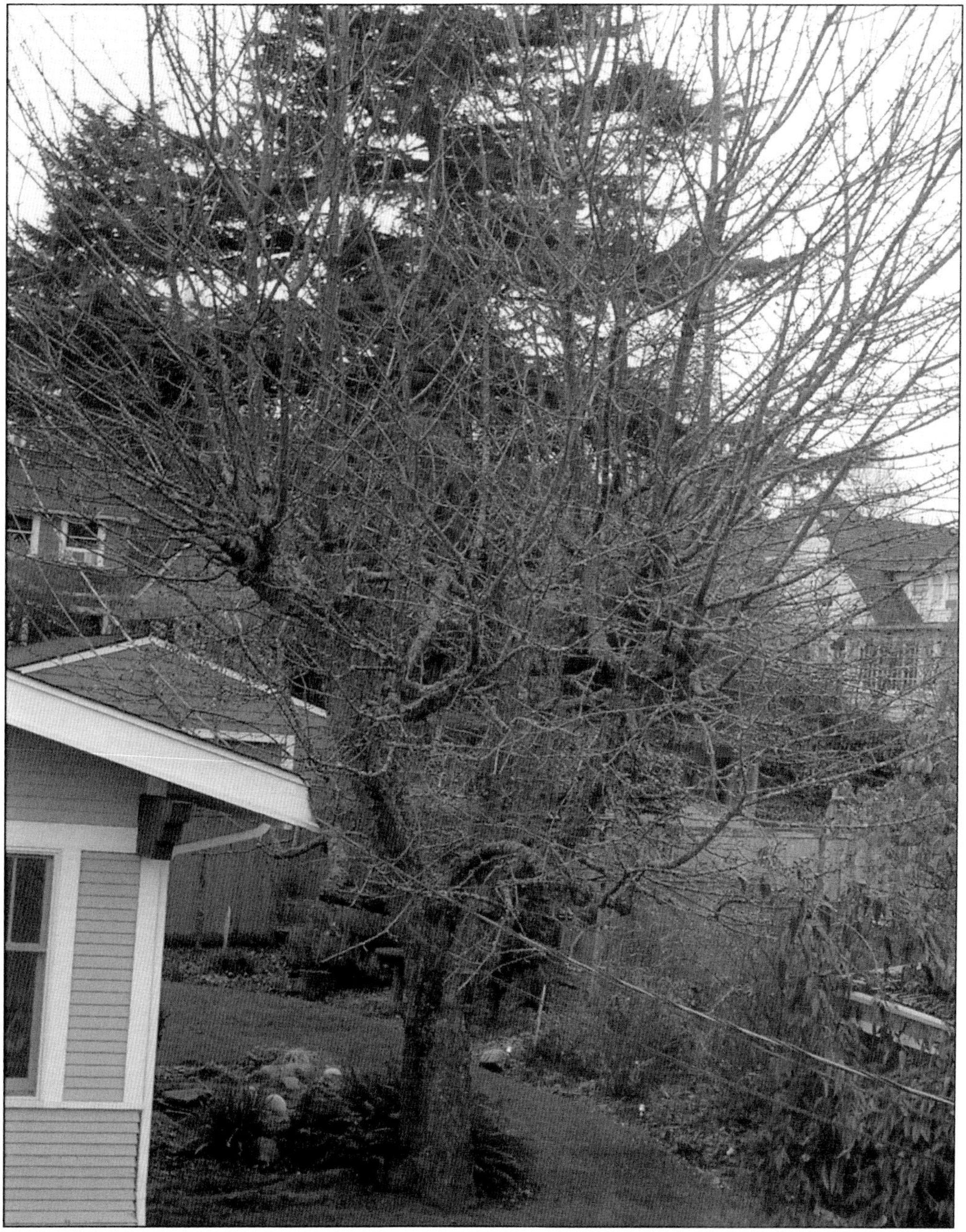

Among his many talents, Job Carr was a nurseryman, skilled in growing and pruning apple trees. When he went to Iowa in 1864, he wanted Rebecca to join him at the nursery he had purchased, but she refused. As was well known, Job did not argue with anyone, and Rebecca was a very strong-willed woman. Soon, he sold the nursery and went west, where he briefly stayed on the Puyallup Indian reservation on Commencement Bay. Howard Carr Jr., the grandson of Job Carr, sold this property. In 1910, it had a main corner house on North Seventh and M Streets and a smaller structure, probably a carriage house. In 1924, two houses were built. The cherry tree pictured in the winter of 2010 in the backyard is probably one of the original trees in Job Carr's orchard. Hopefully, more original hidden fruit trees are in the area. (Gyda May photograph.)

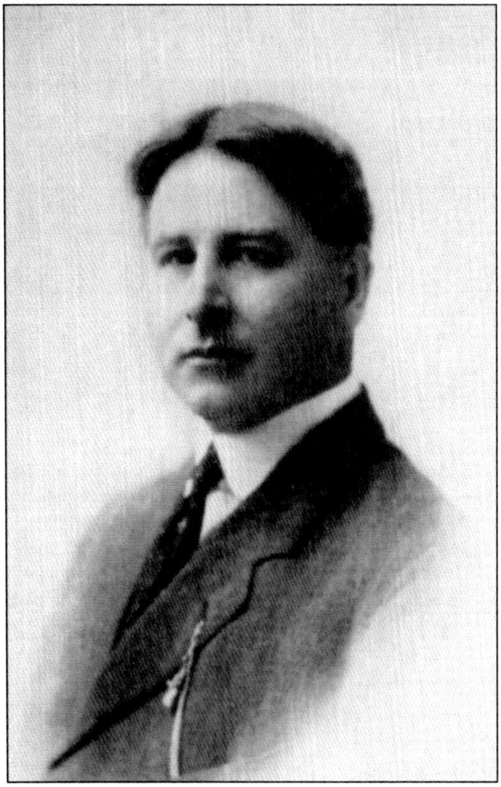

This photograph, about 1915, is of Caleb "Calvin" Carr, a son of Howard Carr. He was Pierce County's treasurer from 1913 to 1917 and also treasurer for the board of education. On January 1, 1907, he married Emma Marschke, from Wisconsin. They had two sons, Roy and Maxwell. In 1923, they would build a new house at 1420 North Fifth Street. Howard Carr had been successful in buying and selling real estate. He died in 1891, and Calvin and his siblings inherited his property.

The Foursquare house at 514 North Ainsworth Street was home to Clarence E. Griffin in 1904. Calvin and Emma Carr lived there from about 1905 to 1915. His brothers, Howard Jr. and Anthony, also lived in the neighborhood. In 1907, Calvin's grandmother Rebecca Staley was listed in the city's directory as head of the household at 2515 North Thirtieth Street in Old Tacoma. Rebecca died in 1908 at age 86.

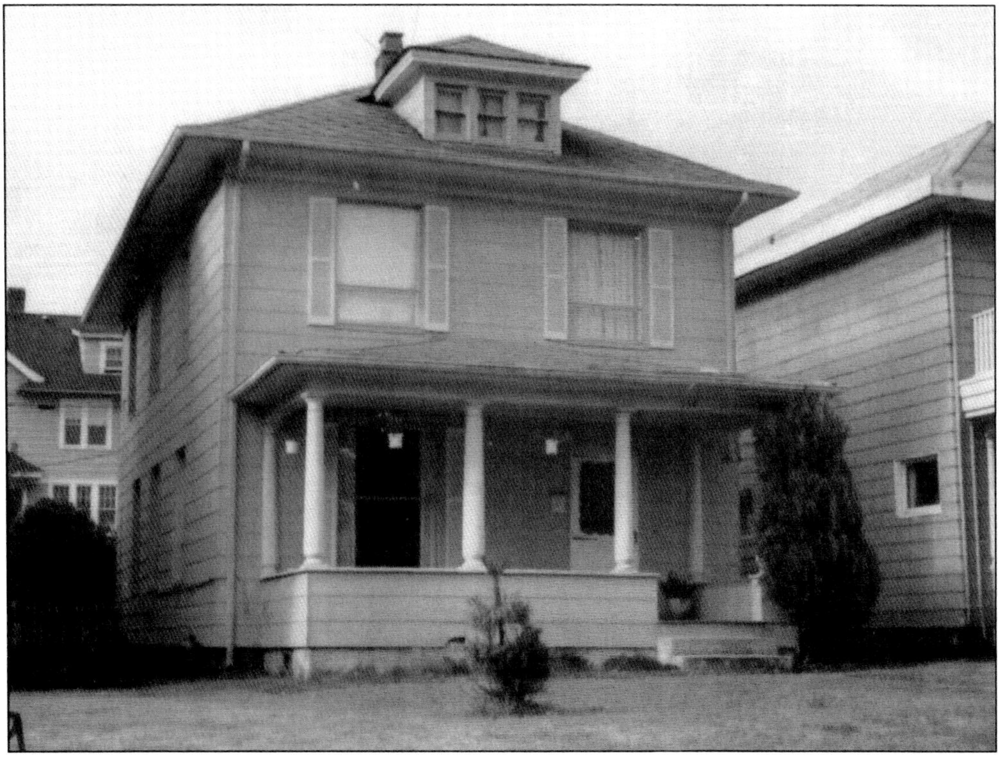

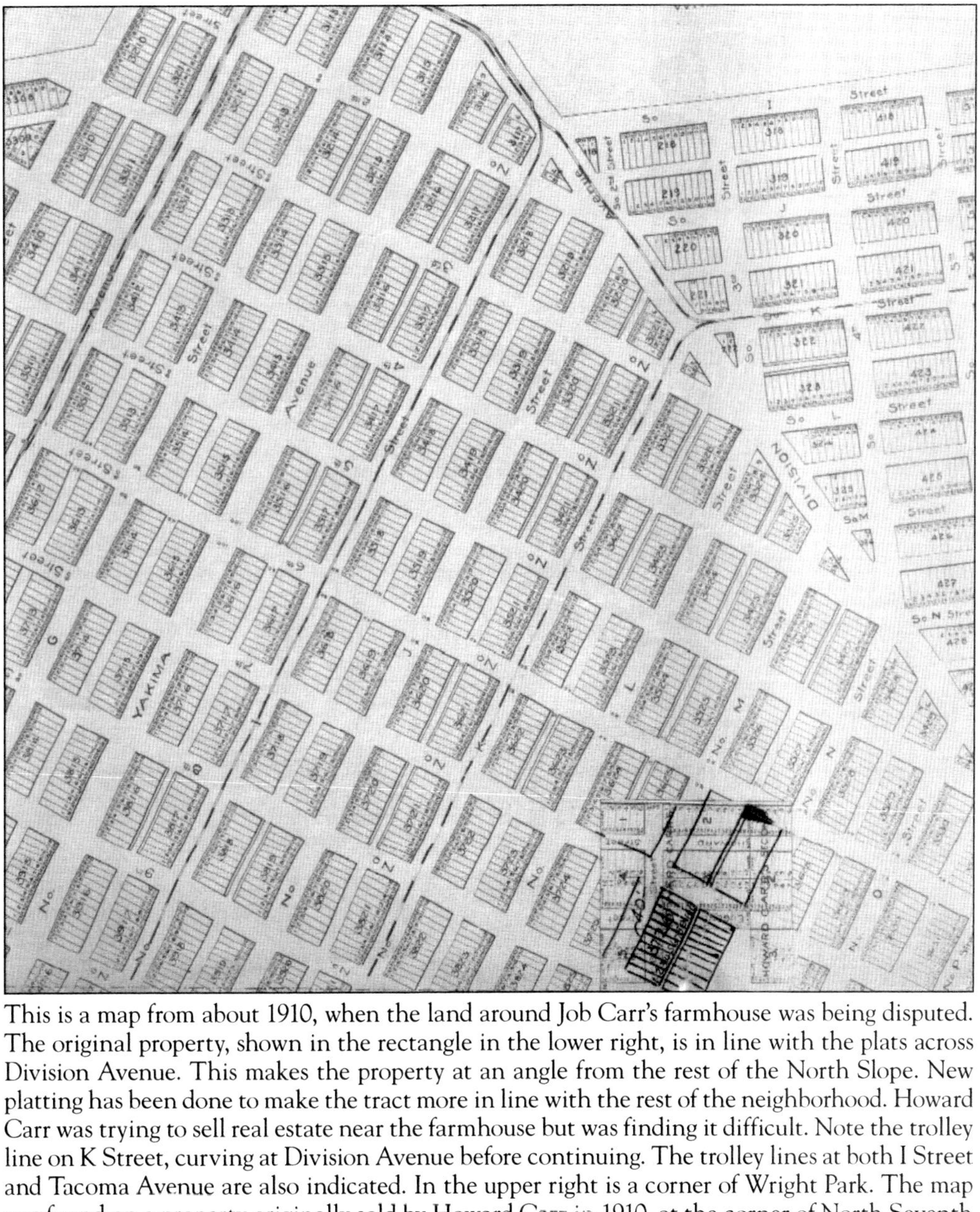

This is a map from about 1910, when the land around Job Carr's farmhouse was being disputed. The original property, shown in the rectangle in the lower right, is in line with the plats across Division Avenue. This makes the property at an angle from the rest of the North Slope. New platting has been done to make the tract more in line with the rest of the neighborhood. Howard Carr was trying to sell real estate near the farmhouse but was finding it difficult. Note the trolley line on K Street, curving at Division Avenue before continuing. The trolley lines at both I Street and Tacoma Avenue are also indicated. In the upper right is a corner of Wright Park. The map was found on a property originally sold by Howard Carr in 1910, at the corner of North Seventh and M Streets. (Gyda May photograph.)

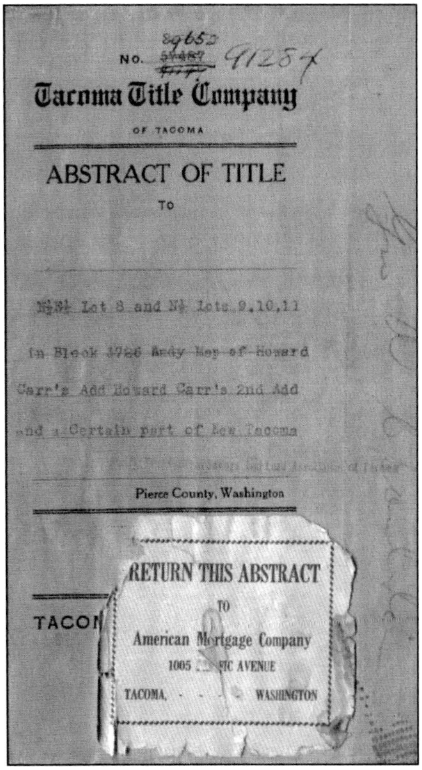

No.

Tacoma Title Company

OF TACOMA

ABSTRACT OF TITLE

TO

N½E½ Lot 8 and N½ Lots 9,10,11

in Block 3726 Amdy Map of Howard

Carr's Add Howard Carr's 2nd Add

and a Certain part of New Tacoma

Pierce County, Washington

RETURN THIS ABSTRACT

TO

American Mortgage Company

1005 [illegible] AVENUE

TACOMA, WASHINGTON

George A. Chamberlain bought the corner house at 1303 North Seventh Street m Katherine Clifford. Property in the title (left) is listed as follows: "N1/2E1/2 Lot 8 and N1/2 Lots 9,10,11, in Block 3726 Amdy (Amendatory) Map of Howard Carr's Add Howard Carr's 2nd Add and a Certain part of New Tacoma." The image below is from an abstract that describes property formerly within the Carr farm: "Lots Five (5) to eleven (11) inclusive, in Block Thirty-seven Hundred and Twenty-six (3726), as the same are designated upon a certain plat entitled, 'Amendatory Map of Howard Carr's Addition-Howard Carr's 2nd Addition, and a certain part of New Tacoma,' which was filed for record in the office of the Auditor of said County, May 16th, 1910." The California bungalow was built in 1924 after the original house was demolished. (Both, courtesy of Katie Dean.)

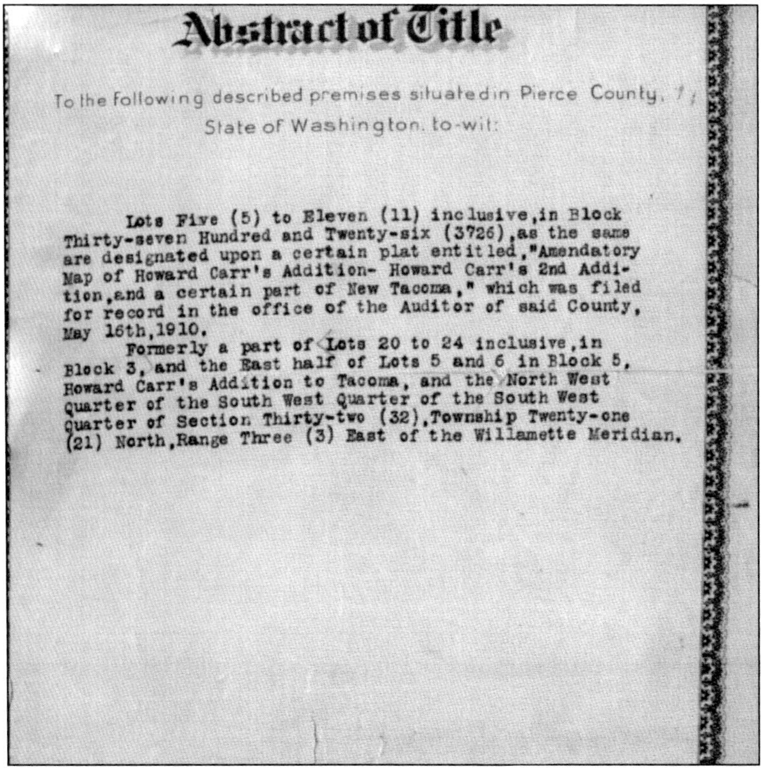

Abstract of Title

To the following described premises situated in Pierce County, State of Washington, to-wit:

Lots Five (5) to Eleven (11) inclusive, in Block Thirty-seven Hundred and Twenty-six (3726), as the same are designated upon a certain plat entitled, "Amendatory Map of Howard Carr's Addition- Howard Carr's 2nd Addition, and a certain part of New Tacoma," which was filed for record in the office of the Auditor of said County, May 16th, 1910.

Formerly a part of Lots 20 to 24 inclusive, in Block 3, and the East half of Lots 5 and 6 in Block 5, Howard Carr's Addition to Tacoma, and the North West Quarter of the South West Quarter of the South West Quarter of Section Thirty-two (32), Township Twenty-one (21) North, Range Three (3) East of the Willamette Meridian.

If these stone stairs leading up to the old Carr orchard could talk, they would have plenty of stories to tell. The *Tacoma Daily Ledger* on April 4, 1920, reports the following: "One of Tacoma's oldest landmarks, the home of Job Carr on North Sheridan Avenue between North Seventh and Eighth Streets, is now passing. Work of tearing down the house, which has stood for more than 40 years, began last week and will make way for a modern residence. The house is a two-story frame structure . . . surrounded by a large orchard of fine bearing trees. About 30 of the trees still remain . . .. The original abstract for the property conveys the land from the United States government to Job Carr . . . and bears the signature of Pres. Ulysses S. Grant. The property commands one of the best views in the city." (Right, Gyda May photograph.)

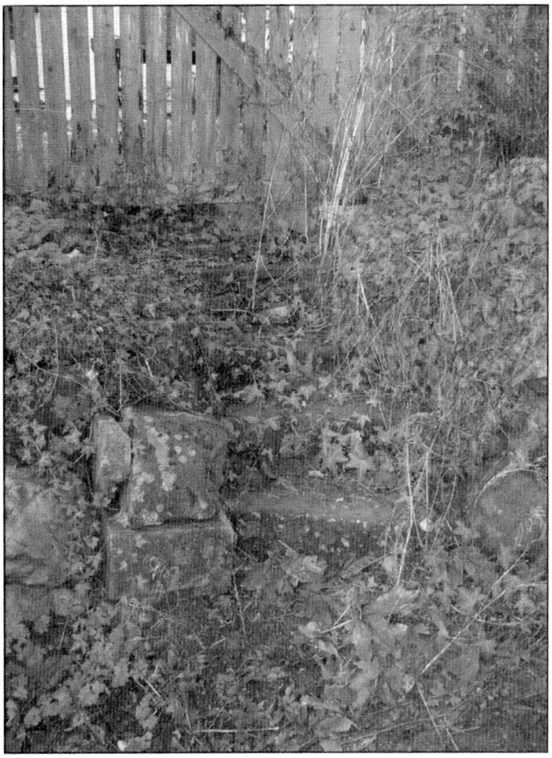

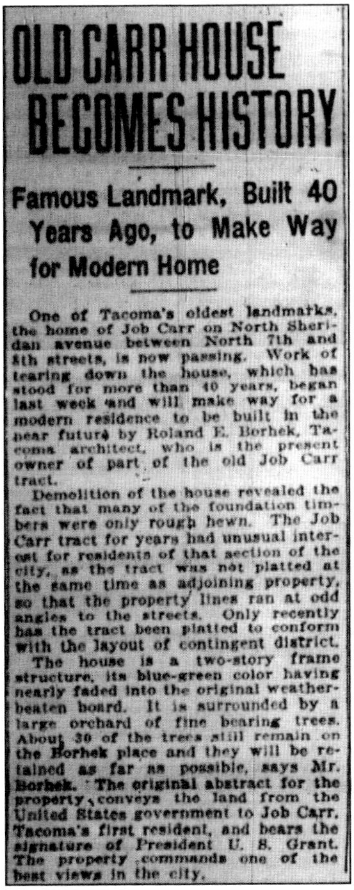

OLD CARR HOUSE BECOMES HISTORY

Famous Landmark, Built 40 Years Ago, to Make Way for Modern Home

One of Tacoma's oldest landmarks, the home of Job Carr on North Sheridan avenue between North 7th and Sth streets, is now passing. Work of tearing down the house, which has stood for more than 10 years, began last week and will make way for a modern residence to be built in the near future by Roland E. Borhek, Tacoma architect, who is the present owner of part of the old Job Carr tract.

Demolition of the house revealed the fact that many of the foundation timbers were only rough hewn. The Job Carr tract for years had unusual interest for residents of that section of the city, as the tract was not platted at the same time as adjoining property, so that the property lines ran at odd angles to the streets. Only recently has the tract been platted to conform with the layout of contingent district.

The house is a two-story frame structure, its blue-green color having nearly faded into the original weather-beaten board. It is surrounded by a large orchard of fine bearing trees. About 30 of the trees still remain on the Borhek place and they will be retained as far as possible, says Mr. Borhek. The original abstract for the property conveys the land from the United States government to Job Carr, Tacoma's first resident, and bears the signature of President U. S. Grant. The property commands one of the best views in the city.

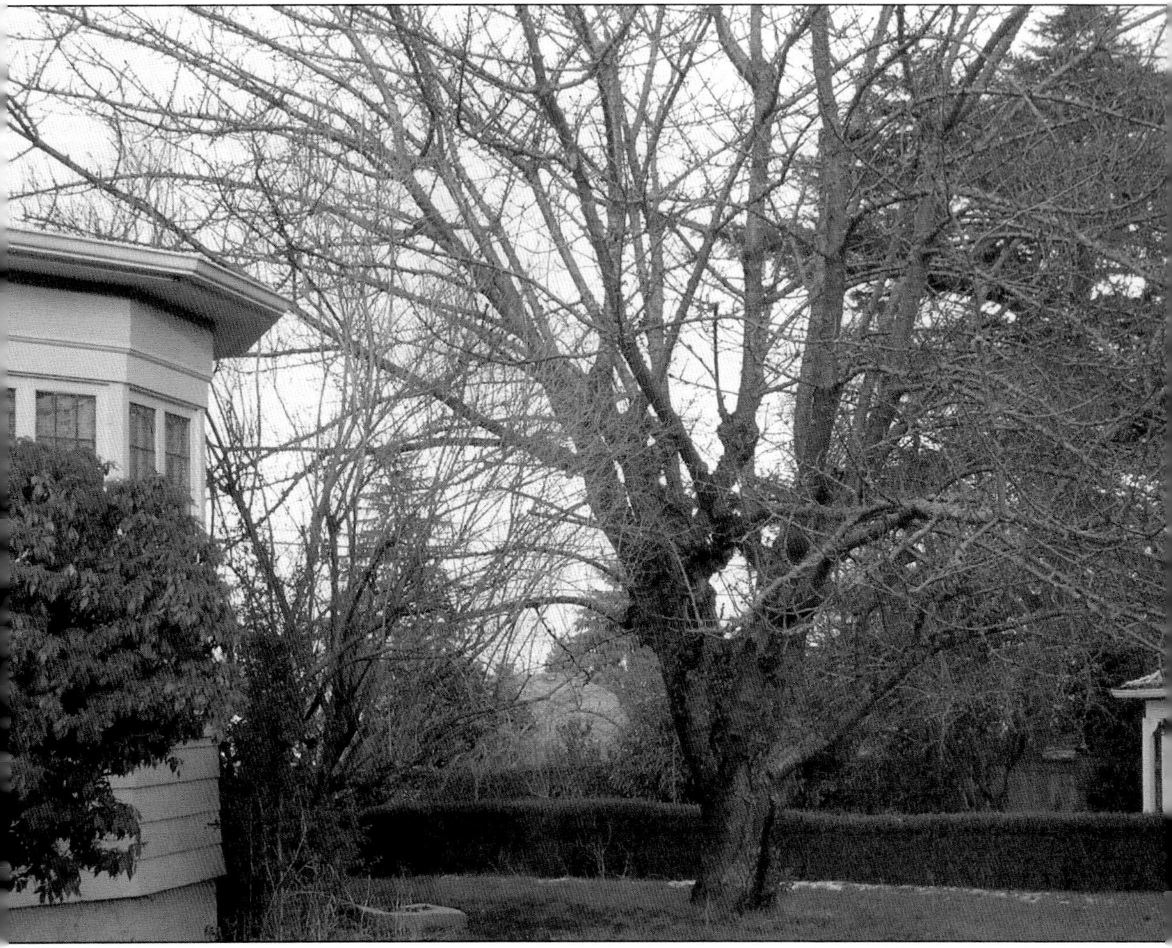

A majestic cherry tree almost fills this photograph of the garden at 715 North Sheridan Avenue. Perhaps it is one of the fruit trees lovingly planted by Job Carr on his farm on the North Slope. Maybe the Carr family enjoyed these fruits of his labor when they visited him there. People in the North Slope Historic District are interested in these historic trees. To the left is a corner of the house, modern in 1920, built by Tacoma architect Roland Borhek. Borhek built the Rialto Theater and Jason Lee Middle School, as well as many buildings in Seattle, Tacoma, and Spokane. He was president of the Tacoma Architects Association. The trees surrounding the garden dwarf the small gazebo to the right in the photograph. It is a peaceful setting, at the pinnacle of Job Carr's Hill. (Gyda May photograph.)

Three

Religion and Learning

Worship and education provided a solid foundation for the daily lives of families in the North Slope. It was here that Job Carr studied his Bible by the light of the lantern. It was here that Rev. Victor Morgan spoke of healing. And children of these various congregations and organizations held the future in their hands.

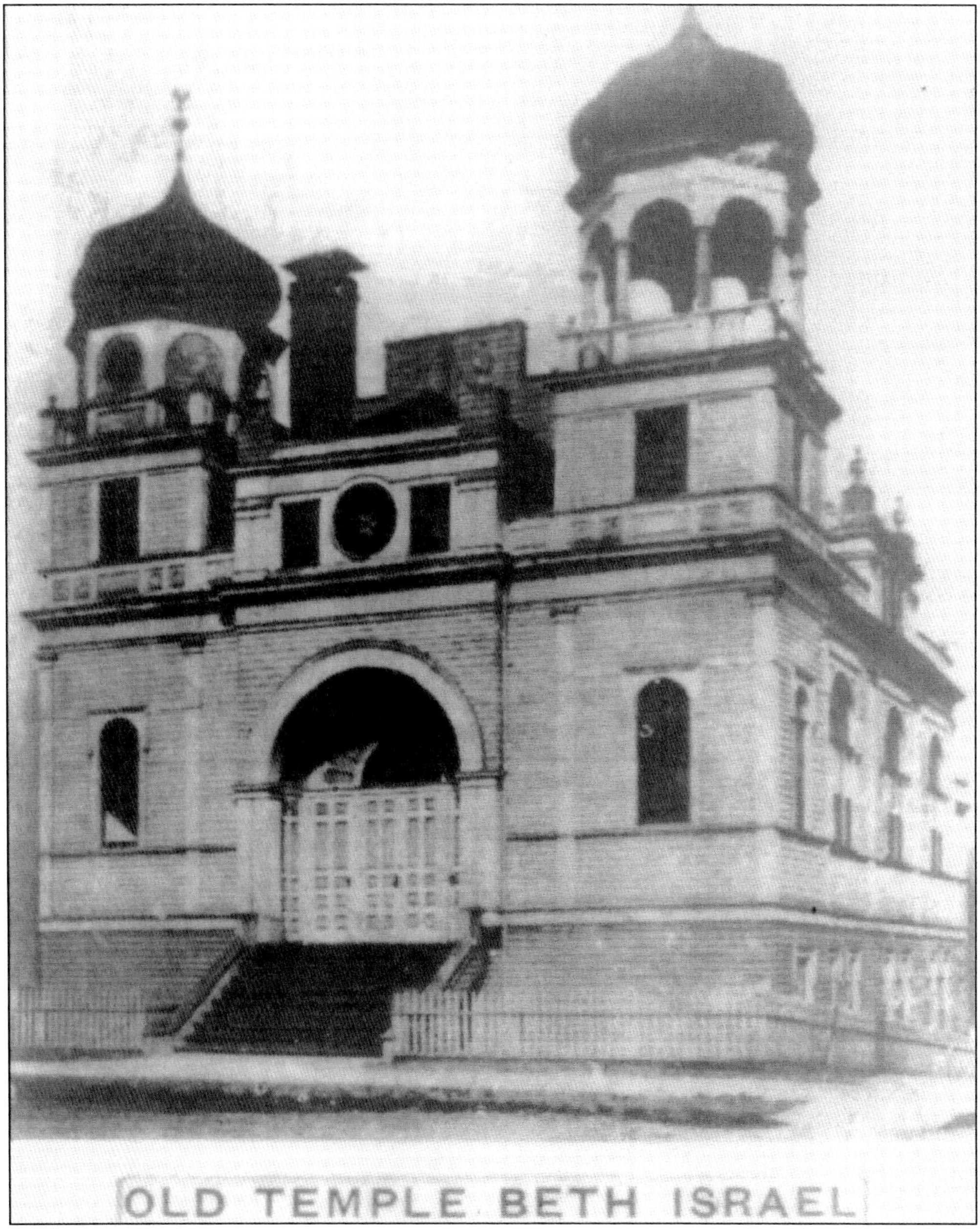

According to an article in the *Tacoma Daily Ledger* on October 1, 1892, the Jewish feast of the atonement, Yom Kippur, was being celebrated by Orthodox Hebrews in the Elks Hall and by the Reform sect in the Unitarian church. Tacoma's Jewish community had grown large enough to agree to disagree. Those who met that year in the Unitarian church had formally organized as a congregation, Beth Israel. Tacoma's first synagogue, designed by local architect C.A. Darmer, was located downtown on South Tenth and I Streets. The building was dedicated in September 1893. The new congregation chose to affiliate with the Reform movement. Members worshipped in this synagogue until 1919. Henry Hunt writes in 1915 that Theophil Feist, a local merchant, was synagogue president and Meyer Jacob, also in dry goods, was secretary. Both of these men were very active in Jewish charities and other organizations.

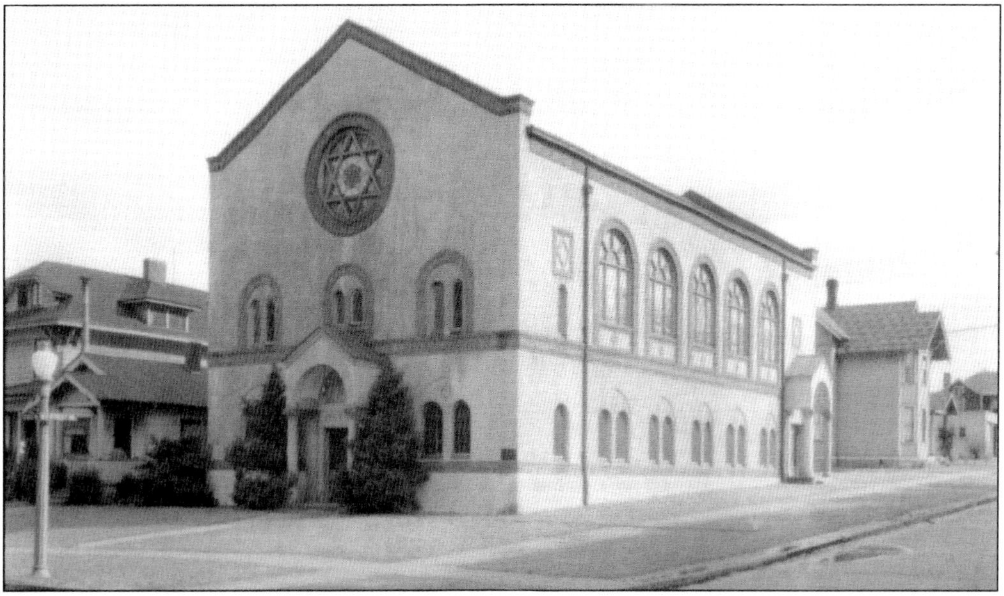

In 1918, Temple Beth Israel sold the old synagogue downtown and dedicated a new temple (above) on 324 North J Street in the North Slope neighborhood in 1922. Three years later, the Orthodox Jews of Chevra Talmud Torah built a similar temple on South Fourth and I Streets. For 42 years, the Reform Jews of the North Slope worshipped at the stucco synagogue with its unusual stained-glass windows, created as memorials to pioneer families. In 1956, Rabbi Richard Rosenthal came to serve at Temple Beth Israel. He and his wife, Barbara, lived at 409 North Sheridan Avenue (below). After much discussion, arguing, and compromise, Tacoma's two temples voted to merge in 1960 as Temple Beth El. The building at North J Street was sold in 1964. Rabbi Rosenthal led the merged temples until his retirement in 1997.

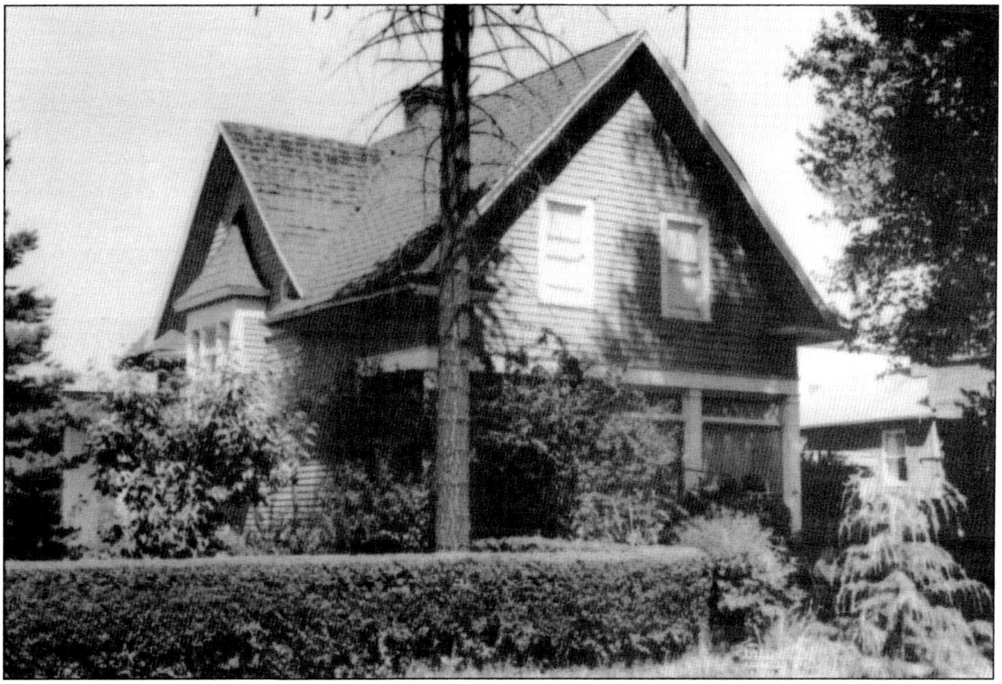

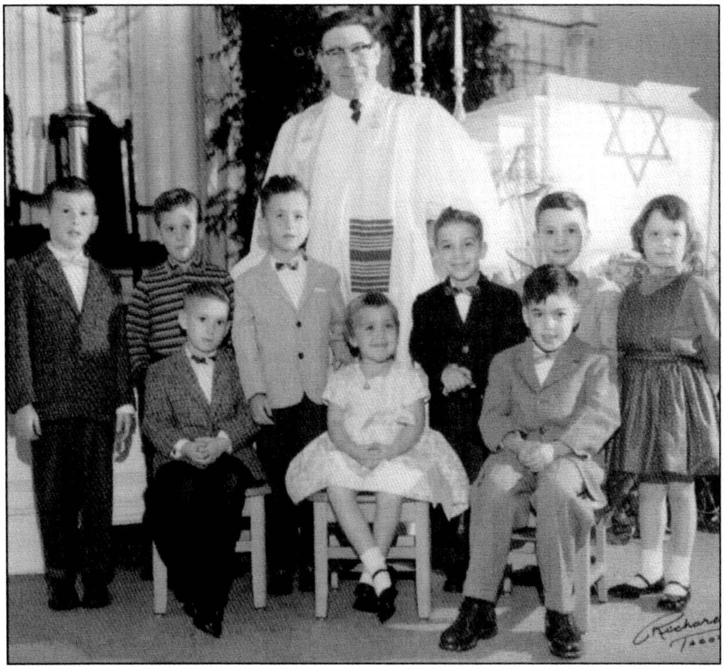

Nine children, seven boys and two girls, pose with Rabbi Richard Rosenthal in 1959 for their Consecration photograph. Born in Germany, Rabbi Rosenthal came to the United States in 1939 and settled in Shreveport, Louisiana. He was a graduate of the Centenary College in Shreveport and was ordained at the Hebrew Union College in Cincinnati in 1954. He served as an army chaplain for two years before he arrived in Tacoma.

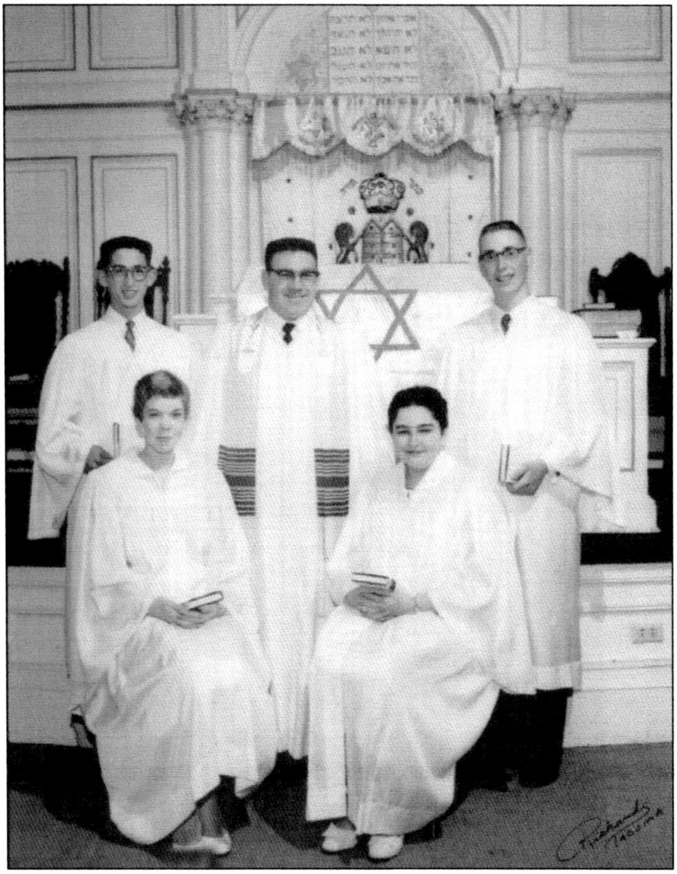

Four young confirmands are being welcomed into the congregation in June 1959. Rabbi Rosenthal will accept their vows of faith, and each will be presented with a certificate of confirmation and an inscribed prayer book. Reform Judaism had reintroduced the ceremony of confirmation. Those pictured are, from left to right, (first row) Marilyn Aqua and Leslie Apstein; (second row) Gary Donion, Rabbi Rosenthal, and Ronald Diamond.

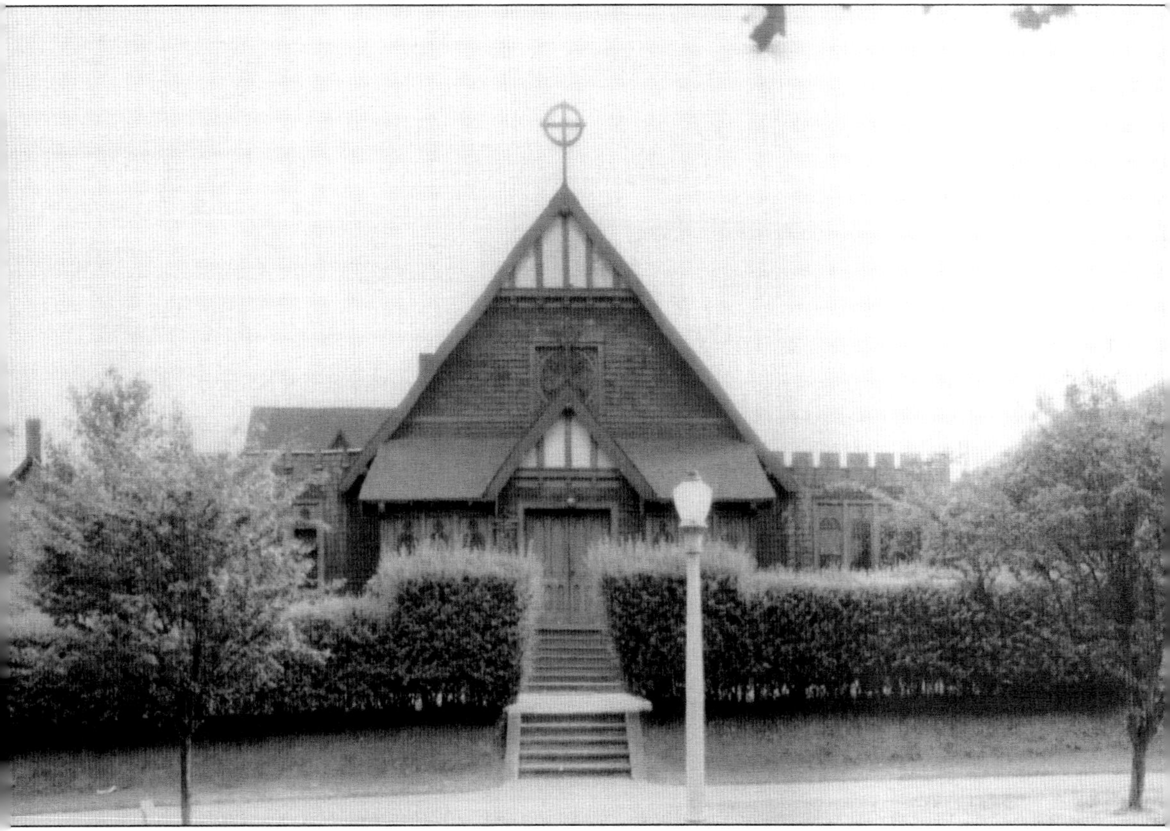

Christ Episcopal Church was located at 316 North K Street. It was designed by architects Daniels and Cook and built in 1889. Tacoma's population had expanded due to the railroad and timber industry booms, and the church formed a new parish. The church purchased nine lots on the corner of North Third and K Streets—at that time in the forested North Slope—and started building. The new church, Trinity Chapel, held its first service in December 1889. The Gothic-style church held 300 people. St. Luke's was a downtown Tacoma Episcopal congregation organized in the late 1870s. In 1926, both St. Luke's and Trinity were facing financial difficulties, so they merged under the name of Christ Episcopal Church, or Christ Church. In the late 1960s, the building was demolished to make way for a new, modern sanctuary designed by architect Paul Thiry.

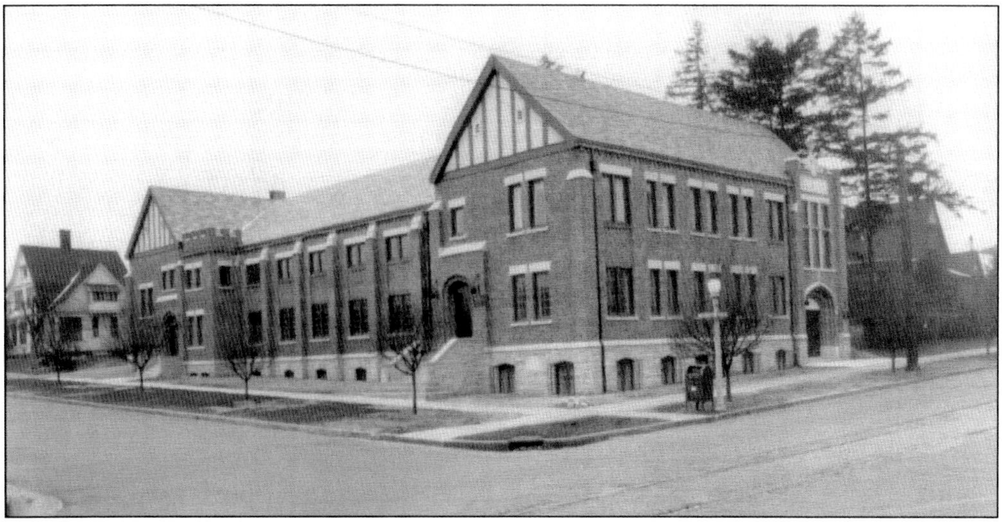

Wells Hall, 316 North K Street, was the new parish meetinghouse erected in 1927 and named after Bishop Lemuel H. Wells, the first rector of Trinity Parish. Ambrose J. Russell was the architect, and the building was constructed in the Tudor Revival style of brick with Wilkeson sandstone. When first built, Wells Hall contained an assembly room and stage, large gymnasium, Sunday school space, kitchen, sewing room, library, and a "retiring room" for men.

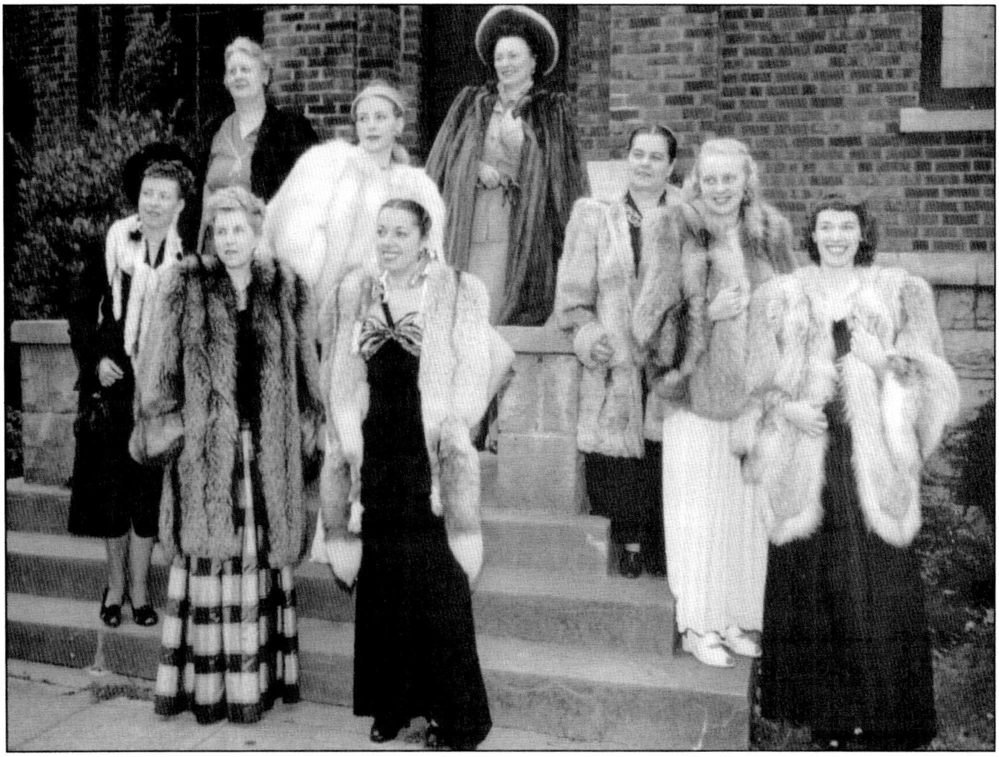

In 1947, the Tacoma Women's Club had a "Furgatta" fashion show at Wells Hall. The event featured the latest in fur fashions. Dora B. Smith was the show's commentator. Club members are shown modeling coats, stoles, and scarves in fox, China mink, chinchilla, Persian paw, and Persian lamb. The names of attendees were on page nine of the *Tacoma Times* on October 11.

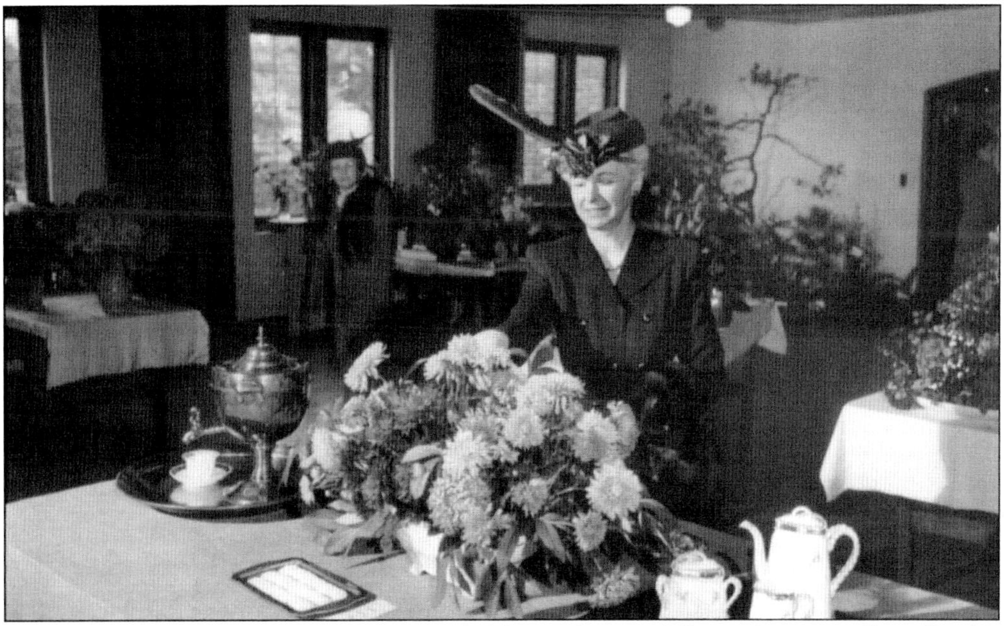

In the fall of 1947, the Tacoma Garden Club held its 24th annual flower show at Wells Hall. Club members demonstrated their artistic skills in flower arranging. Florence Gullickson and Ione M. Wright were chairpersons. Gertrude Peck is shown arranging a centerpiece for the table. In 1957, Trinity House was added to the hall. The expansion included a chapel, columbarium, offices, meeting rooms, classrooms, and a library.

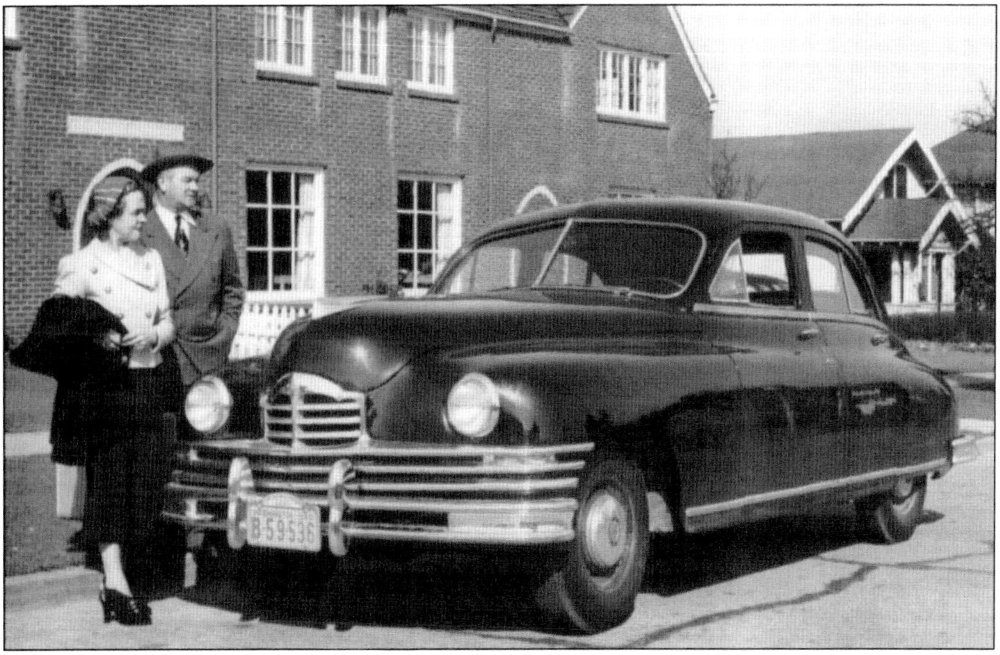

Prior to leaving on a tour of France, England, Belgium, the Netherlands, Germany, Switzerland, and Norway in spring and summer of 1949, Lolly and Gunnar Leggerini pause by their Packard in front of Wells Hall. In 1945, Wells Hall held a mortgage-burning ceremony. Residents of the North Slope enjoyed postwar prosperity.

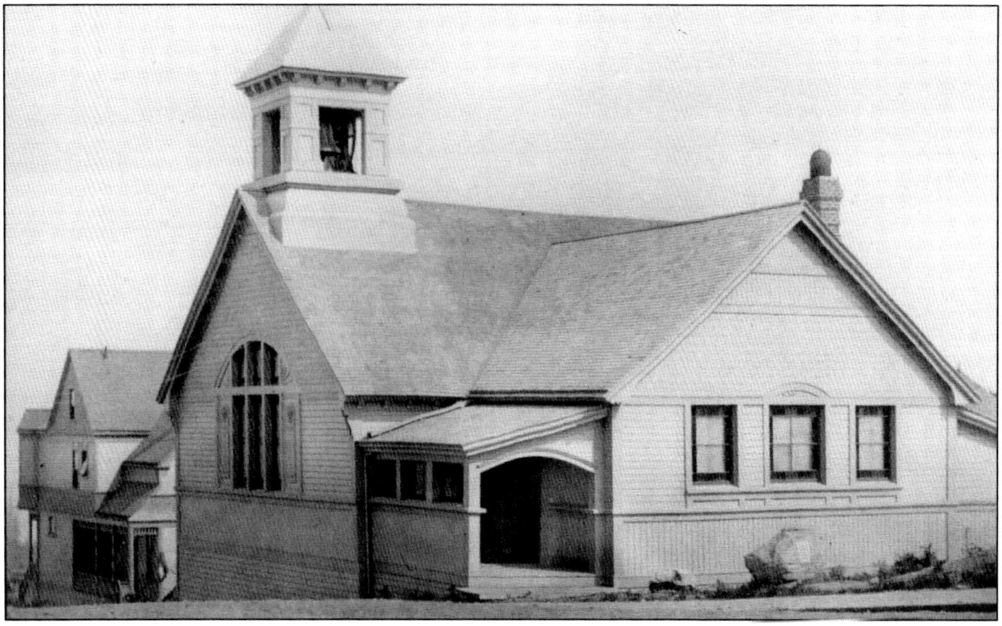

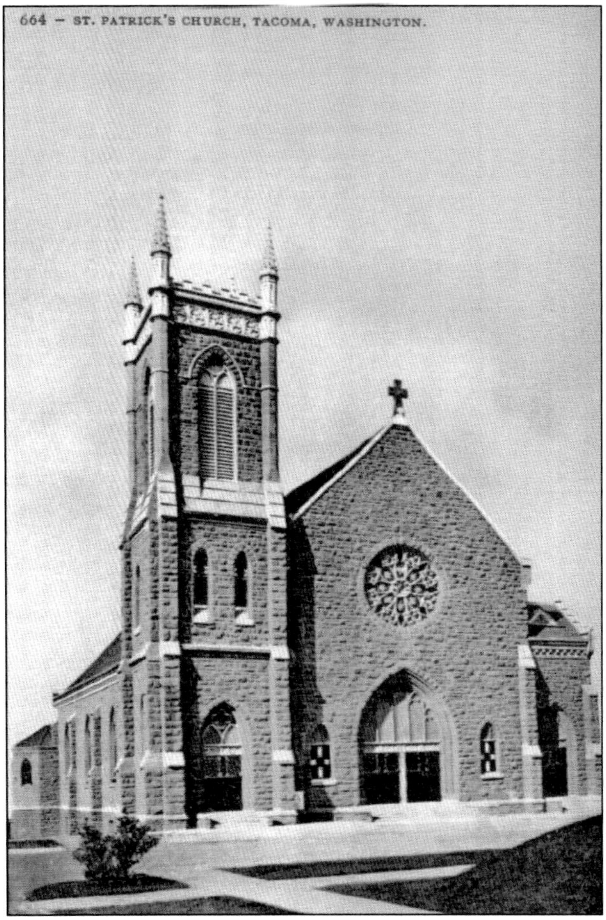

The Atkinson Memorial Church was a Congregational church funded by Rev. Dr. G.H. Atkinson and designed by Charles Talbott. In 1890, Reverend Sims was minister, and from 1893 to 1895, Reverend Gallagher served. According to Herbert Hunt, it was "one of the handsomest little church buildings Tacoma ever had." The church, however, was short-lived. The Roman Catholics later purchased the real estate. (Courtesy of Charlotte Medlock.)

In 1905, the wooden St. Patrick Church in Old Town was destroyed by fire. St. Patrick Church at North Twelfth and J Streets was designed by architect Frederick Heath and built of stone in 1906. The cornerstone was laid on St. Patrick's Day 1906, and the church was dedicated in June 1907. A bell tower graced one corner, and a rose window was centered above the main doors. (Courtesy of Karen May.)

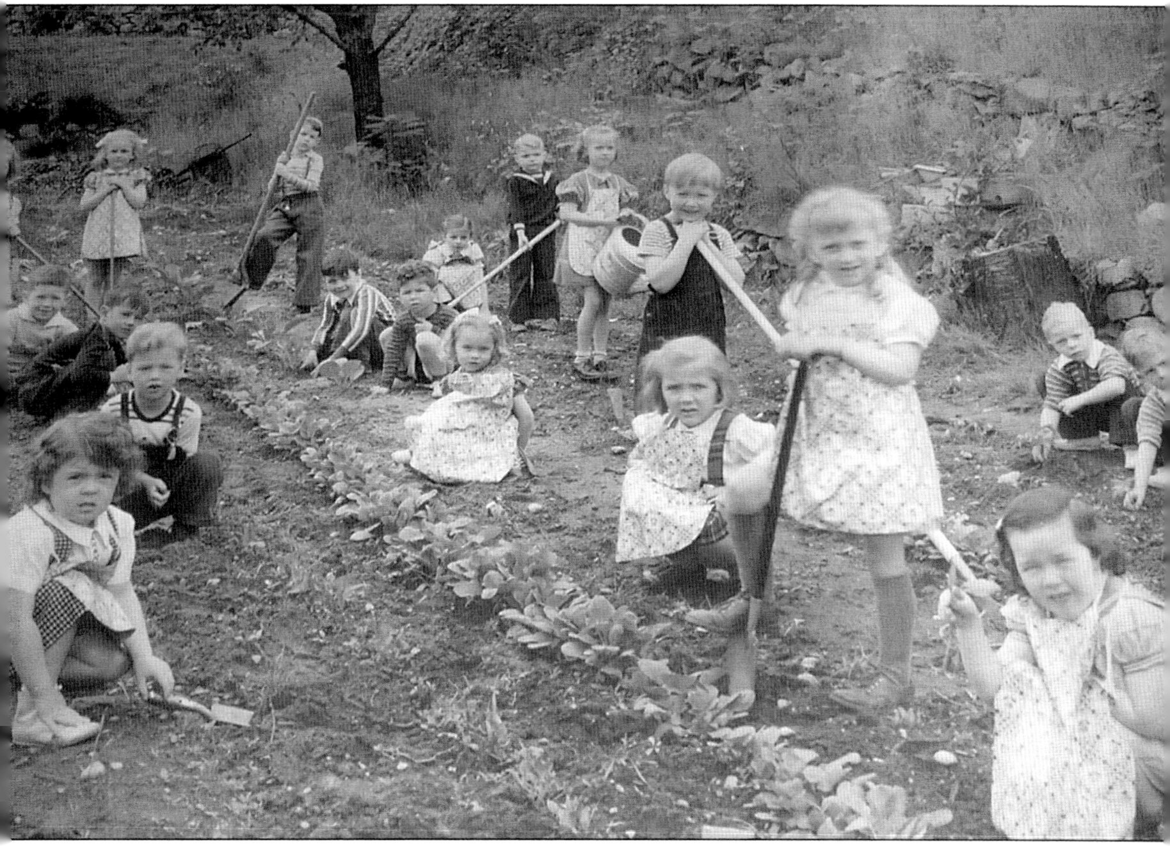

Children from St. Patrick Church are tending their victory garden on the grounds behind the school, located on the slope down the hill. According to archivist Sister Esther, of the Tacoma Dominicans, the year was 1945, and the children were all about five years old. Victory gardens were part of the war effort, and all ages took part during World War II to help the Allies win. The two boys on the far right are, from left to right, Bill and John Rankos, whose father owned the pharmacy in the Stadium District. The other children are unidentified but probably members of the parish. All of the youngsters have gardening tools, and some are wearing special aprons. They were proud to be growing vegetables and doing their part. The church owned the entire block and other property in the neighborhood. (Courtesy of Tacoma Dominican archives.)

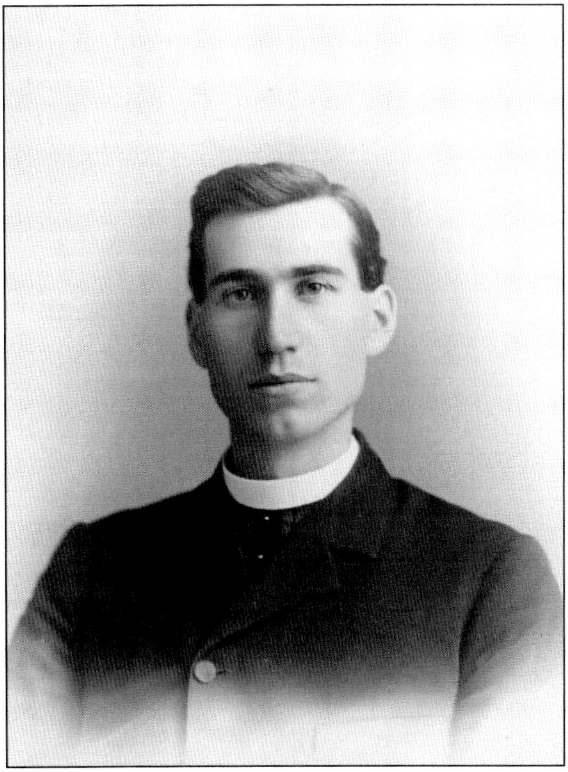

Joseph Francis McGrath was born in Kilmacow, County Kilkenny, in 1871, and studied at the Grand Séminaire de Montreal, Quebec, Canada. He became a priest in 1895 and was a missionary among the Native Americans in northern Michigan for two years. He was rector of St. Patrick Church in Tacoma from 1906 to 1918. Father McGrath next was bishop of Baker, Oregon, for 31 years. (Courtesy of Tacoma Dominican archives.)

Born in 1878 in County Limerick, Msgr. William J. Noonan arrived in the Diocese of Seattle direct from Ireland in 1906. He spent 11 years at St. James Cathedral. In 1918, Monsignor Noonan was pronounced the "Irremovable Rector" of St. Patrick Church in Tacoma. He died in 1953, after 34 years at St. Patrick Church. At his funeral, there were 150 priests, plus sisters and laymen. (Courtesy of Tacoma Dominican archives.)

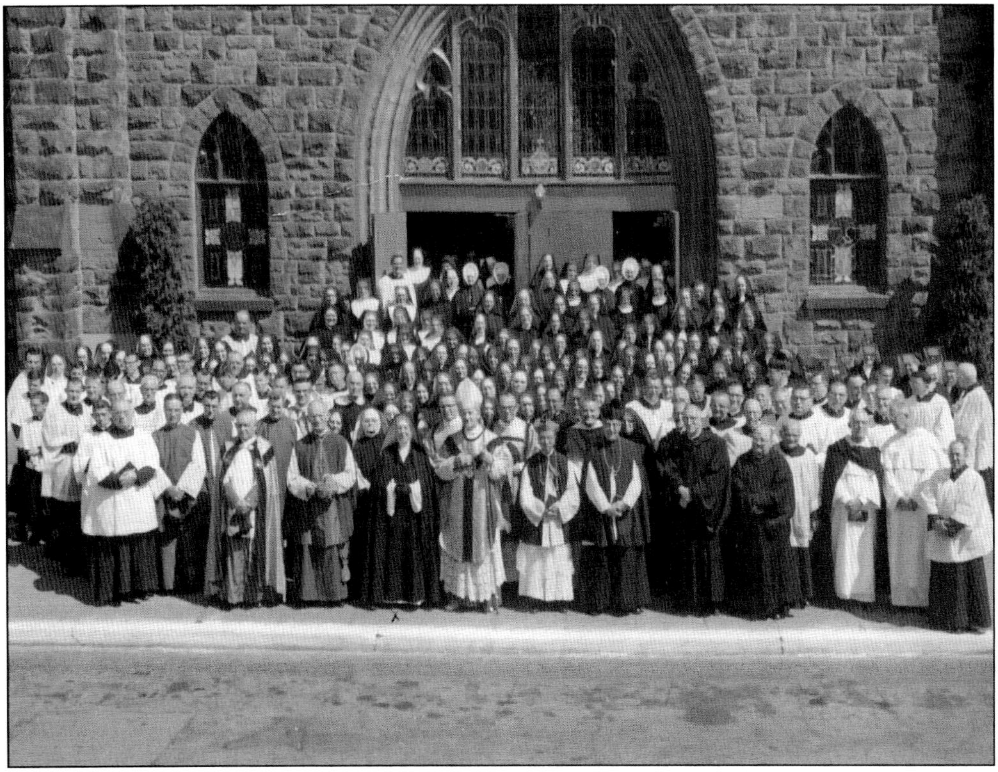

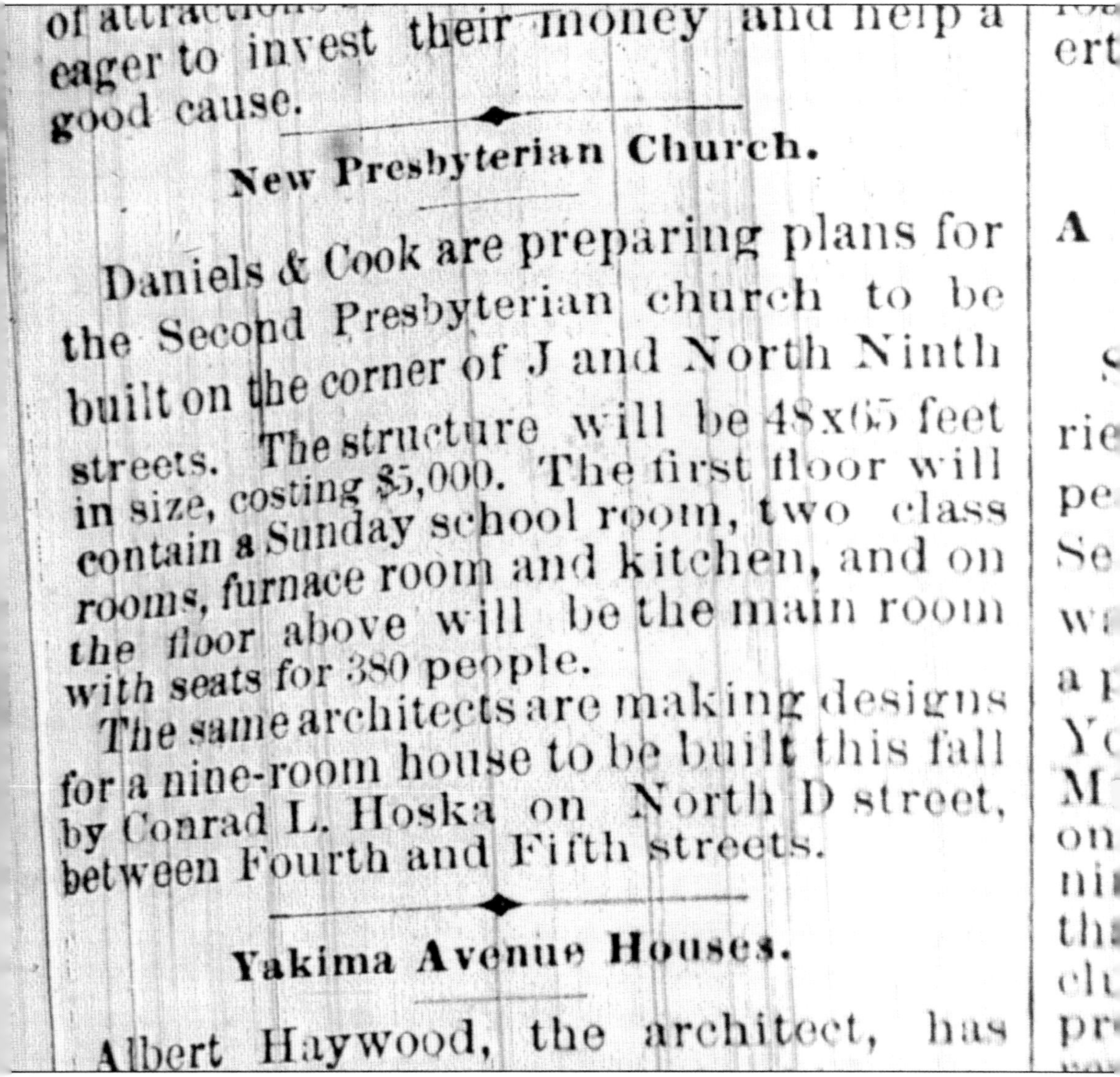

eager to invest their money and help a good cause.

New Presbyterian Church.

Daniels & Cook are preparing plans for the Second Presbyterian church to be built on the corner of J and North Ninth streets. The structure will be 48x65 feet in size, costing $5,000. The first floor will contain a Sunday school room, two class rooms, furnace room and kitchen, and on the floor above will be the main room with seats for 380 people.

The same architects are making designs for a nine-room house to be built this fall by Conrad L. Hoska on North D street, between Fourth and Fifth streets.

Yakima Avenue Houses.

Albert Haywood, the architect, has

In Old Town in 1888, Immanuel Presbyterian was organized as a mission church and called Second Presbyterian Church. In 1889, the church bought the lots at North Ninth and J Streets. For a while, the congregation worshipped in a tent on the property. In 1890, members hired architects Daniels and Cook to design a substantial wooden church, which was built and dedicated in 1891. It was renamed Immanuel Presbyterian Church. There were stained-glass windows, which were dedicated to members and friends of the congregation. With beauty, warmth, and glowing colors, each tells a story of unusual human interest. Over the years, several additions were made to the original building, but the congregation was still growing in size. Only 17 years after the wooden church was constructed, the structure was razed to make way for the Mission-style, reinforced concrete church. (Courtesy of Immanuel Presbyterian Church.)

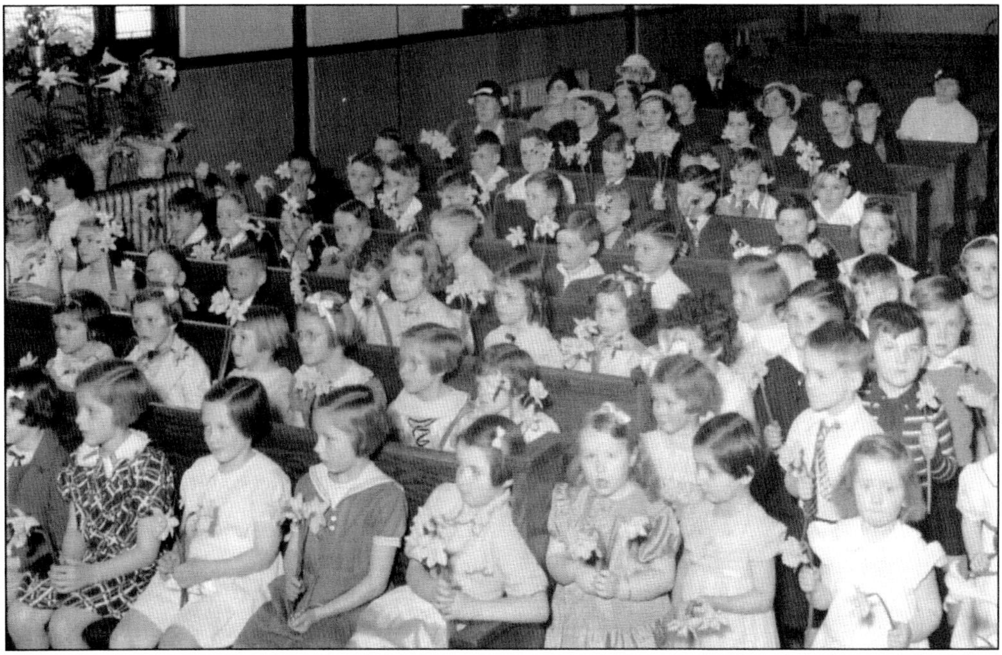

Easter morning 1935 found young children at Immanuel Presbyterian Church holding daffodils, a flower very well known to Tacoma residents. In 1929, a new educational wing, designed by Shaw and Shaw, was added to the church building. Based on the amount of children in the photograph, there were sufficient pupils for the new school.

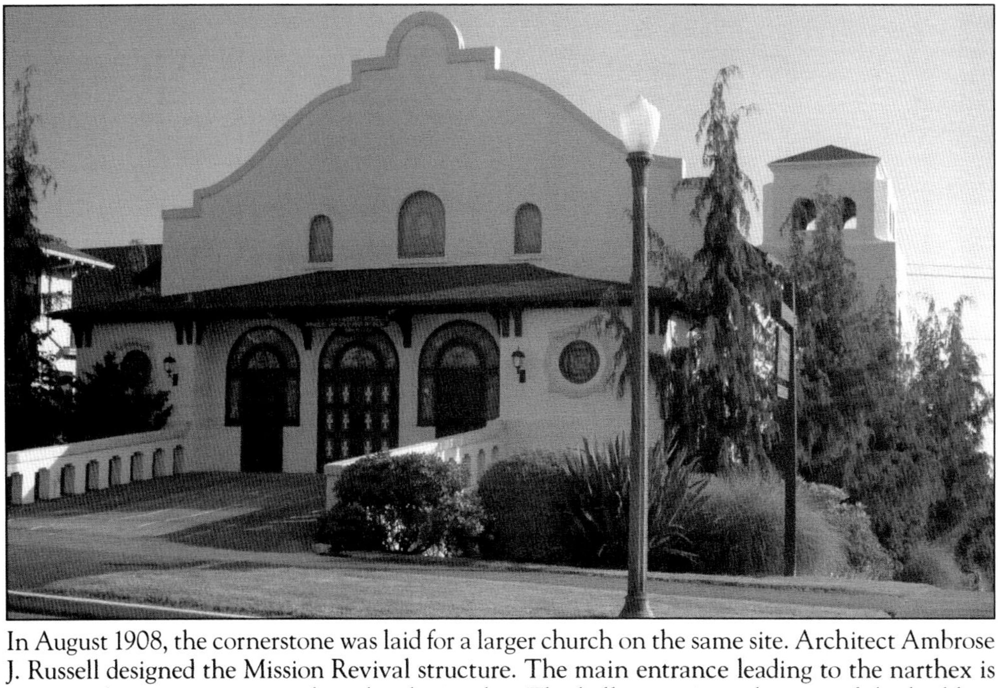

In August 1908, the cornerstone was laid for a larger church on the same site. Architect Ambrose J. Russell designed the Mission Revival structure. The main entrance leading to the narthex is a ramp, chosen to accommodate the sloping lot. The bell tower is at the rear of the building because of the hillside. The beautiful stained-glass windows from the old church light the nave. (Courtesy of Immanuel Presbyterian Church.)

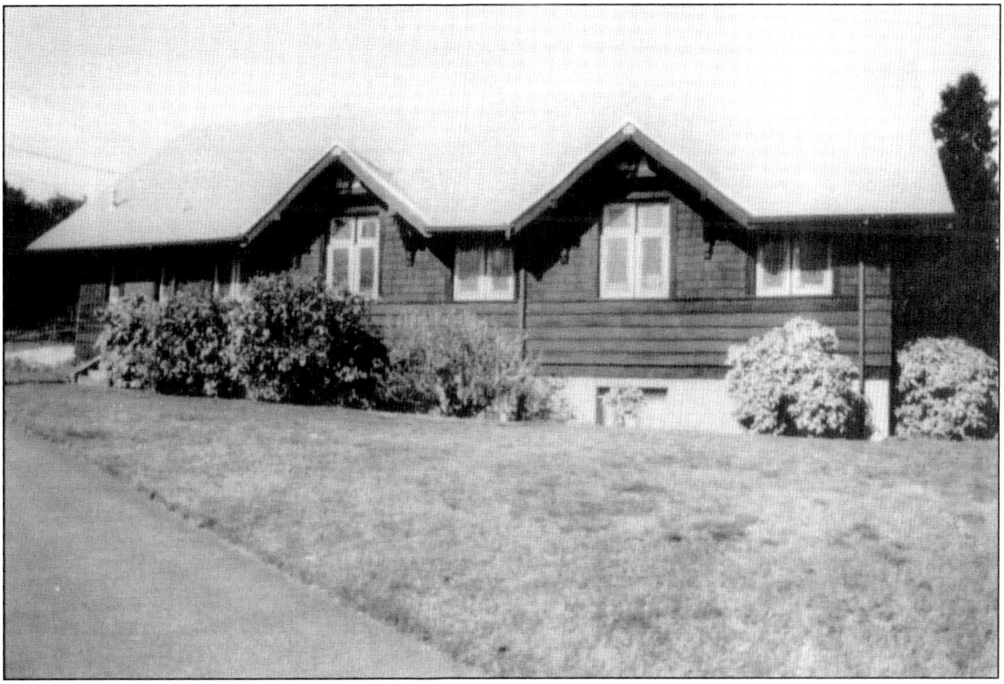

The Park Universalist Church at North J Street and Division Avenue is a rare example of Craftsman-style church architecture and was designed by Woodroofe and Constable. The building was completed in 1909. Originally, the church was located at the corner of North I and Division Avenue on lots donated by Charles Wright. After 1893, the new church had struggled until Abbie Danforth reorganized the group and Rev. William Buchanan was installed.

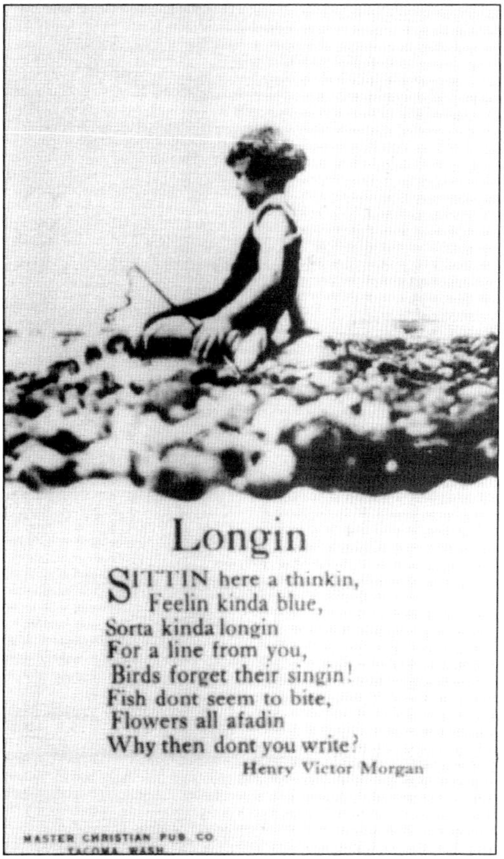

In 1912, Rev. Henry Victor Morgan became the minister. He changed the church from Universalist to Divine Science and was directed toward an international healing ministry that applied universal principles to daily living. Reverend Morgan served until his death in 1952. He had two sons, Murray Morgan and Victor Henry Morgan. Young Murray, in the photograph, inspired his father's poem. Both were published around the world.

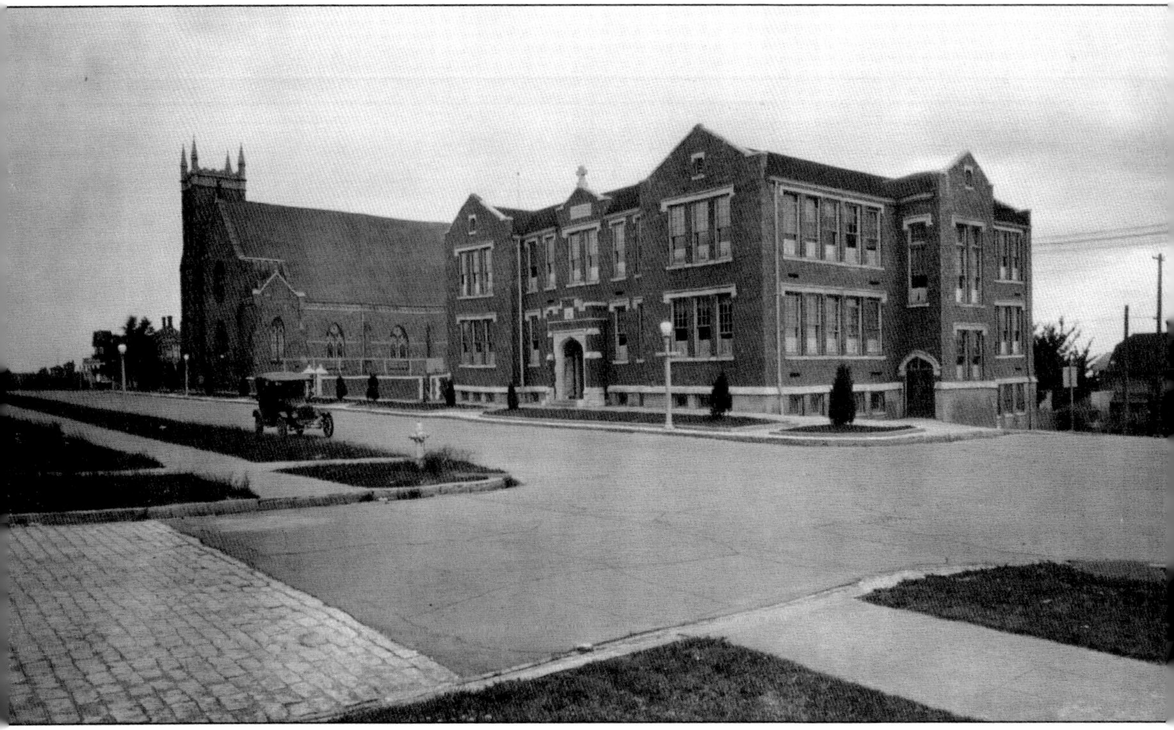

The three-story St. Patrick School on North Eleventh and J Streets was completed on November 12, 1919, with 325 students in the elementary grades. St. Patrick Church is on the left. The school continued at this location for 55 years. The original goal of the Dominican sisters was maintained, providing a quality Catholic education that instructs the mind and the soul. The sisters staffing St. Patrick School lived in the Aquinas Convent until 1940, when they moved closer to the school. In 1921, a Normal School Department was inaugurated under the direction of Mary E. Doyle, former supervisor of the Wisconsin State Normal School. Mother Thomasina was born in New York City in 1859. She had come to Washington Territory in 1888 with Sister de Chantal and Sister Aloysia to found a new congregation of Dominican sisters. Teachers at St. Patrick School followed the wise guidance of these three foundresses. (Courtesy of Tacoma Dominican archives.)

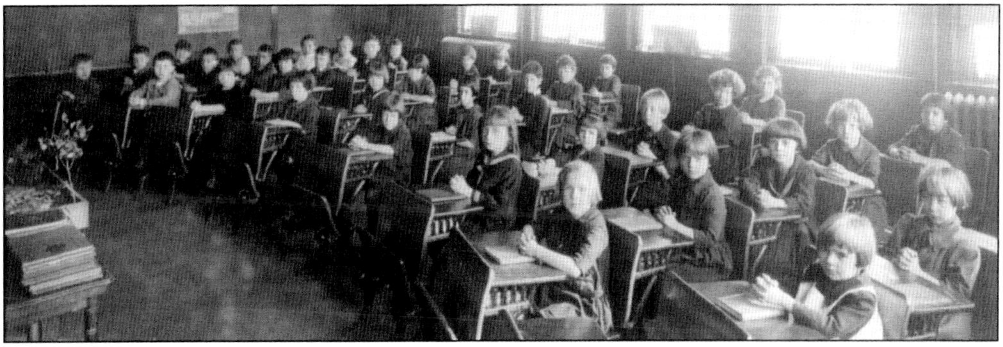

With hands clasped respectfully, students at the St. Patrick Elementary School, probably in the 1920s, focus on the photographer. Sun streams in the windows, and the wood floor is brightly polished. Carved wooden desks are linked, five children to a row, each with a copybook. On the left, behind primers on the table, is a planter holding flowers for a botany lesson. (Courtesy of Tacoma Dominican archives.)

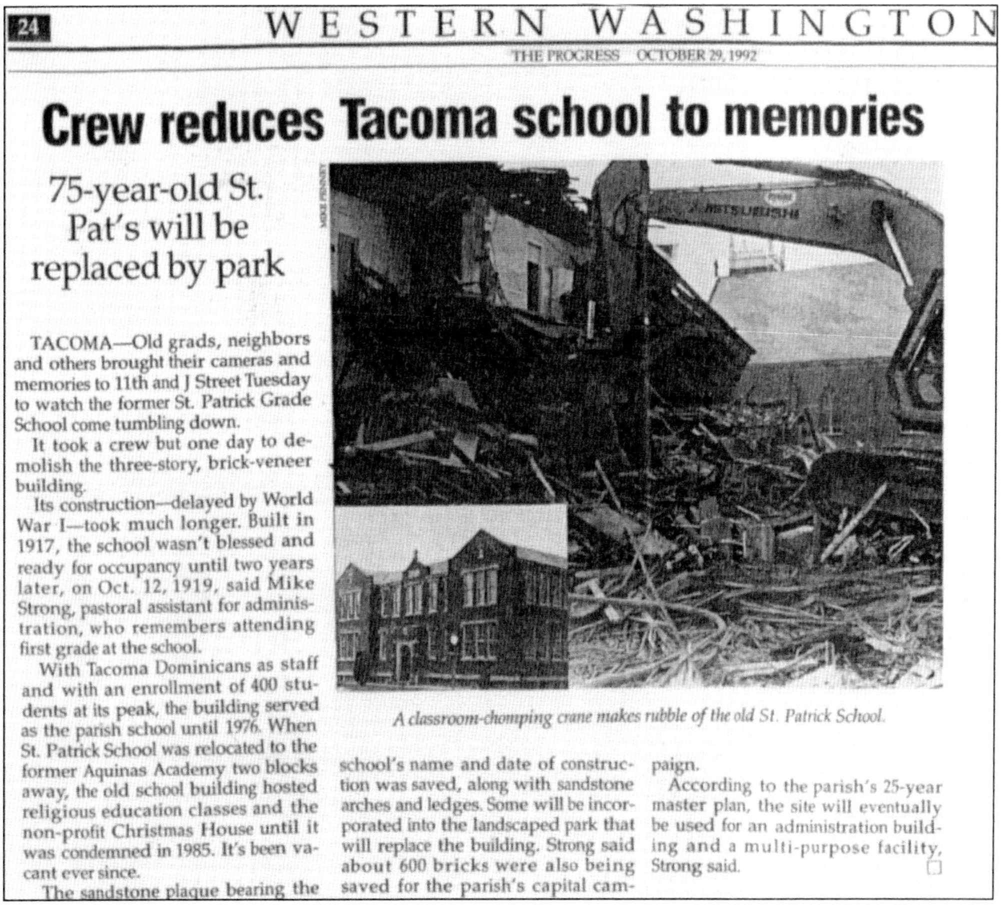

24 WESTERN WASHINGTON

THE PROGRESS OCTOBER 29, 1992

Crew reduces Tacoma school to memories

75-year-old St. Pat's will be replaced by park

TACOMA—Old grads, neighbors and others brought their cameras and memories to 11th and J Street Tuesday to watch the former St. Patrick Grade School come tumbling down.

It took a crew but one day to demolish the three-story, brick-veneer building.

Its construction—delayed by World War I—took much longer. Built in 1917, the school wasn't blessed and ready for occupancy until two years later, on Oct. 12, 1919, said Mike Strong, pastoral assistant for administration, who remembers attending first grade at the school.

With Tacoma Dominicans as staff and with an enrollment of 400 students at its peak, the building served as the parish school until 1976. When St. Patrick School was relocated to the former Aquinas Academy two blocks away, the old school building hosted religious education classes and the non-profit Christmas House until it was condemned in 1985. It's been vacant ever since.

The sandstone plaque bearing the school's name and date of construction was saved, along with sandstone arches and ledges. Some will be incorporated into the landscaped park that will replace the building. Strong said about 600 bricks were also being saved for the parish's capital campaign.

According to the parish's 25-year master plan, the site will eventually be used for an administration building and a multi-purpose facility, Strong said.

A classroom-chomping crane makes rubble of the old St. Patrick School.

In 1974, Aquinas, St. Leo, and Bellarmine consolidated to form one high school, at Bellarmine. With the Aquinas Building now empty, St. Patrick School moved down the hill. The old St. Patrick School was torn down in 1992, and the area was later used to build a home for the St. Patrick parish priest. A small park now contains sandstone arches and ledges from the school. (Courtesy of Tacoma Dominican archives.)

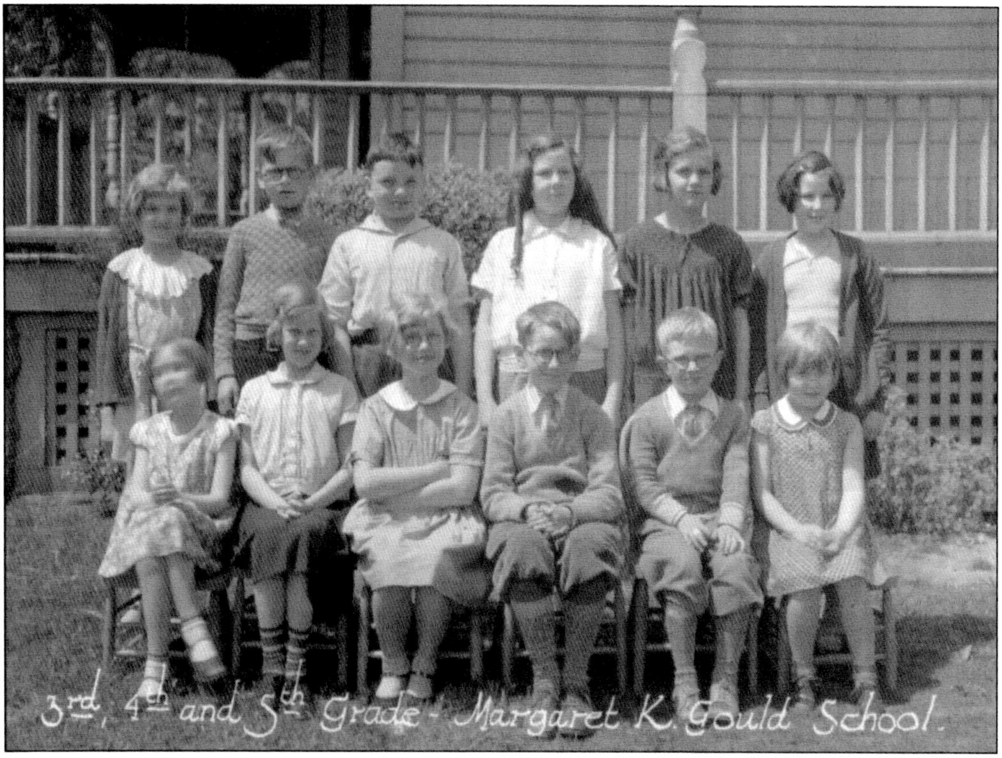

The Margaret K. Gould School was located in a 12-room house at 223 North J Street. Built in 1890 by Ruehr and Bergfeld, the Foursquare house had several owners before Gould purchased it and placed her advertisement for students in 1930. This photograph is of the third-, fourth-, and fifth-grade students in 1932. The school also had kindergarten, first, and second grades.

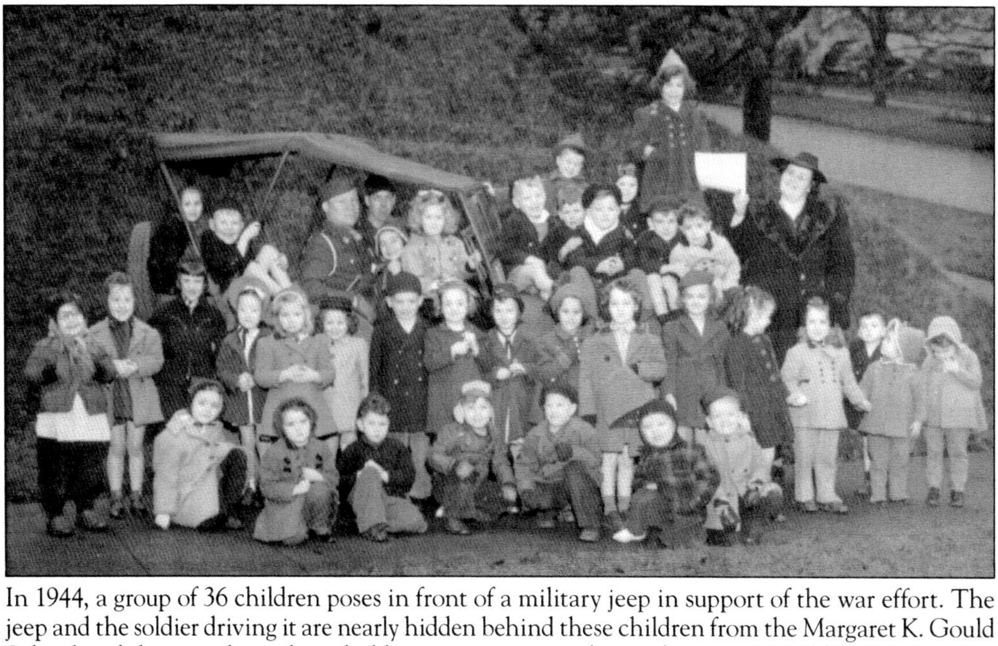

In 1944, a group of 36 children poses in front of a military jeep in support of the war effort. The jeep and the soldier driving it are nearly hidden behind these children from the Margaret K. Gould School and their teacher, who is holding up a poster, perhaps advertising World War II bonds.

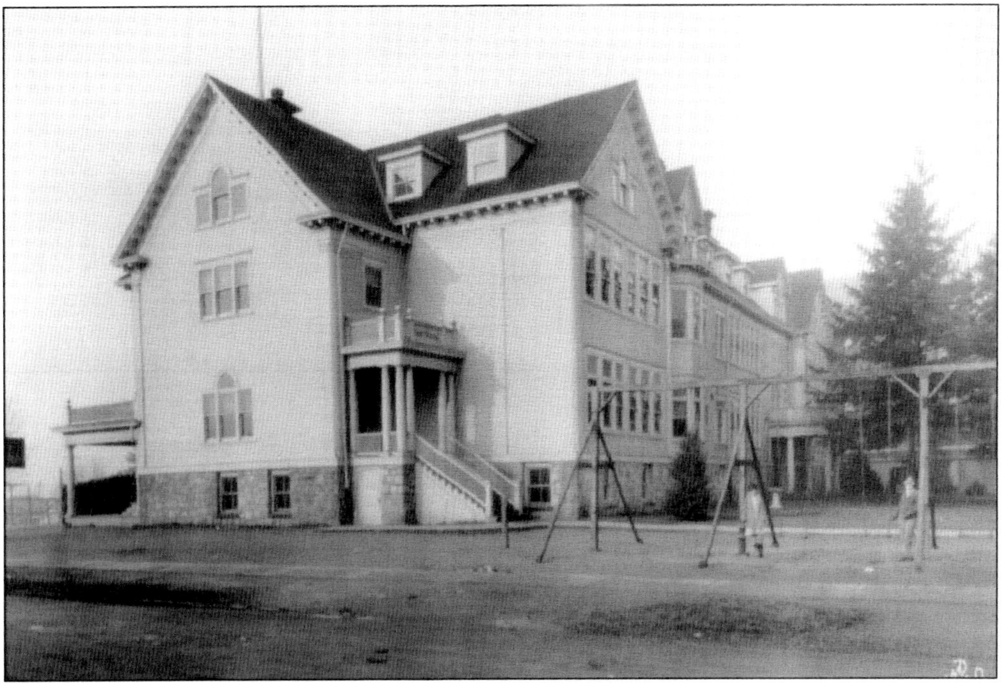

Overcrowded almost as soon as it opened, the wood-framed Grant School opened in 1900 at 1018 North Prospect Street in the Job Carr's Hill area. It was named in honor of Ulysses S. Grant. At this time, two other Tacoma schools, Sheridan and Sherman, were built and named after Union generals.

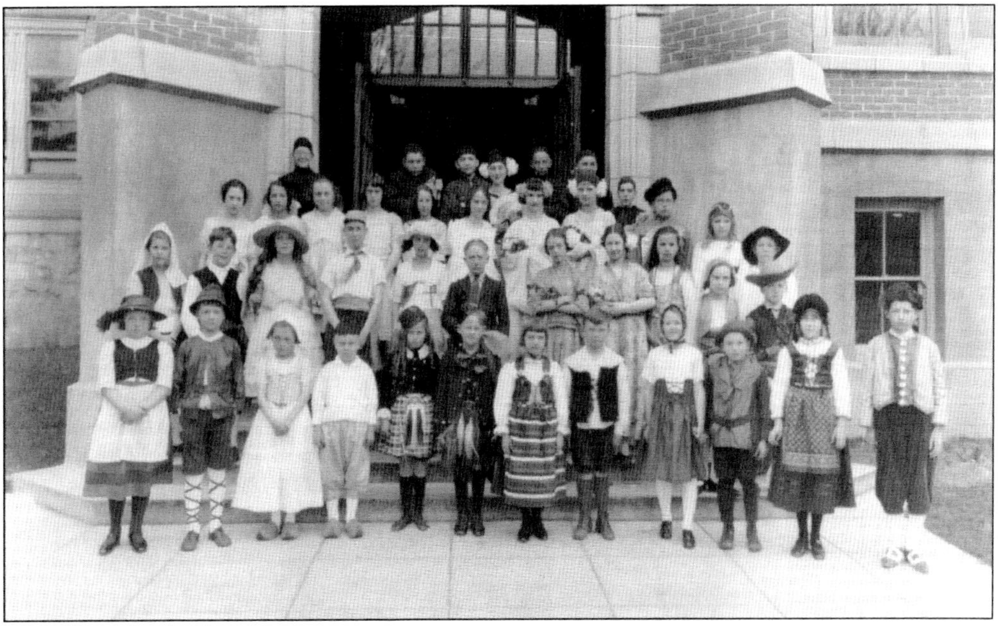

In 1920, a brick school building was added, but the wooden school was not removed until 1955, when it had deteriorated and more space was needed. In April 1922, a total of 40 schoolchildren stand on the steps of the brick schoolhouse. They are dressed in costumes from other countries, probably on the day that they sang and danced in a musical play, *A Meeting of Nations*, before the Grant Parent-Teacher Association (PTA).

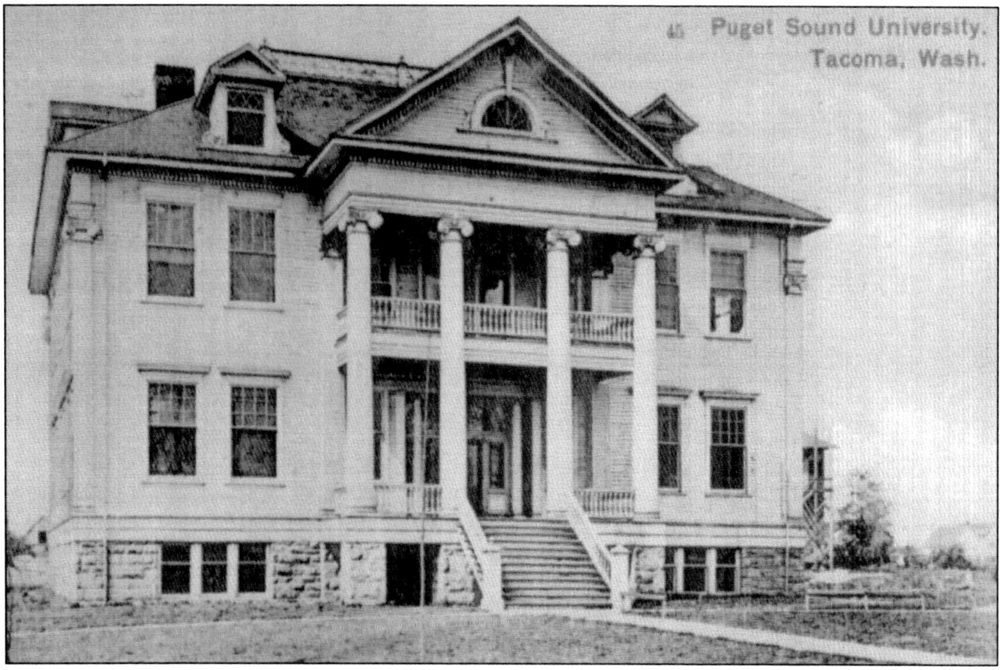

In 1888, the Methodist Episcopal Church founded Puget Sound University. In 1903, architect George W. Bullard designed the buildings, and the first permanent campus was opened at 602 North Sprague Avenue in the Job Carr's Hill neighborhood. This postcard was sent in 1908 from a student to his sister during finals week. In 1924, the college, then called the College of Puget Sound, moved, and the buildings were demolished.

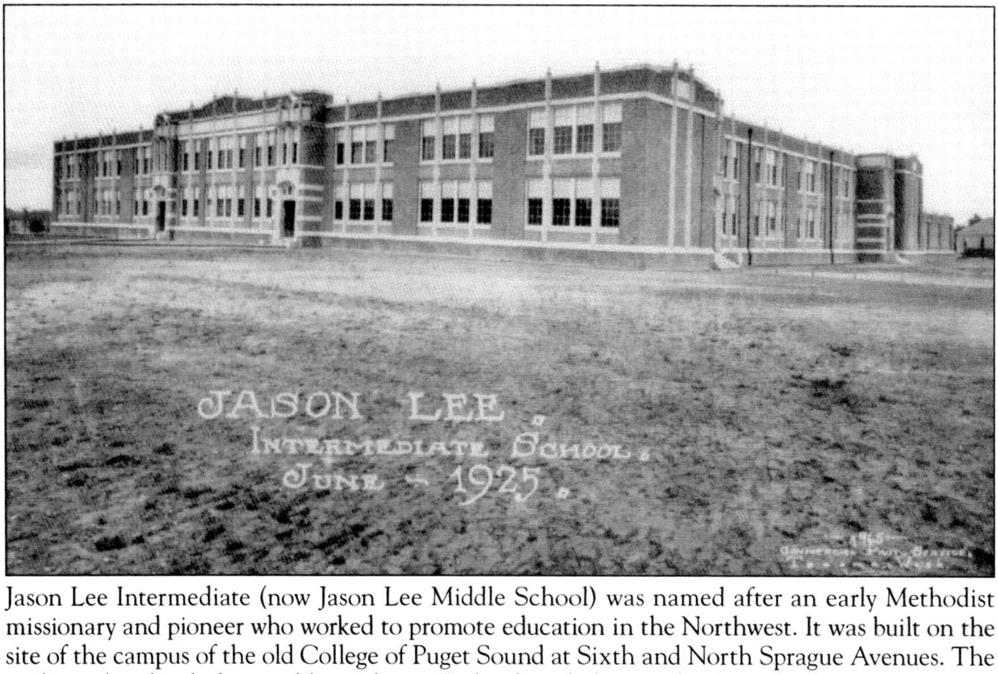

Jason Lee Intermediate (now Jason Lee Middle School) was named after an early Methodist missionary and pioneer who worked to promote education in the Northwest. It was built on the site of the campus of the old College of Puget Sound at Sixth and North Sprague Avenues. The Tudor-style school, designed by architect Roland Borhek, was the first and largest of six new intermediate schools built to relieve overcrowding.

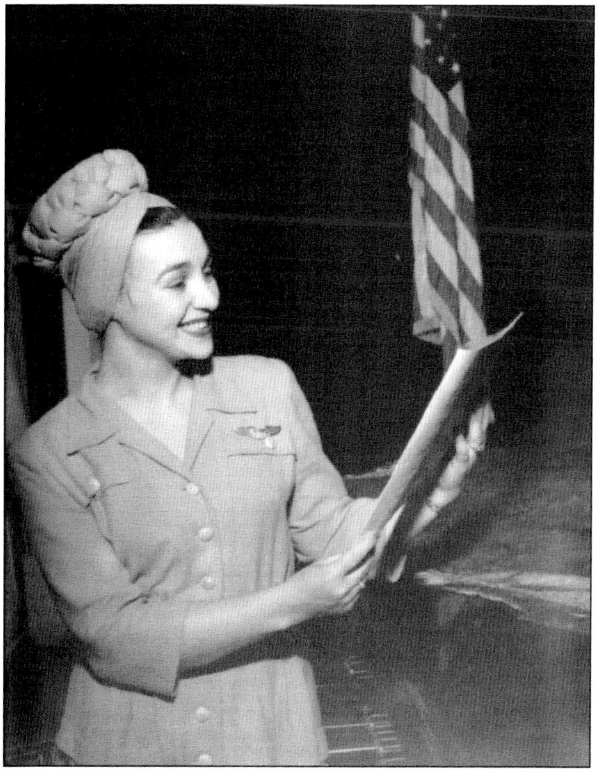

In 1942, mezzo-soprano Mona Paulee (right) performed as the guest artist of the Tacoma Philharmonic at the opening concert at Jason Lee. The petite and vivacious star of the Metropolitan Opera is shown at rehearsal before she sang selections from *Carmen*. While in town, Paulee attended the War Chest luncheon at the Elks Lodge. In 1949, Jason Lee was still hosting the Tacoma Philharmonic. Jean Winter's students at the junior high sit two to a seat for voice class (below). One of the students directs at the front of the classroom, while Winter accompanies on the piano. In 2001, Jason Lee Middle School received awards for its restoration of this historic building.

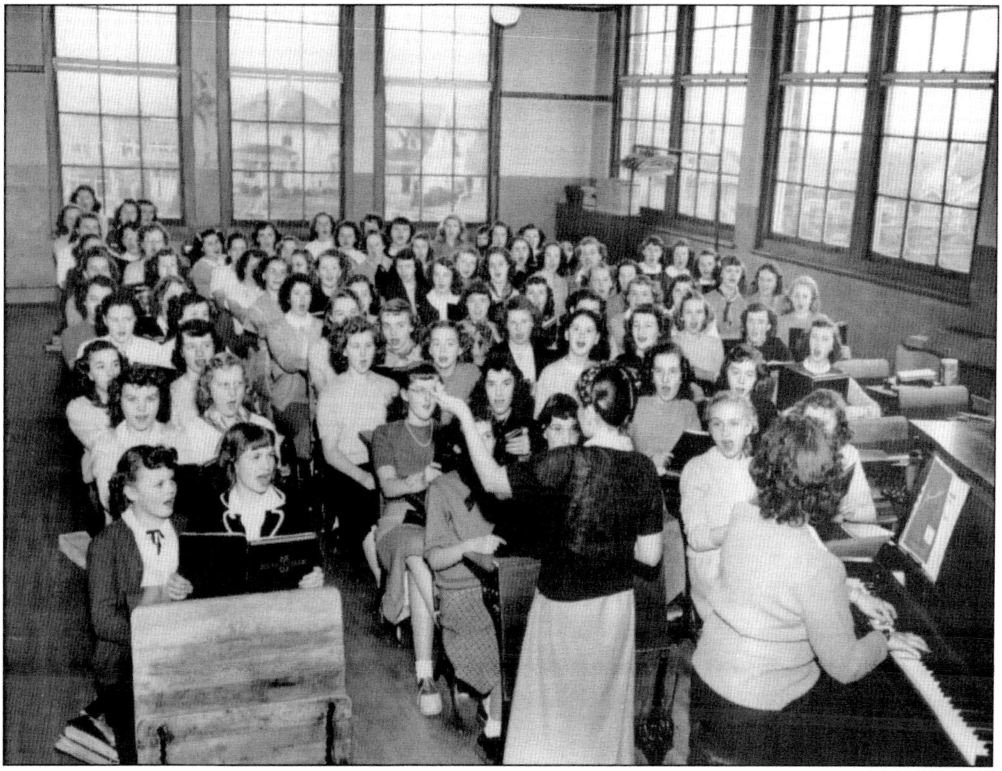

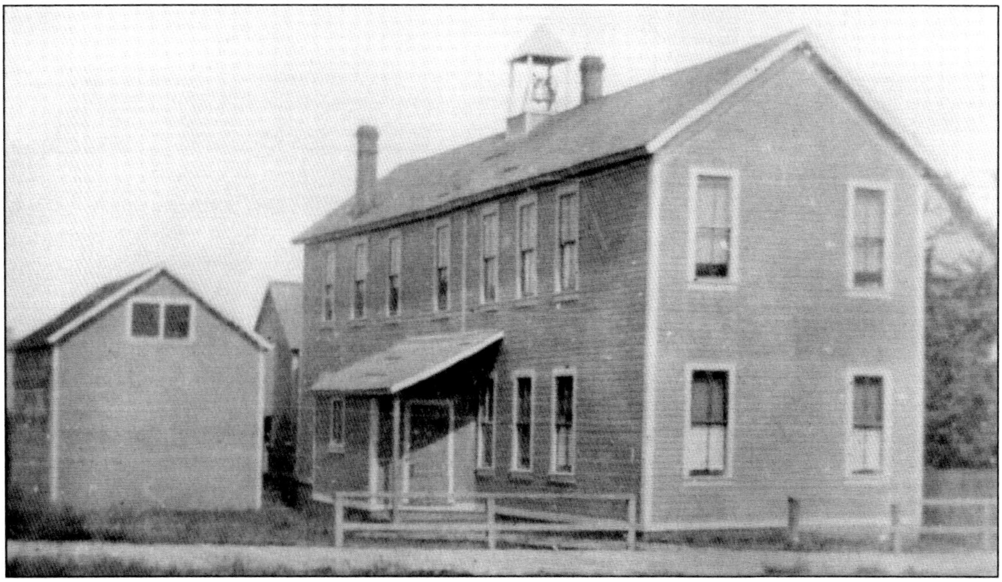

At 313–315 North K Street was Tacoma Academy. Built in 1890 as a day and boarding school, for 13 years it provided classical and scientific courses to prepare high school students for college. It was highly regarded, and eventually its founder and principal, Dr. A.P. Powelson, discussed with other prominent individuals the possibility of a college in Tacoma. (Courtesy of Charlotte Medlock.)

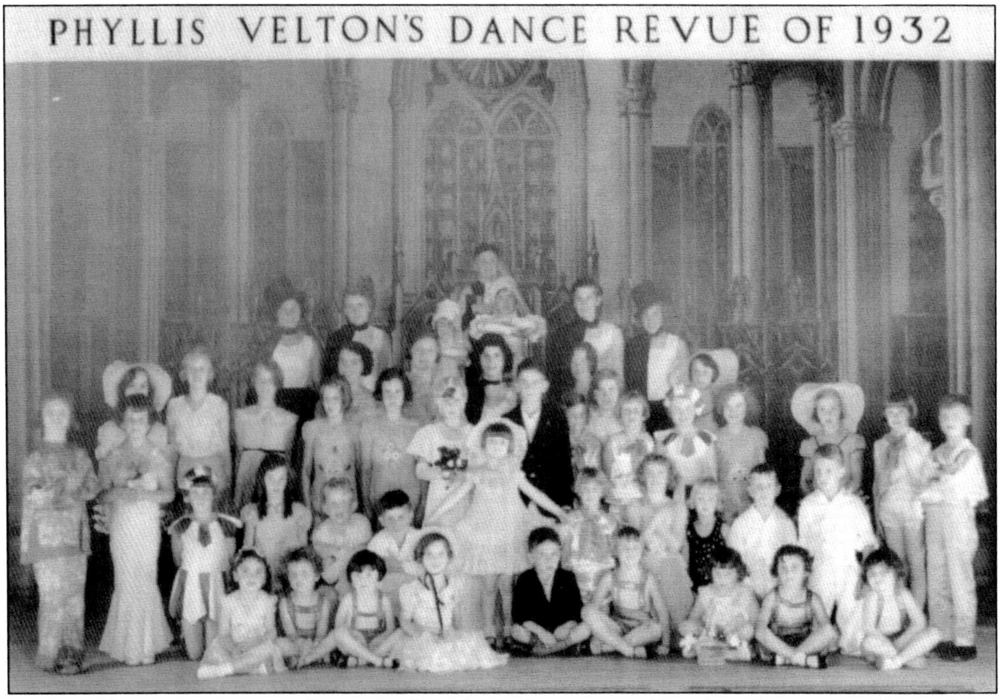

Phyllis Velton was a Tacoma dancer and teacher. She presented her first dance revue for students in 1931. In 1935, the city's directory lists her studio at 220 North I Street. Velton taught both classical and modern dance and was known for her "ultra-modern" dance interpretations using Egyptian and Assyrian themes. The faces of the young dancers in 1932 glow under the bright lights, with costumes and a Gothic backdrop.

Four

Movers and Shakers

The essence of the North Slope was its residents. And the people who energized the neighborhood were the industrialists, the bankers, the land agents, and the business owners. Also vital were the architects and the builders who completed their designs of dwellings befitting the dynamic and creative men and women who lived on Job Carr's Hill.

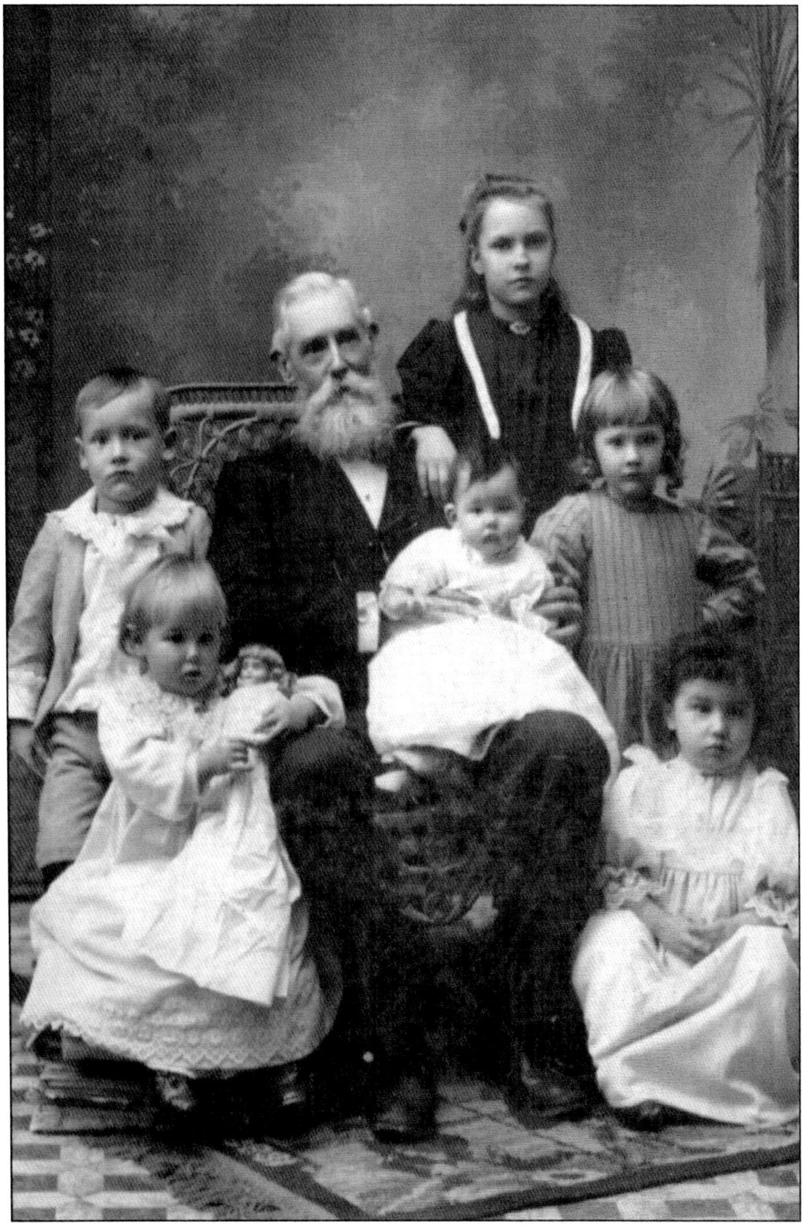

Jeremiah Hartley "J.H." Lister had come from England to visit his brother David Lister, who was the first mayor of New Tacoma. In 1876, David had started the Tacoma Foundry, which was usually called Lister's Foundry. The foundry made sawmill machinery, steamboat engines, and other equipment vital to the region. J.H. Lister went back to England and in 1884 returned to Tacoma with his family, which included his wife, Ellen; his four sons, Arthur, Ernest, Albert, and Alfred; and daughter Sarah Jane. Another daughter, Ada, stayed in England. After 10 days crossing the Atlantic, they took a train across the United States and arrived at the Northern Pacific station in Tacoma. In 1886, J.H., with two of his sons, founded Standard Iron Works on East Twenty-third Street. While visiting relatives in 1904, J.H. Lister died in Kings Cross, Halifax, Yorkshire, England. In the photograph, J.H. Lister is shown with some of his first grandchildren in the mid-1890s. On his lap is Florence, the daughter of Ernest Lister. (Courtesy of Sherry Munson.)

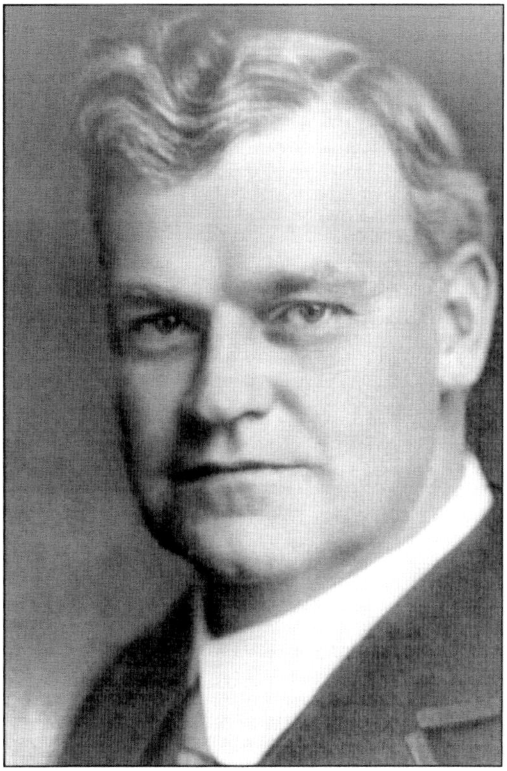

Ernest Lister was born in Halifax, Yorkshire, England, on June 15, 1871. The youngest child of J.H. and Ellen Lister, he came to Tacoma when he was only 13. According to Alfred Lister's great-granddaughter Sherry Munson, Ernest was a strong supporter of John R. Rogers in his candidacy for governor in 1896 and was one of his closest friends and advisers. After Governor Rogers's death, Ernest resigned as commissioner of state institutions and entered, with his brother Albert, the contracting and building trades, which resulted in the organization of the Lister Manufacturing Company, a lumber business. As the Democratic candidate in 1912, Ernest Lister was elected the governor of Washington. In 1916, he was reelected. In Tacoma's 1910 city directory, his daughter Florence (below) was listed as living in the household at 1402 North Fifth Street. (Both, courtesy of Sherry Munson.)

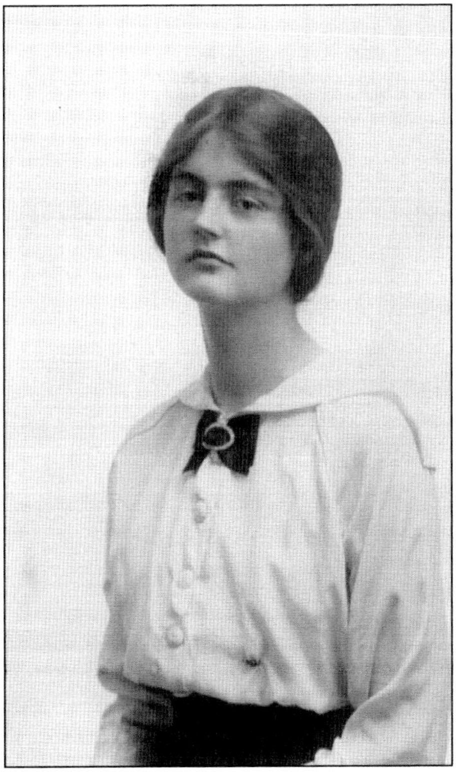

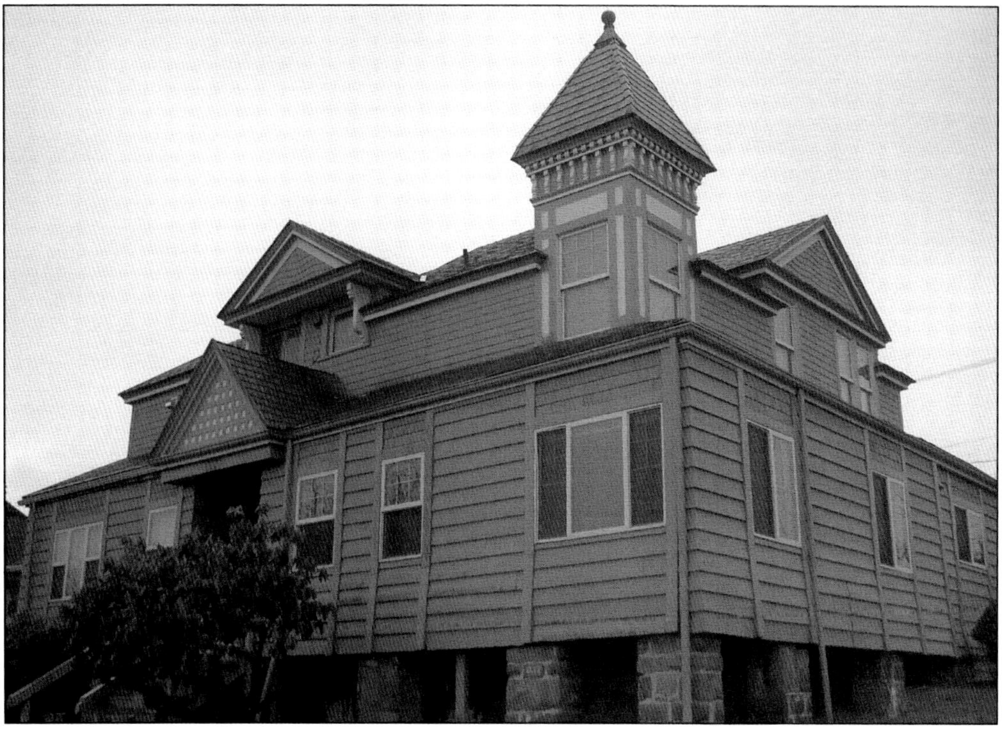

Ernest Lister's uncle David S. Lister Sr. became New Tacoma's first mayor in 1881. There would be a second mayor, and then New and Old Tacoma would merge to become Tacoma in 1884. David Lister accumulated considerable property and decided to retire to rest and travel. In 1890, the house on 1022 North I Street was built and occupied by Mr. and Mrs. David Lister. He died in 1894. (Gyda May photograph.)

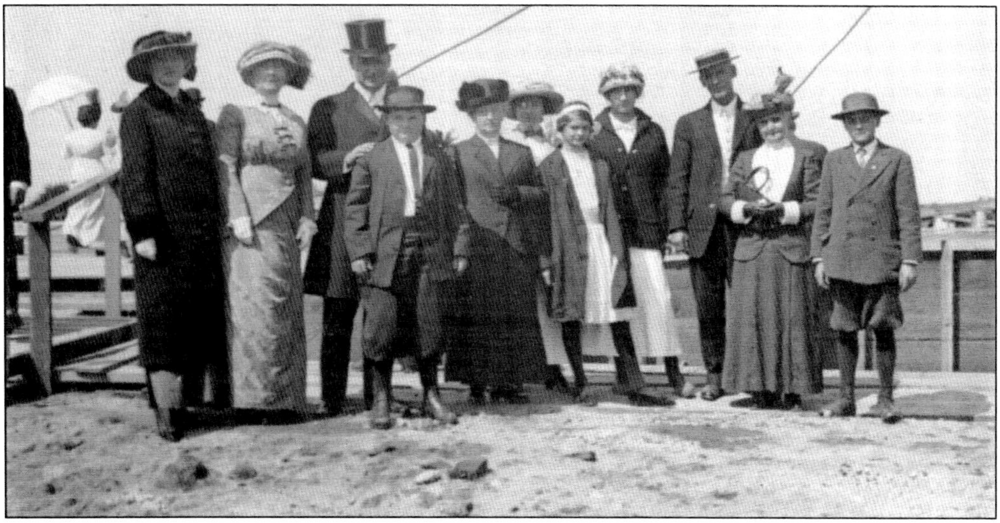

During his duties as governor, Ernest Lister, third from left in the top hat, takes a rare pause for a photograph with his family. In front of the governor is his son John. Those standing next to John are, from left to right, his mother, Ellen; his sister, Florence (partially hidden); and Alfred's family—Dorothy, Lillian, Alfred, wife Clara, and Kingston. The two ladies on the left are unidentified. (Courtesy of Sherry Munson.)

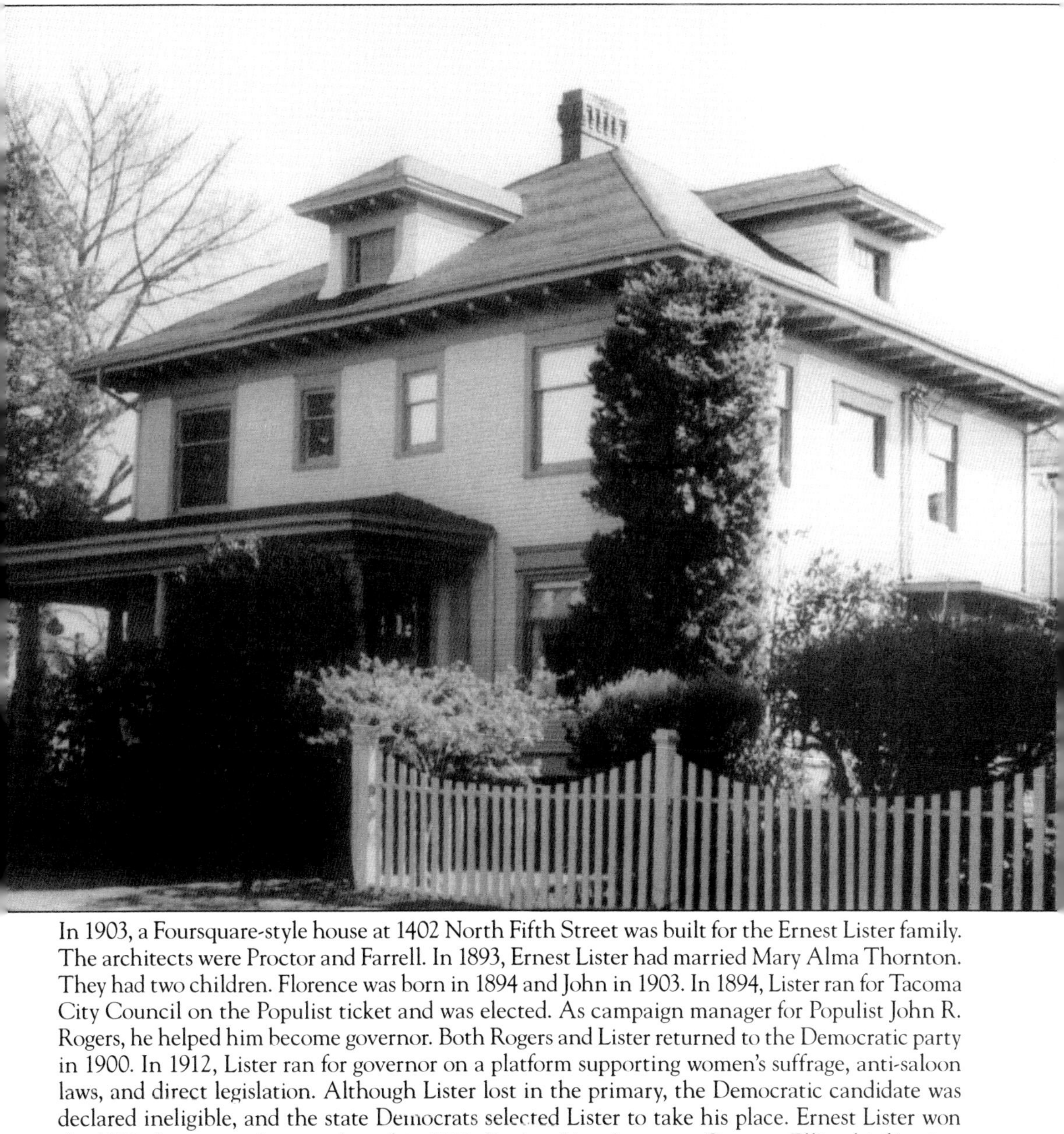

In 1903, a Foursquare-style house at 1402 North Fifth Street was built for the Ernest Lister family. The architects were Proctor and Farrell. In 1893, Ernest Lister had married Mary Alma Thornton. They had two children. Florence was born in 1894 and John in 1903. In 1894, Lister ran for Tacoma City Council on the Populist ticket and was elected. As campaign manager for Populist John R. Rogers, he helped him become governor. Both Rogers and Lister returned to the Democratic party in 1900. In 1912, Lister ran for governor on a platform supporting women's suffrage, anti-saloon laws, and direct legislation. Although Lister lost in the primary, the Democratic candidate was declared ineligible, and the state Democrats selected Lister to take his place. Ernest Lister won the 1912 election and was reelected in 1916. During Lister's tenure, Overton Ellis, chief justice, lived at 613 North K Street; Guy Kelley, the speaker, lived at 924 North L Street; and Louis F. Hart, lieutenant governor (and governor upon Lister's death), lived at 617 North Oakes Street.

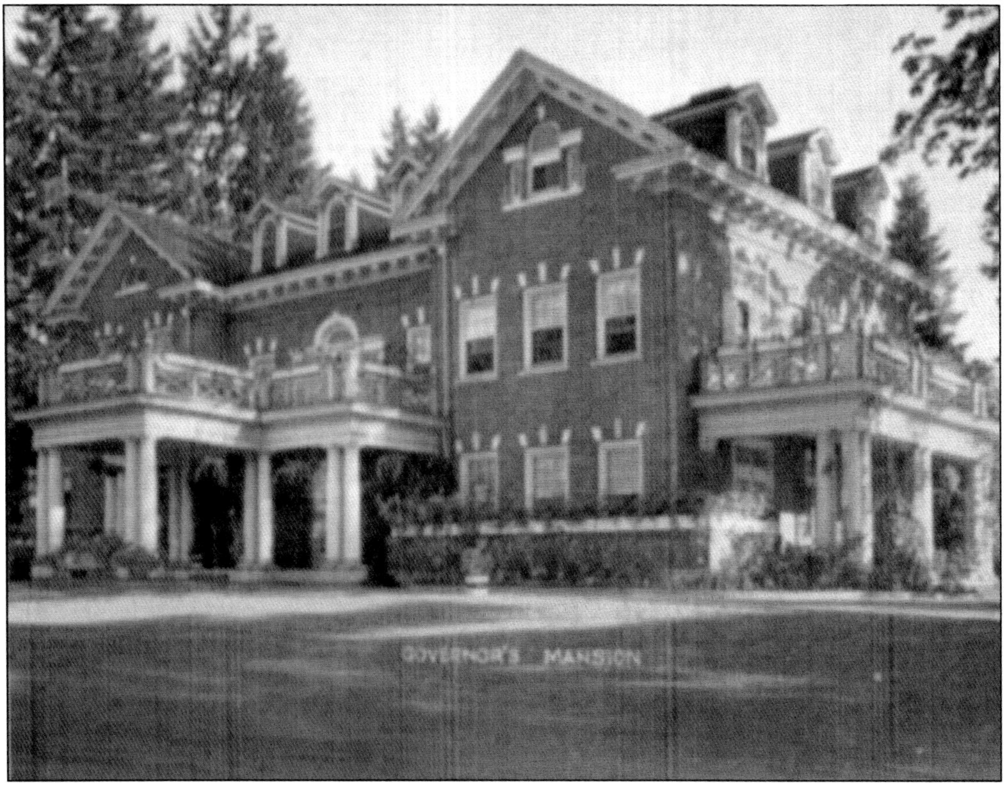

The Georgian-style governor's mansion in Olympia was designed and built by Tacoma architects Russell and Babcock and has 19 rooms and sloping lawns with flowering shrubs surrounded by evergreen trees. It has a panoramic view of Olympia, Puget Sound, and the Olympic Mountains. As governor, Ernest Lister helped establish the eight-hour workday in Washington. He was active in the state effort to help win World War I. (Courtesy of Sherry Munson.)

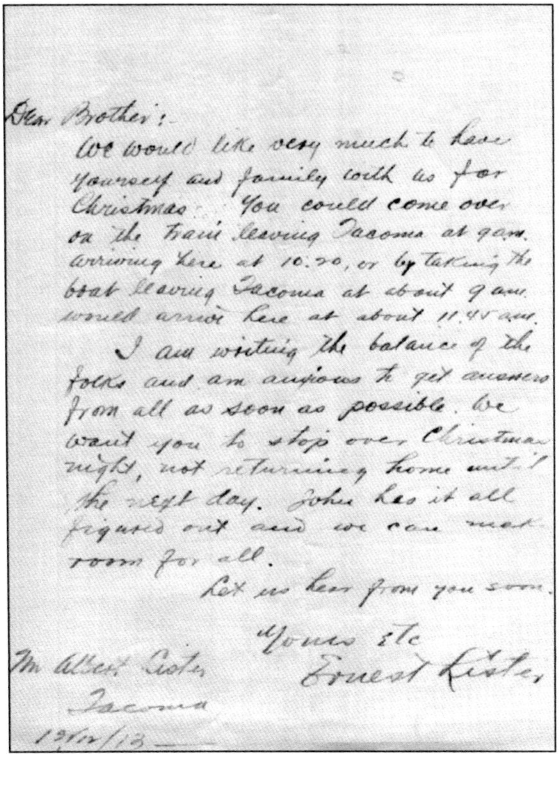

Dear Brother:-
We would like very much to have yourself and family with us for Christmas. You could come over on the train leaving Tacoma at 9 a.m. arriving here at 10.20, or by taking the boat leaving Tacoma at about 9 a.m. would arrive here at about 11.45 a.m.
I am writing the balance of the folks and am anxious to get answers from all as soon as possible. We want you to stop over Christmas night, not returning home until the next day. John has it all figured out and we can make room for all.
Let us hear from you soon.
Yours etc
Ernest Lister
Mr Albert Lister
Tacoma
19/12/13 —

This letter to Albert was written December 19, 1913. Note the British date, with the day written before the month. The governor included his brother in the guests invited for a Lister family Christmas at the mansion. He mentions the train or boat leaving Tacoma in the morning. He assures Albert that he can stay overnight, as John "has it all figured out"—John was 10 years old at this point in time. (Courtesy of Sherry Munson.)

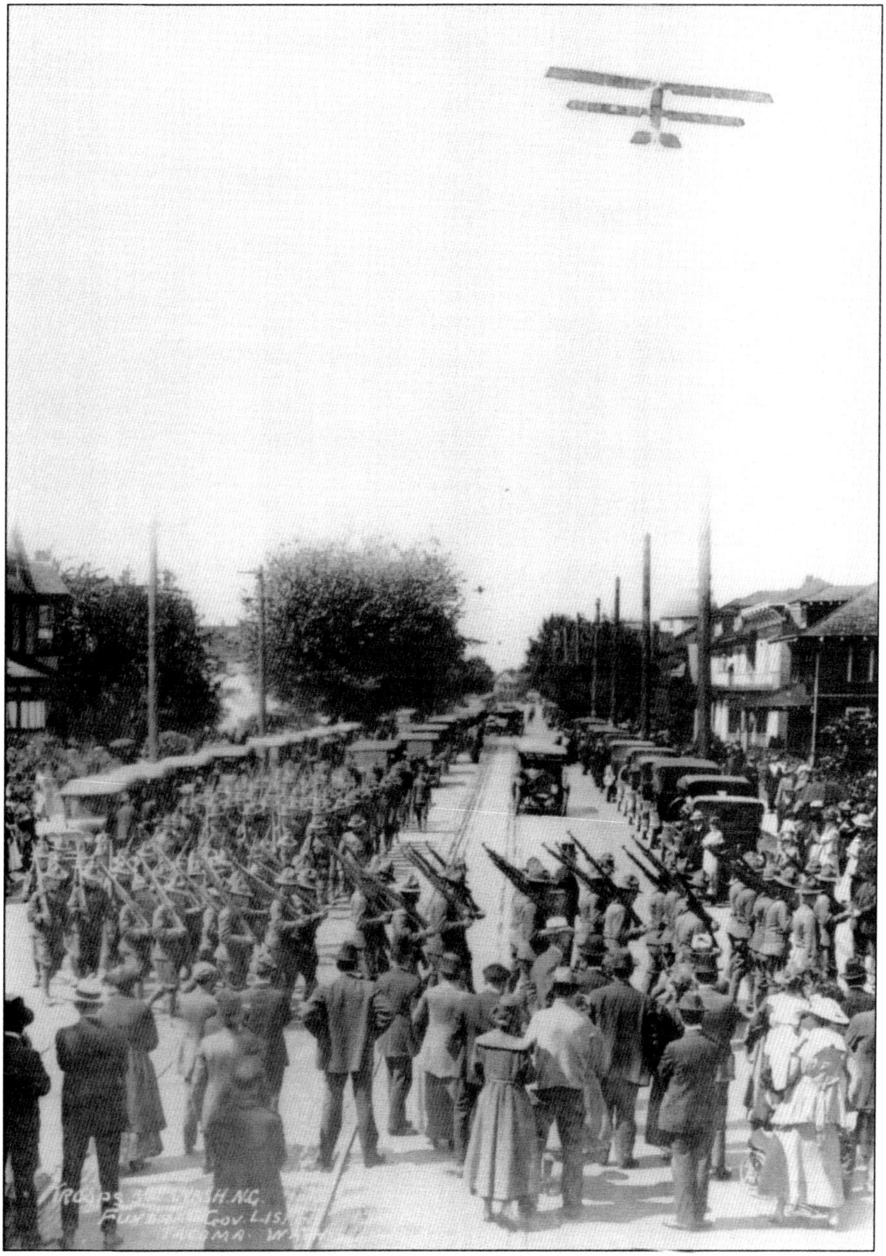

Governor Lister passed away June 14, 1919, one day before his 48th birthday. Sherry Munson writes, "Due to the stress of World War I activities, Governor Lister's health broke down." In spite of a long illness, he fulfilled his duties bravely. The *Tacoma News Tribune* of June 14, 1919, states: "It was his lovable human qualities besides his broad abilities that endeared him to his friends. Success never separated him from his old friends. Pressure of strenuous political duties did not hinder the affection that he gave so freely to his family. He did his duty honestly and fearlessly." A friend stated, "He has always been a man who stood for everything that was honorable and just." Hundreds gathered in Tacoma for the Masonic funeral, shown here on North I Street. The biplane dropped flowers in his memory. Ernest Lister was followed in death by his wife, Alma, in 1923, daughter Florence in 1925 (nearly 33 years old), and son John in 1930 at 27 years of age.

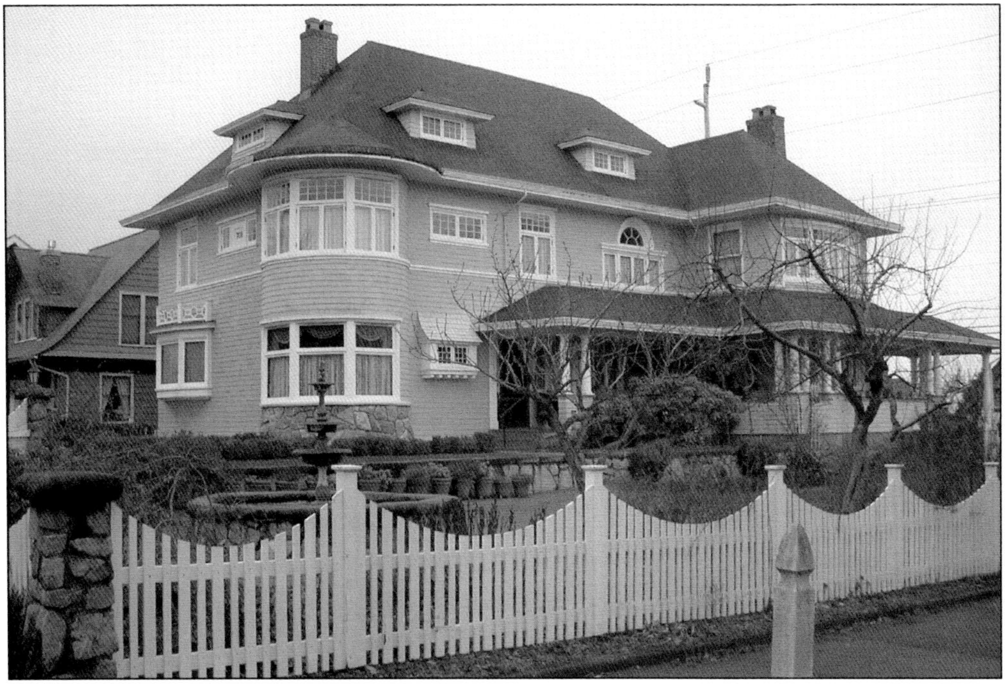

This Queen Anne–style house was built in 1901 at 701 North J Street for Henry A. and Birdella Rhodes. It was distinguished by a circular bay window with a stone foundation. The large front porch faced the Garfield Gulch rather than J Street. The gulch was later filled in, and North Seventh Street came to a dead end, enabling lawns and gardens to be planted. In 1904, Henry's brother Charles William "Will" built a house nearby at 702 North K Street. Albert Rhodes, another brother, lived at 702 North I Street, also on Garfield Gulch and built in 1902. In the photograph below, Henry Rhodes shows off his first automobile, with three unidentified lady passengers enjoying the ride. (Above, Gyda May photograph; below, courtesy of Charlotte Medlock.)

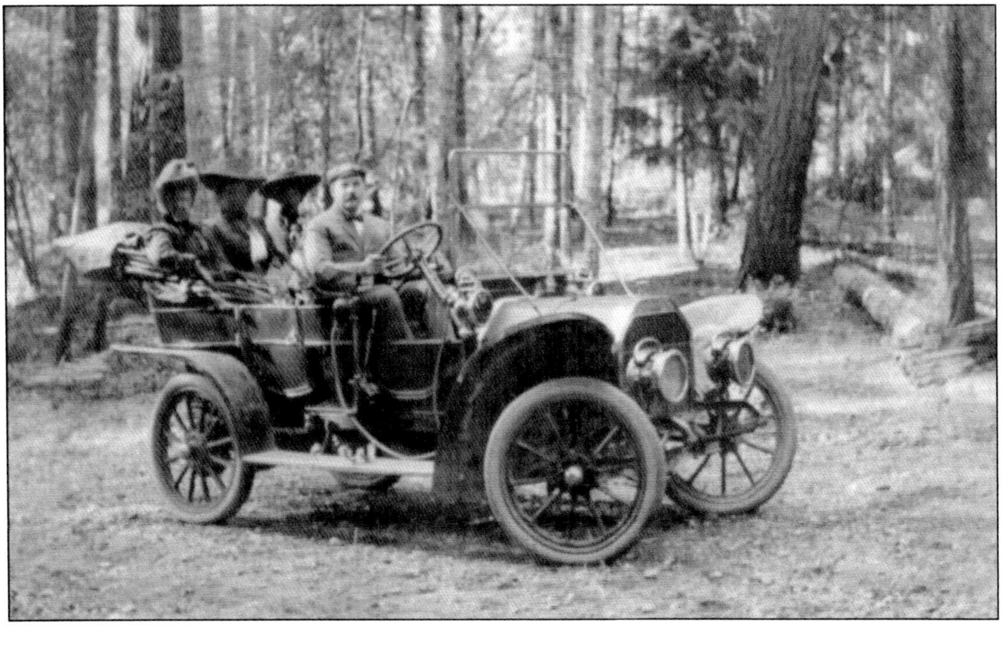

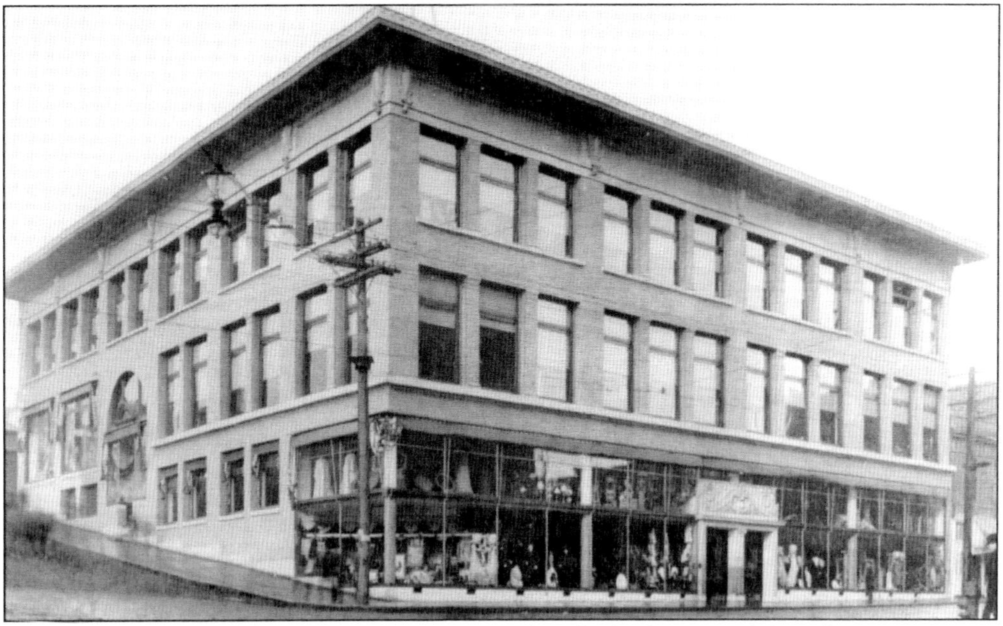

According to author Robert Doubleday, Henry and Will Rhodes opened their first store in 1892 and delivered tea, coffee, spices, extracts, crockery, and china by horse and wagon. They moved twice but kept their inventory small. Competitors with large stocks of imported crockery and china took large losses when tariffs changed. Rhodes Brothers Store flourished, and Henry and Will built a three-story structure designed in 1903 by Ambrose Russell and Frederick Heath.

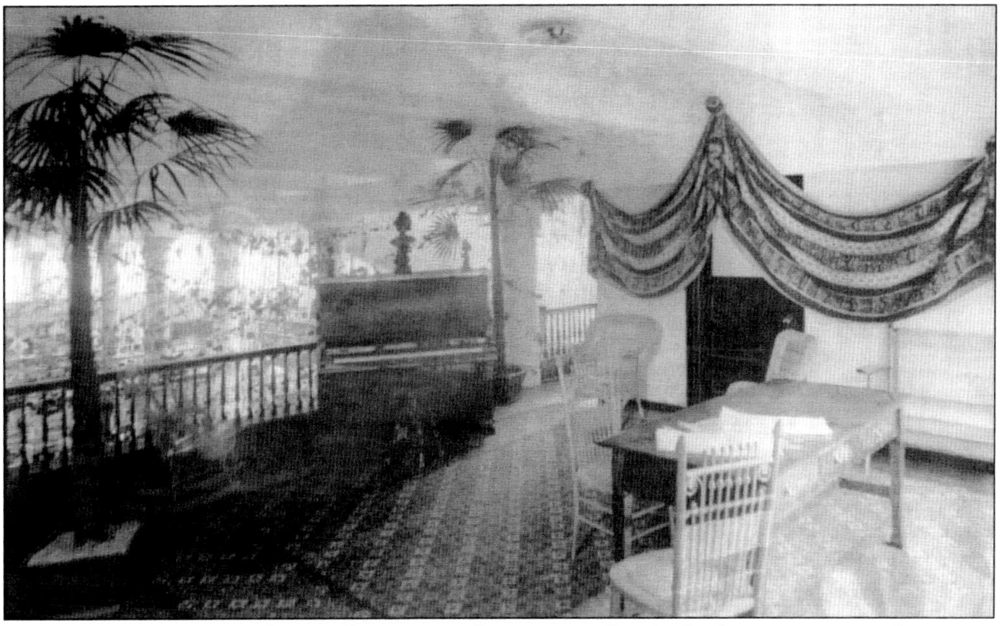

Built for luxury, the Rhodes Brothers Store, shown around 1904, had a mezzanine with a piano overlooking the first floor. The ladies' lounge was located here, with comfortable chairs where shoppers could rest or visit. The piano could be heard throughout the first floor. In 1907, Albert Rhodes moved to Seattle and opened a department store, Rhodes, which obviously had a similar name but was completely separate from the original business.

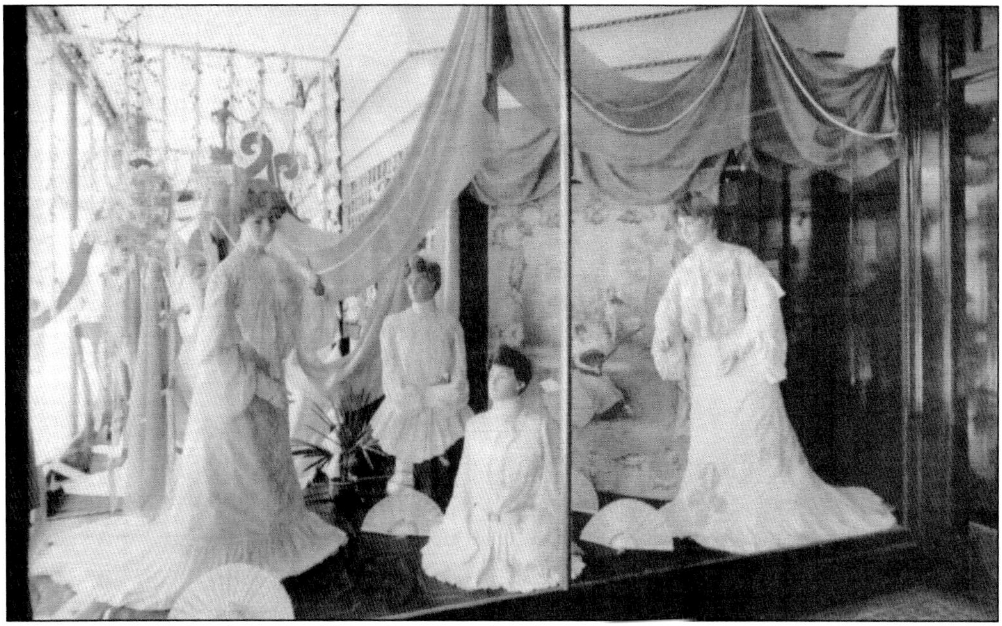

This window display shows wedding dresses at the Rhodes Department Store around 1904. When Henry A. Rhodes opened his three-story grand emporium at 950 Broadway in November 1903, it quickly became famous for its lavish decorations and extensive window displays. Huge plate-glass windows presented the most current fashions by seasons. The store employed a full-time window trimmer and decorator, Herbert A. Foster.

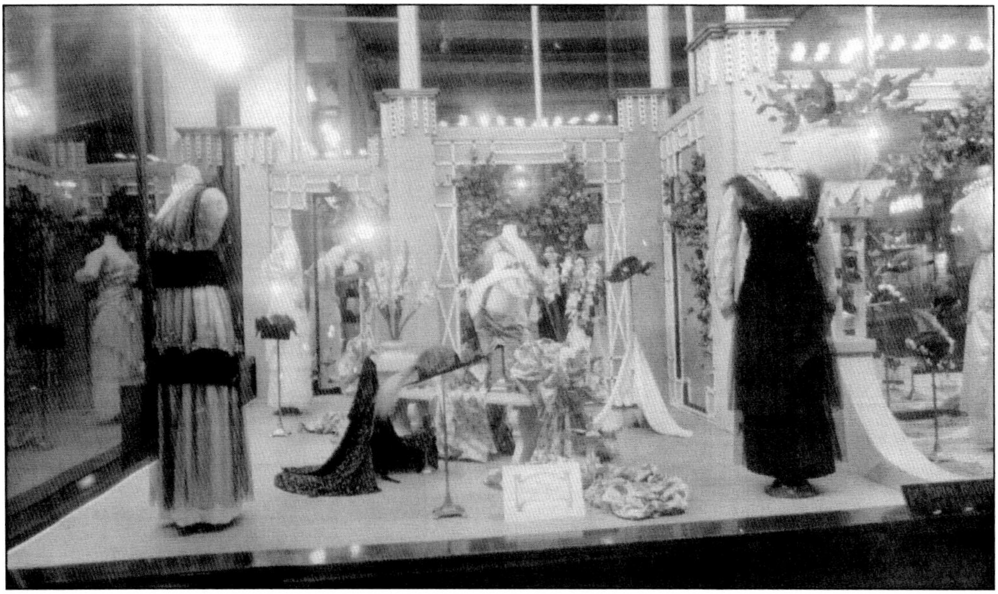

Around 1910, Rhodes Brothers Store displays women's fall fashions in a corner window. Business was booming due to the appeal of current styles, expert merchandising, and advertising. Signs led travelers to the store from miles around, promising them that "all roads lead to Rhodes." Buyers made frequent trips to New York for the latest fashions. In 1911, three stories were added to the building. Rhodes sold the store in 1925 to the Schlesinger chain of Pacific Coast Stores, which retained the Rhodes Brothers name.

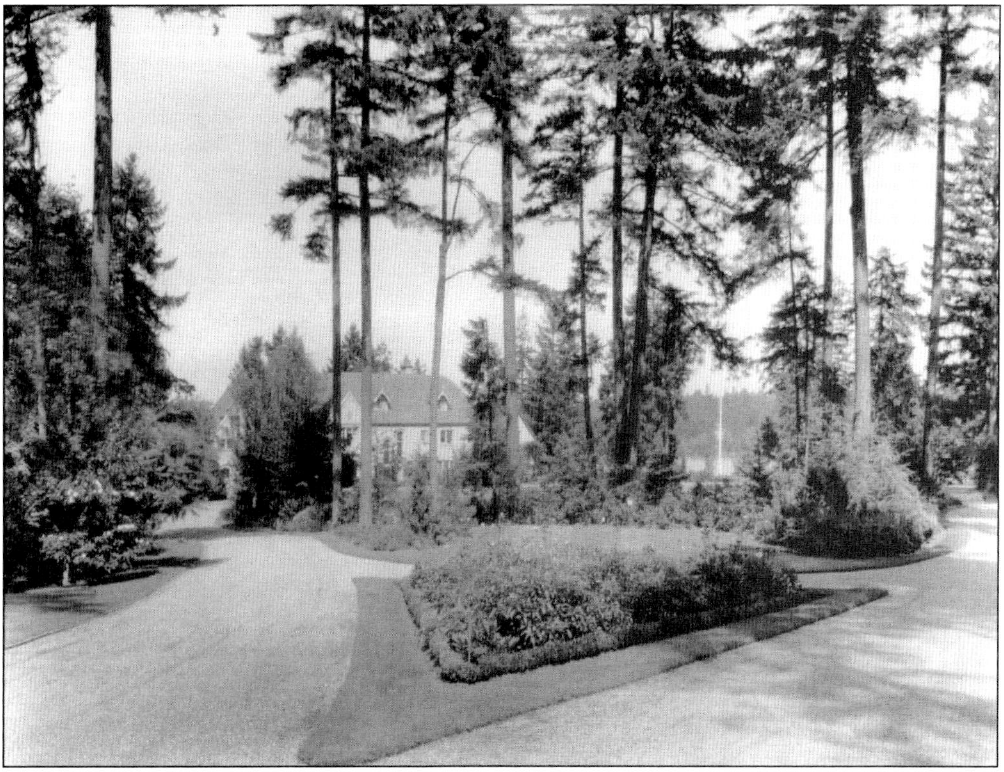

A driveway (above) leads to Rhodesleigh, the Henry A. and Birdella Rhodes estate designed by Heath, Gove and Bell on Lake Steilacoom. The site was originally the location of the Rhodes' summer cottage. A larger home (right) was built in 1921 as a family tribute to son Edward B. Rhodes, who was killed in World War I. Daughter Vera also moved there with her husband, Audsley Fraser. The 12-room Tudor Revival mansion was built of Tufa stone from Oregon. The interior was finished in oak with high paneled walls and ornamental plastered ceilings. A portrait of Lt. Edward B. Rhodes hung over the mantel in the library. (Right, courtesy of Ben Cody.)

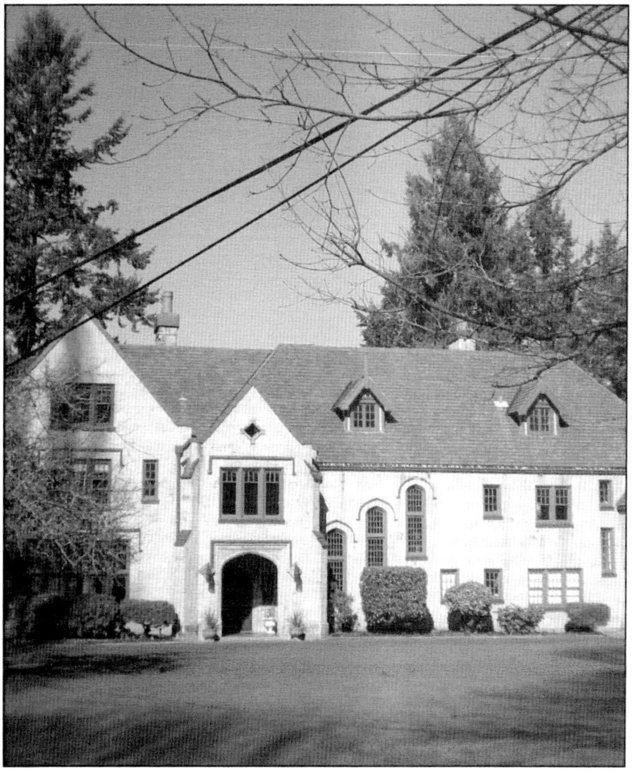

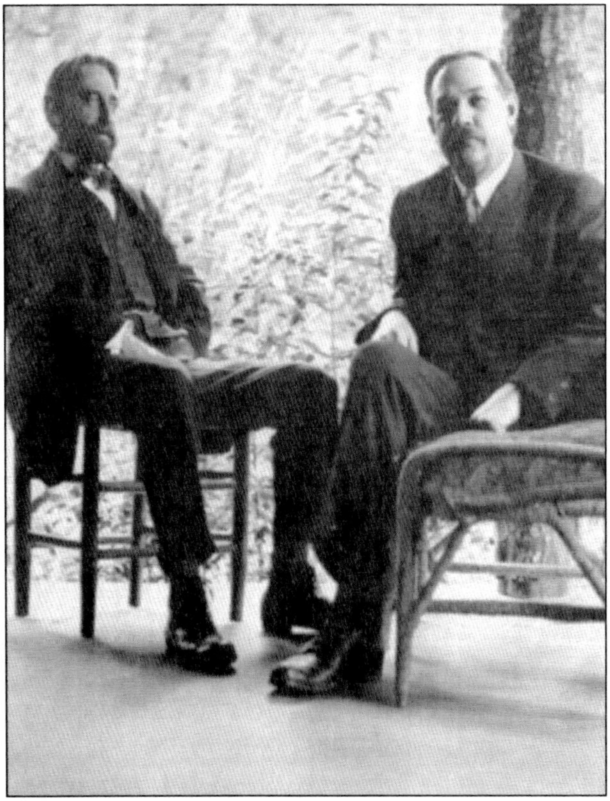

George H. Plummer (left in photograph at left) and Henry A. Rhodes often sat together on the porch to socialize. Each important in his own field of endeavor, Henry Rhodes was president of a very successful department store, and G.H. Plummer was land agent for the Northern Pacific Railroad. They seemed to have little in common except their love for cars, but perhaps that made it easier to be together, considering there was no need for competition. Taking a rest after a leisurely cruise on fat-tire bicycles (below) in Tacoma in 1899 are, from left to right, ? Clark, ? Clark, Margaret Cooper, Leticia Mason, two unidentified people, Emma Fries (later Mrs. G.H. Plummer), and probably Harry Kahler. Families like the Masons and the Plummers were in the social set in the North End of town and were often seen together. (Courtesy of Charlotte Medlock.)

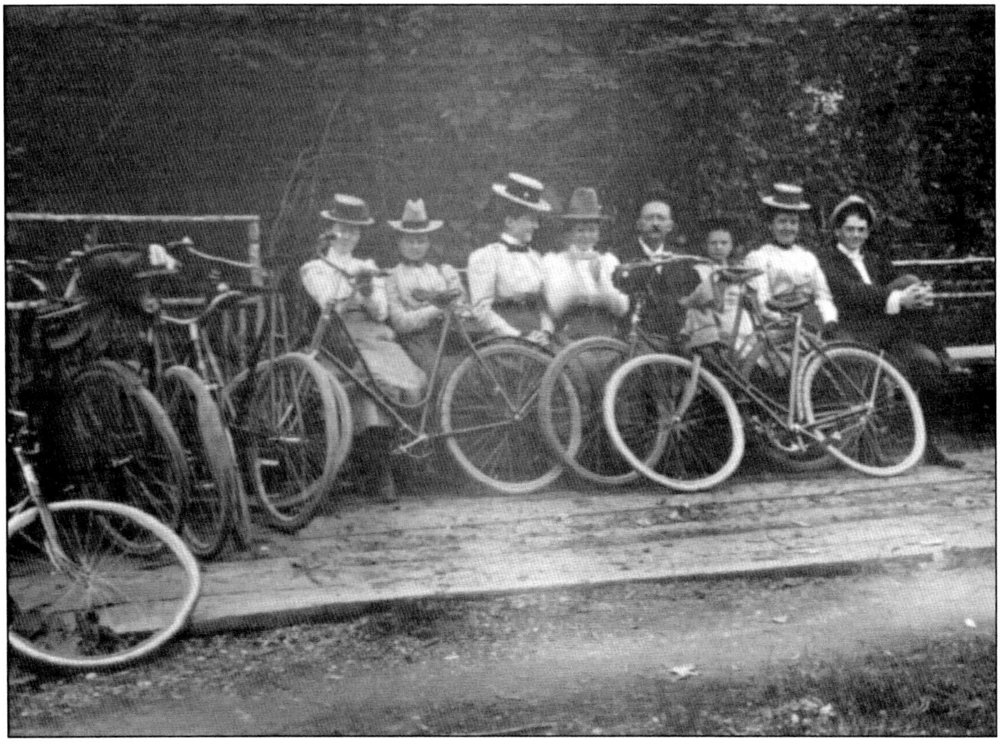

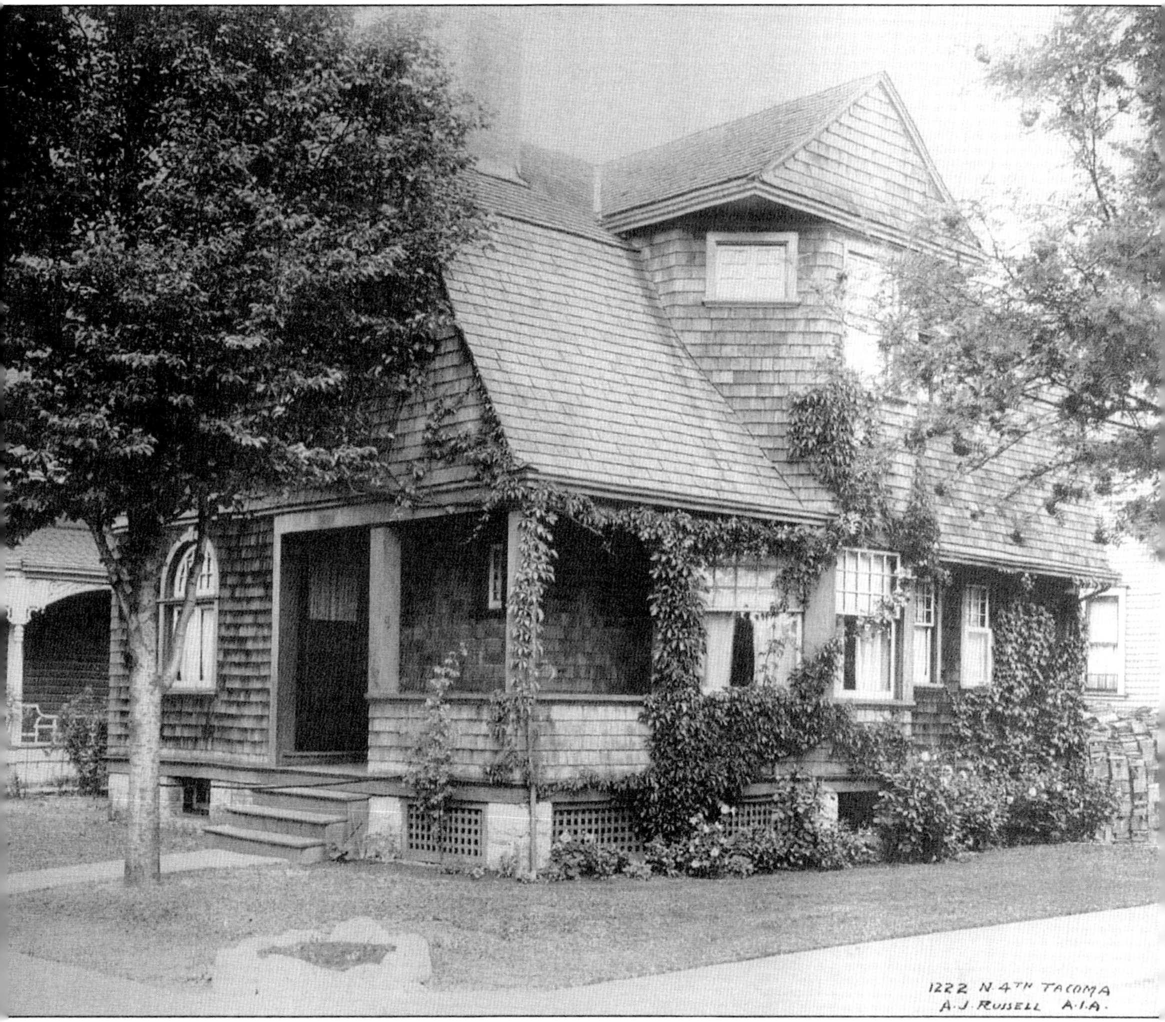

When he was exhorted by famous Rev. Henry Ward Beecher to go west to Tacoma, George W. Plummer spoke to his sons, and gradually the whole family arrived in Tacoma in 1889. George W. dealt in real estate. When he died in 1902, his wife, Harriet Ann, stayed in Tacoma. She moved to 1222 North Fourth Street to live with their son and daughter E.A. and Edith Plummer. E.A. was a dealer in Washington land and timberlands. In 1902, he was in the land department of the Northern Pacific Railway and, in 1910, he resigned and went into real estate. The Queen Anne–Shingle Style house at 1222 North Fourth Street was built and occupied by renowned architect Ambrose J. Russell. He lived there until 1908, when he moved to American Lake. (Courtesy of Charlotte Medlock.)

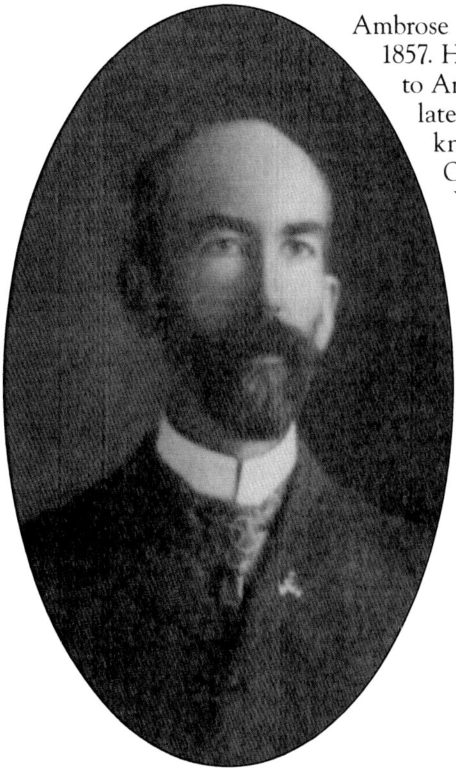

Ambrose J. Russell, a missionary's son, was born in India in 1857. He graduated from the University of Glasgow, came to America, and married Loella Sargent in 1891. A year later, they moved to Tacoma. Ambrose Russell's well-known designs included the governor's mansion in Olympia, the Tacoma Country and Golf Clubhouse, the York Rite Masonic Temple and Temple Theater, and Point Defiance Pavilion, among other buildings and numerous residences. (Courtesy of Julie Turner.)

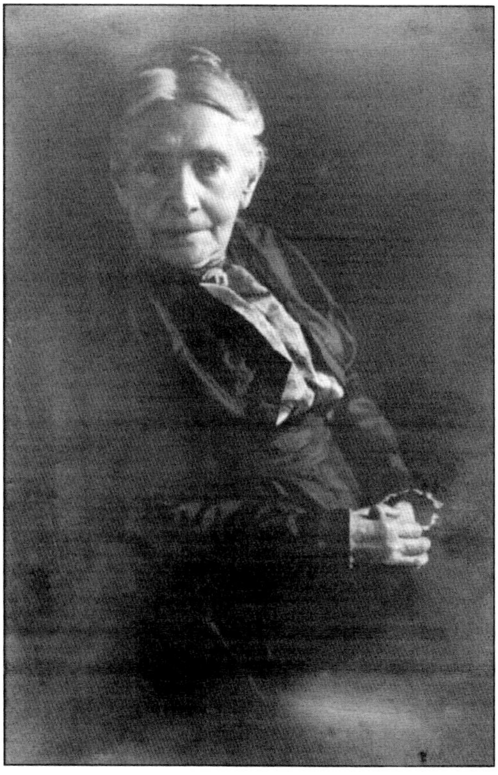

Harriet Ann Plummer was born in New York City in 1839. The daughter of Mr. and Mrs. James Madison Bull, she came to Tacoma at age 50 with her husband, George W. Plummer. They had five sons—Frederick, George H., Henry G., Sidney, and Ernest A.—and a daughter, Edith. Until her death in 1928 at age 89, Harriet Ann lived with Ernest A. Plummer and Edith. (Courtesy of Charlotte Medlock.)

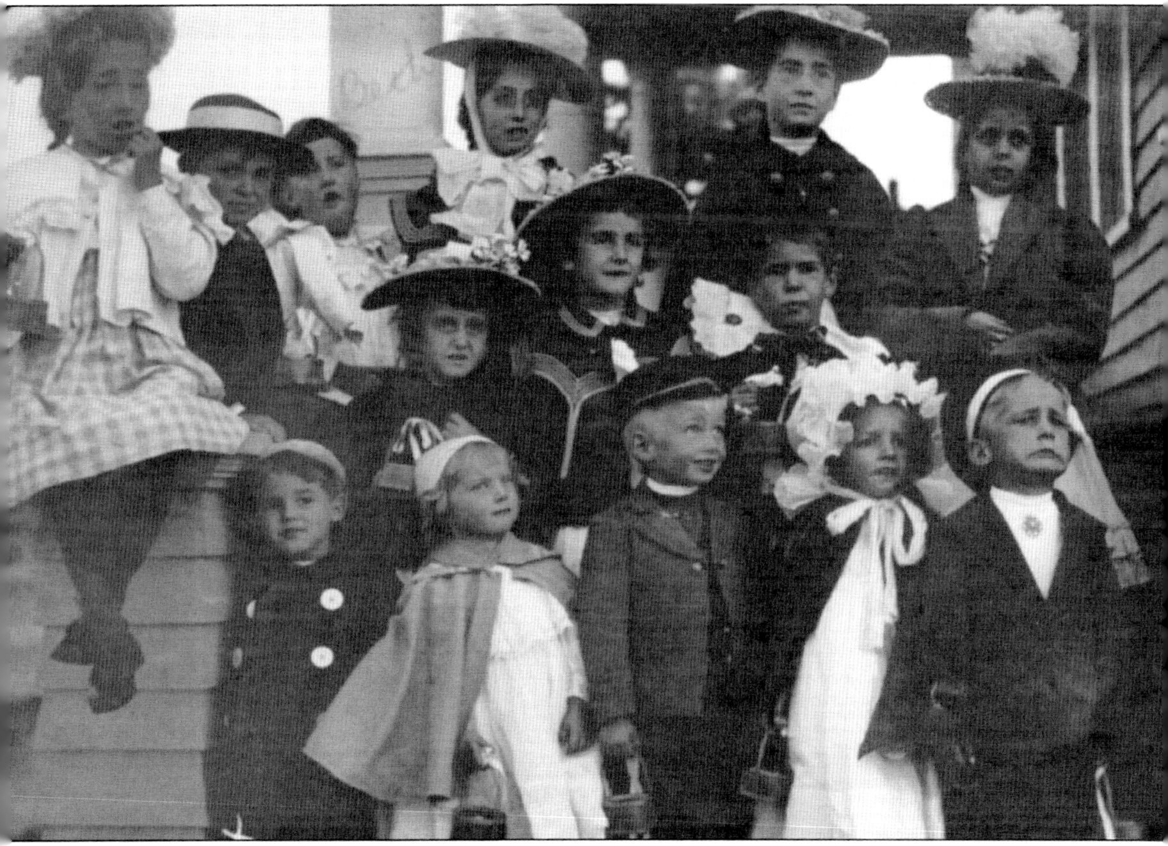

The kindergarten class of 1898 poses on the porch of 502 North L Street for the third annual commencement of the Tacoma Theater Kindergarten Training School. The boy standing on the far left in the first row, with big buttons on his jacket, is Don Plummer, the son of G.H. and Emma Plummer. The attached card reads, "Eile nicht, weile nicht," which is German, freely translated, for "haste not, waste not." Don's neighbor Helen Atkinson lived with her parents, George and Grace Atkinson, at 624 North Ainsworth Avenue, a few blocks from the G.H. Plummers. In 1906, as a young girl, Helen helped milliners Nell V. Wilson and Bertha L. Wilson (her aunts) and her mother, Grace Wilson Atkinson, in their hat shop. Her father George, a bookkeeper, worked full-time at the family business. The hat shop was open from 1906 until 1923. As an adult, Helen had a storage chest full of silks, satins, ribbons, and laces left over from the hats. (Courtesy of Charlotte Medlock.)

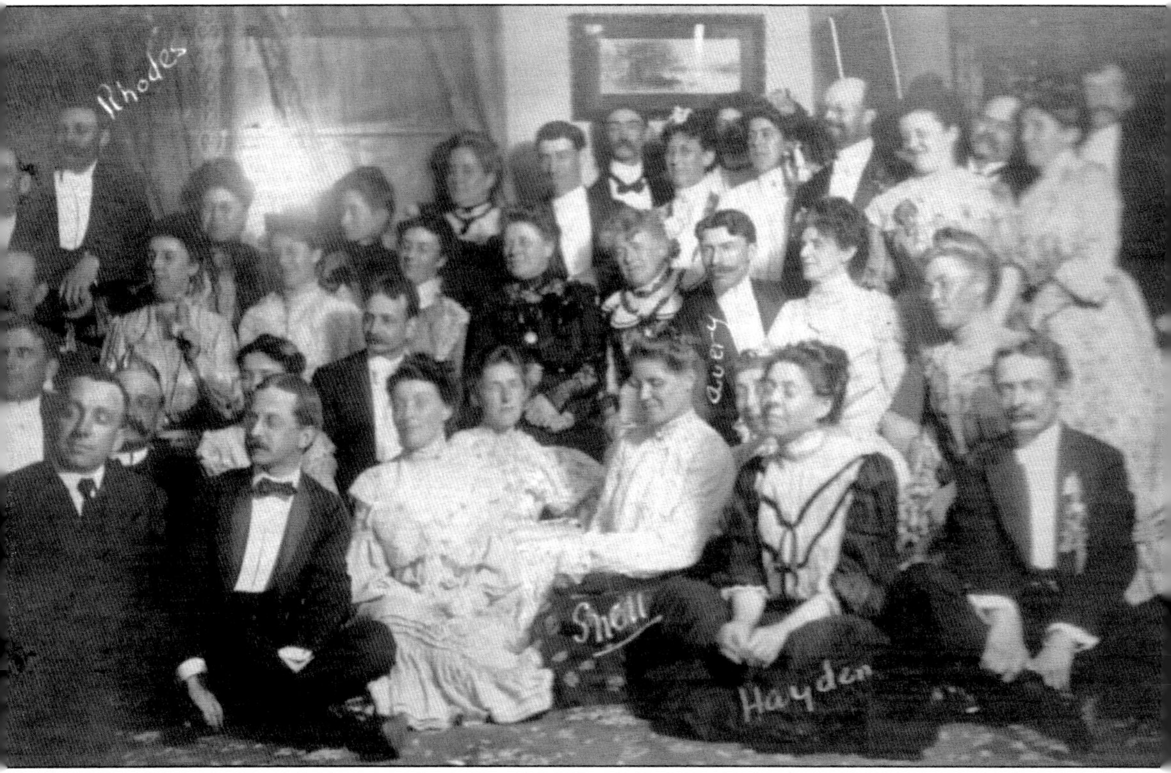

In the G. Howard Plummer home at 502 North L Street, the living room was a setting for entertainment. As the guests came through the columns at the entry, they could see the high ceilings, the carpeted hardwood floors, and a fireplace on the left. Singing was accompanied by piano or guitar. Among the unidentified figures, a few names are noted on the photograph. Standing to the far left in the rear is a Mr. Rhodes. Seated in the second row, third from the right, is probably Alexander Gordon Avery, and in the first row, on the right, are two ladies with the last names of Snell and Hayden. (Courtesy of Charlotte Medlock.)

Donald Plummer is shown in 1918 in his World War I uniform. He served in France during the war. In his diaries during high school, he wrote about dances at home and at Sloan's Academy on I Street and Division Avenue and often mentioned friend Helen Atkinson. He and Helen had attended the University of Washington before he served in World War I. (Courtesy of Charlotte Medlock.)

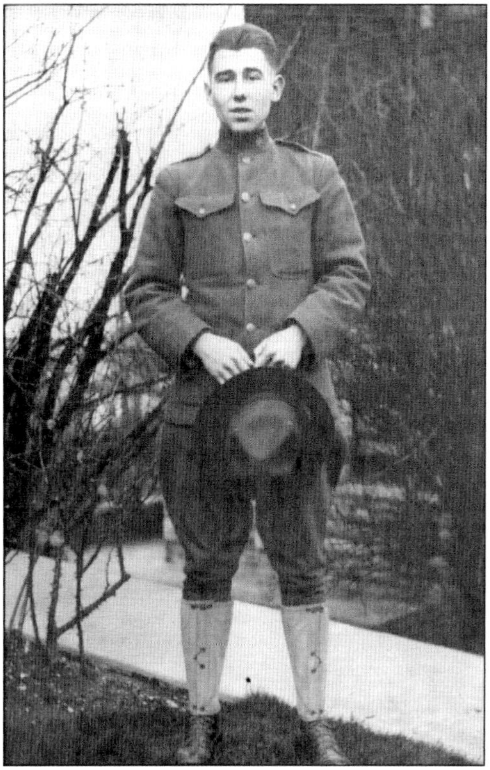

Helen Atkinson lived with her parents on North Ainsworth Avenue. She went to Stadium High School and was a star tennis player. She also enjoyed dancing and socializing with friends, including Don Plummer. After college and his service in the war, Don and Helen were married in the home at 624 North Ainsworth Avenue. It is possible some of the material for her satin gown came from the hat shop. (Gyda May photograph.)

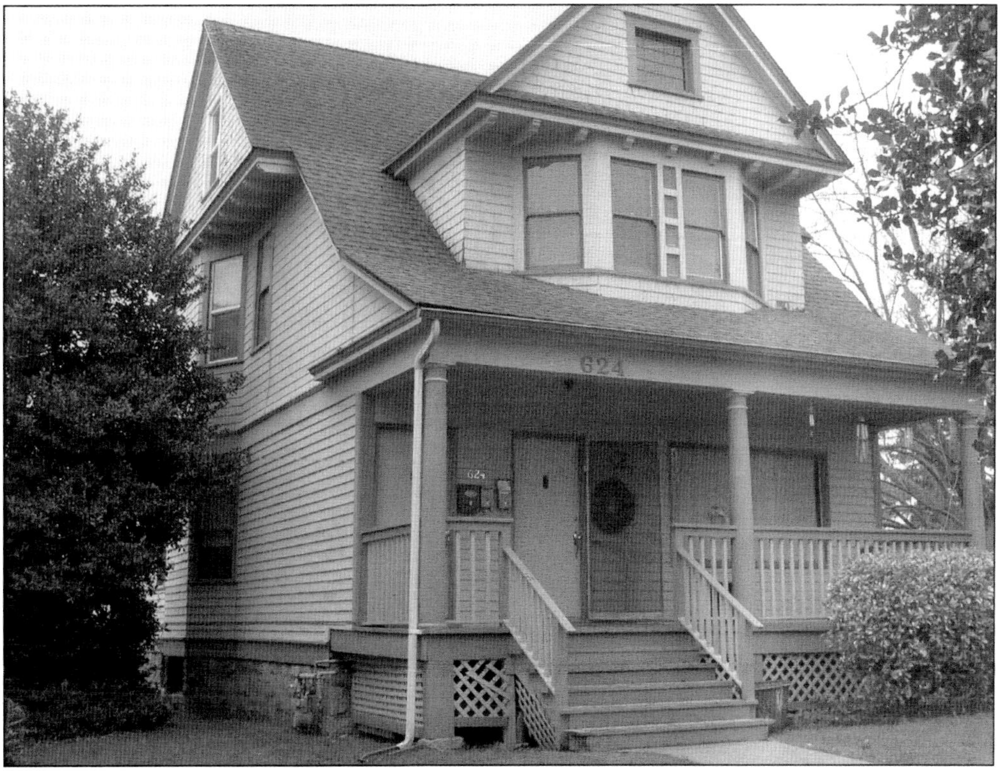

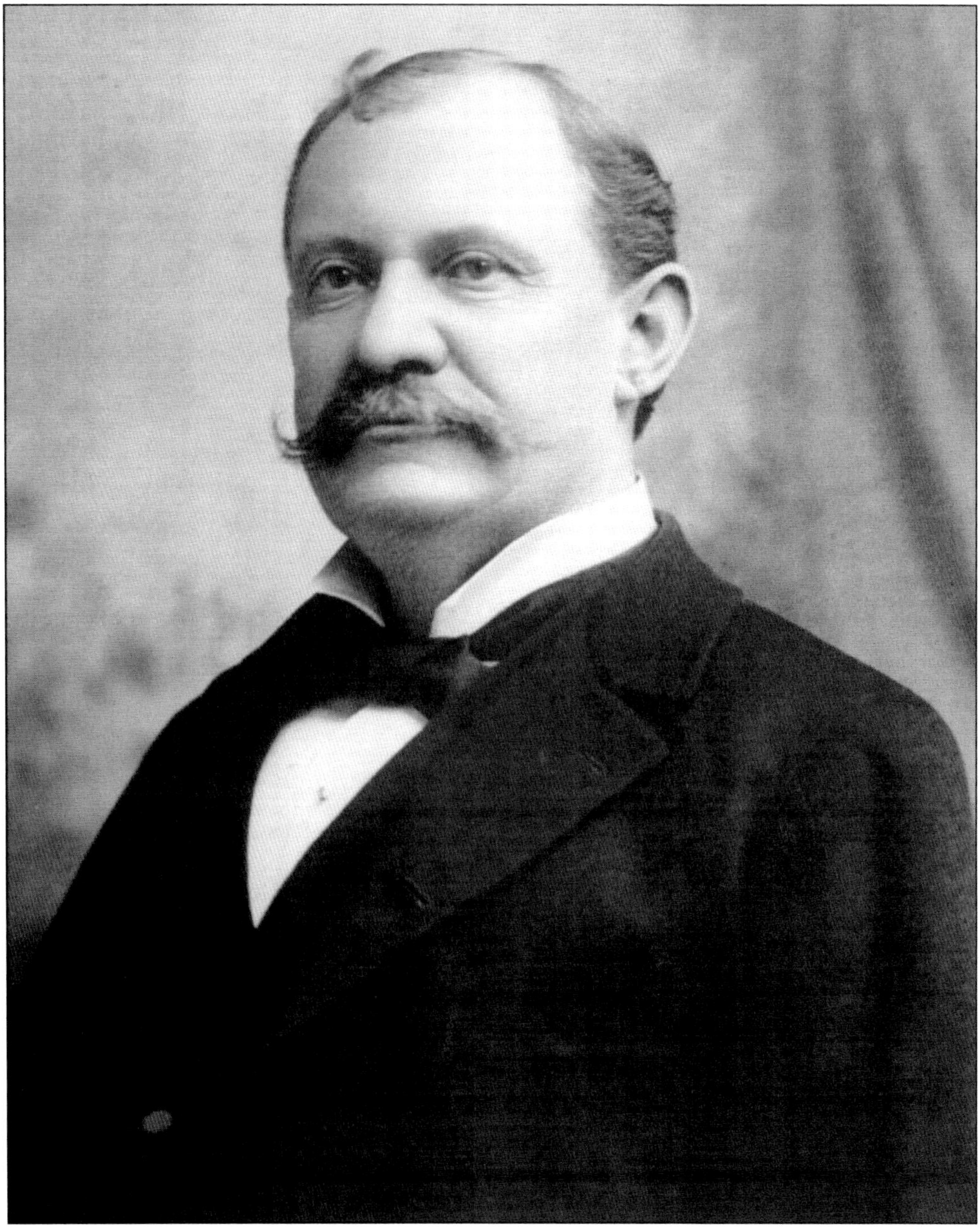

Judge John W. Linck and his wife, Eva, moved into 817 North J Street in 1901. Linck was elected mayor of Tacoma in 1908. Also active in national politics, Linck was a personal friend of three US presidents—Benjamin Harrison, William McKinley, and Theodore Roosevelt. Linck left office in 1910 and went on to serve as a justice of the peace until 1922. He owned a valuable collection of antique clocks. The Linck home was a favorite hangout of the Crosby family children, including toddler Bing Crosby, who lived nearby at 1112 North J Street. Before that, the John Q. Masons lived at the house about 11 years until 1900, when they moved to 912 North I Street. Virginia Mason (not connected to the hospital in Seattle) was a leader in the women's suffrage movement. The Mason home was often the meeting place for civic and cultural events. The Nesika Club was formed at the house in 1892.

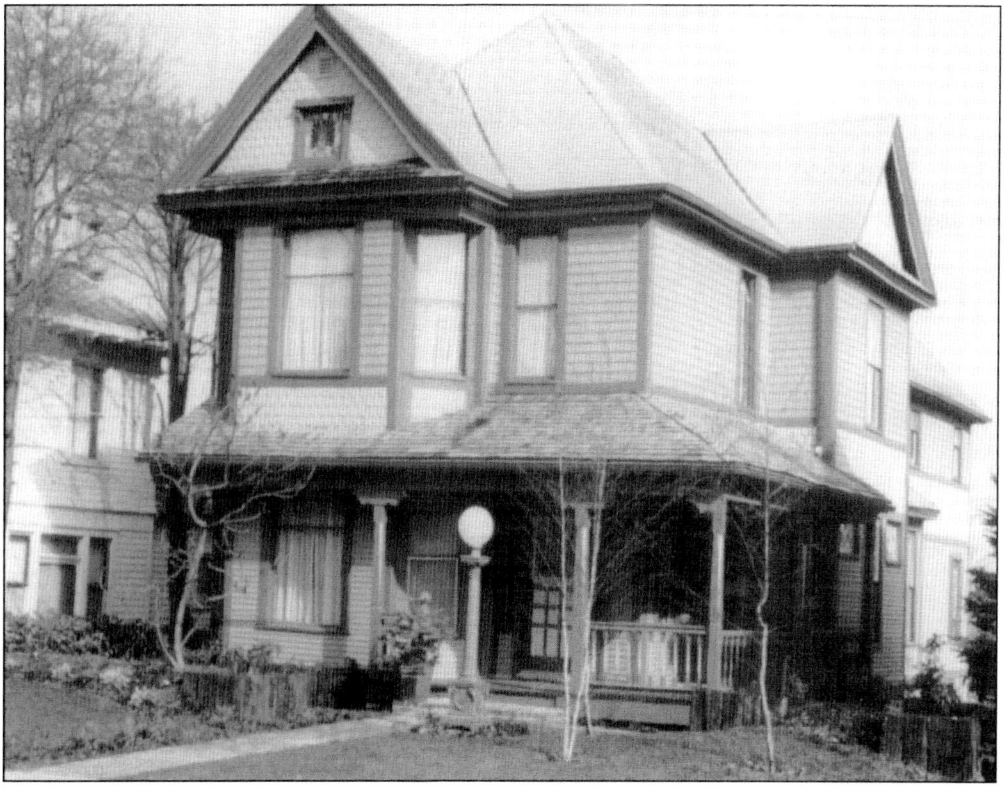

North J Street was still scattered with logging debris when John Q. and Virginia Mason built their home in 1889. People had to follow a trail along the Garfield Gulch that bisected the neighborhood to reach their house. A stairway of 42 steps led to the front door. Having served in the telegraph service during the Civil War, John Mason came to Tacoma from Illinois in 1888 as the assistant superintendent of Northern Pacific Railway's telegraph department. The above photograph shows how the house looked when it was built; it was a Queen Anne home with old-growth fir beams, maple floors, and bay windows. When Jay and Julie Turner purchased the residence, it was in need of extensive repair, which was no small task. At the end, the Virginia Mason home is back and better than ever. (Right, courtesy of Charlotte Medlock.)

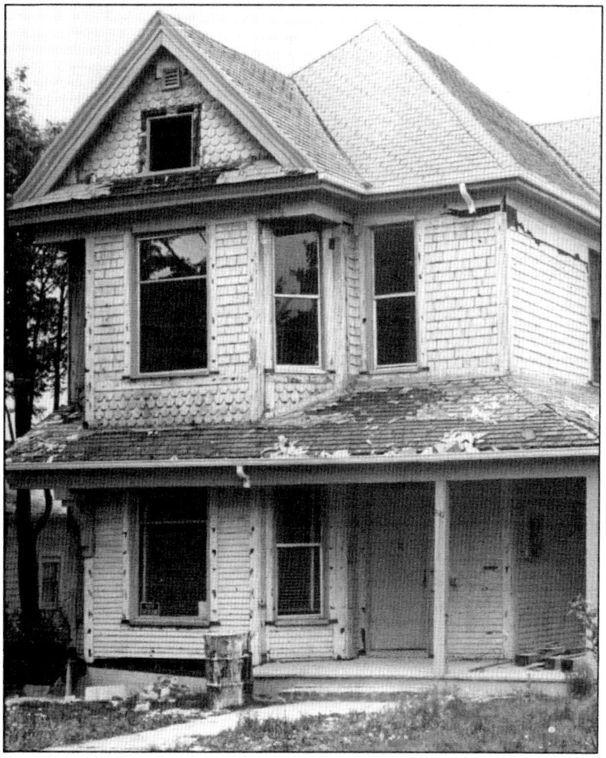

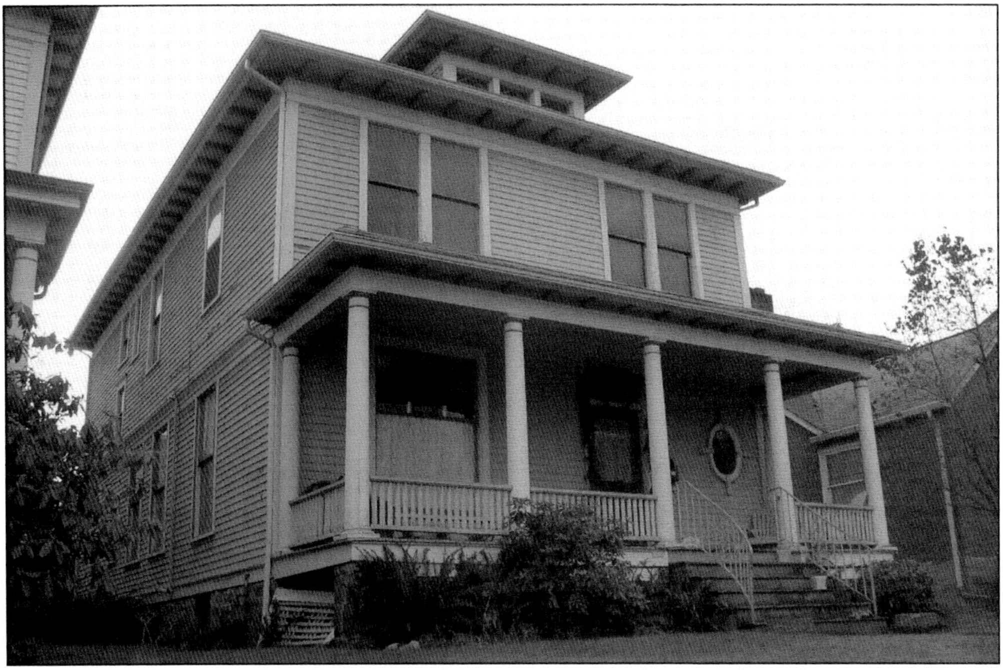

This Colonial Revival–Foursquare home (a twin to 308 North I Street) was built in 1905 at 312 North I Street (above). The owner, Berman Heyman, came to the United States from Germany as a young child. Heyman became a partner of the Schoenfeld family, of Seattle, and in 1902 founded a furniture store, called L. Schoenfeld and Sons, in Tacoma. He was president of the business for more than 20 years. The picture below shows a downtown Tacoma street scene on a spring day in 1920. A streetcar is making a turn onto A Street and has just passed the L. Schoenfeld and Sons store at 105–111 South Eleventh Street. This would be the Schoenfeld furniture store location until 1924, when it would move to the remodeled Sandberg Building at 1423 Pacific Avenue. (Above, Gyda May photograph.)

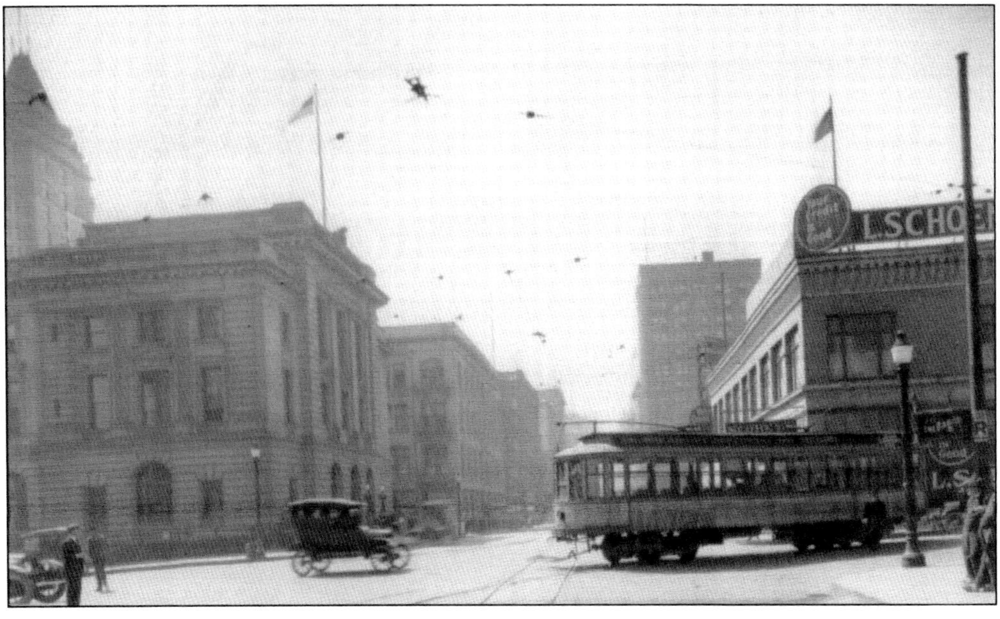

Uniformed delivery drivers for L. Schoenfeld and Sons pose in front of their trucks in June 1924. The men had recently been supplied with uniforms patterned after the military, including knee-high boots. Customers were able to readily identify these Schoenfeld representatives. The home furnishings store had just moved to its new location on Pacific Avenue.

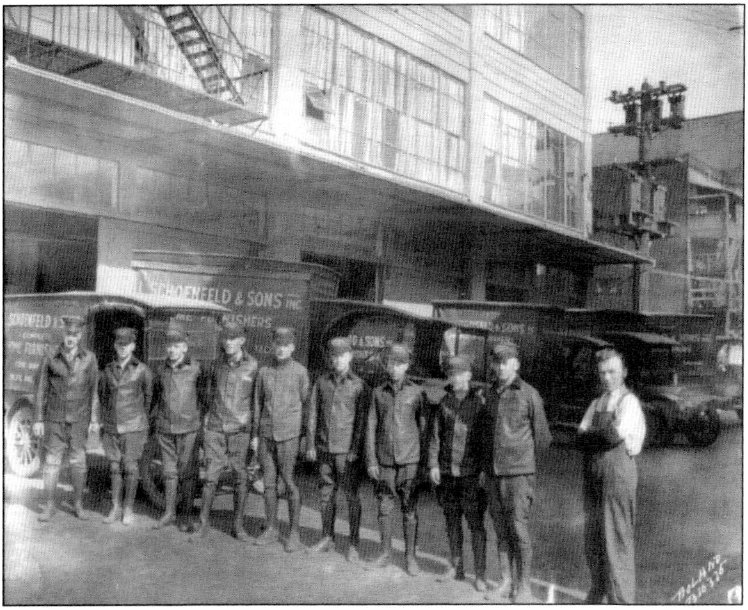

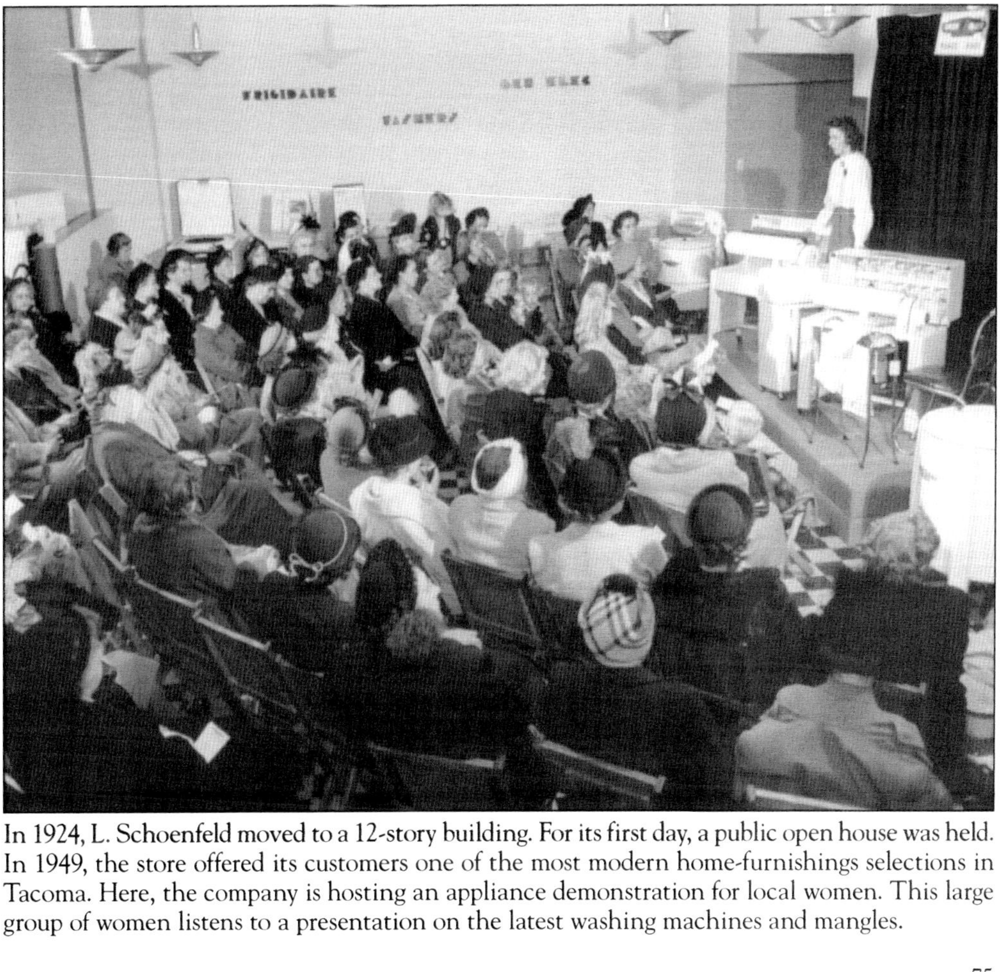

In 1924, L. Schoenfeld moved to a 12-story building. For its first day, a public open house was held. In 1949, the store offered its customers one of the most modern home-furnishings selections in Tacoma. Here, the company is hosting an appliance demonstration for local women. This large group of women listens to a presentation on the latest washing machines and mangles.

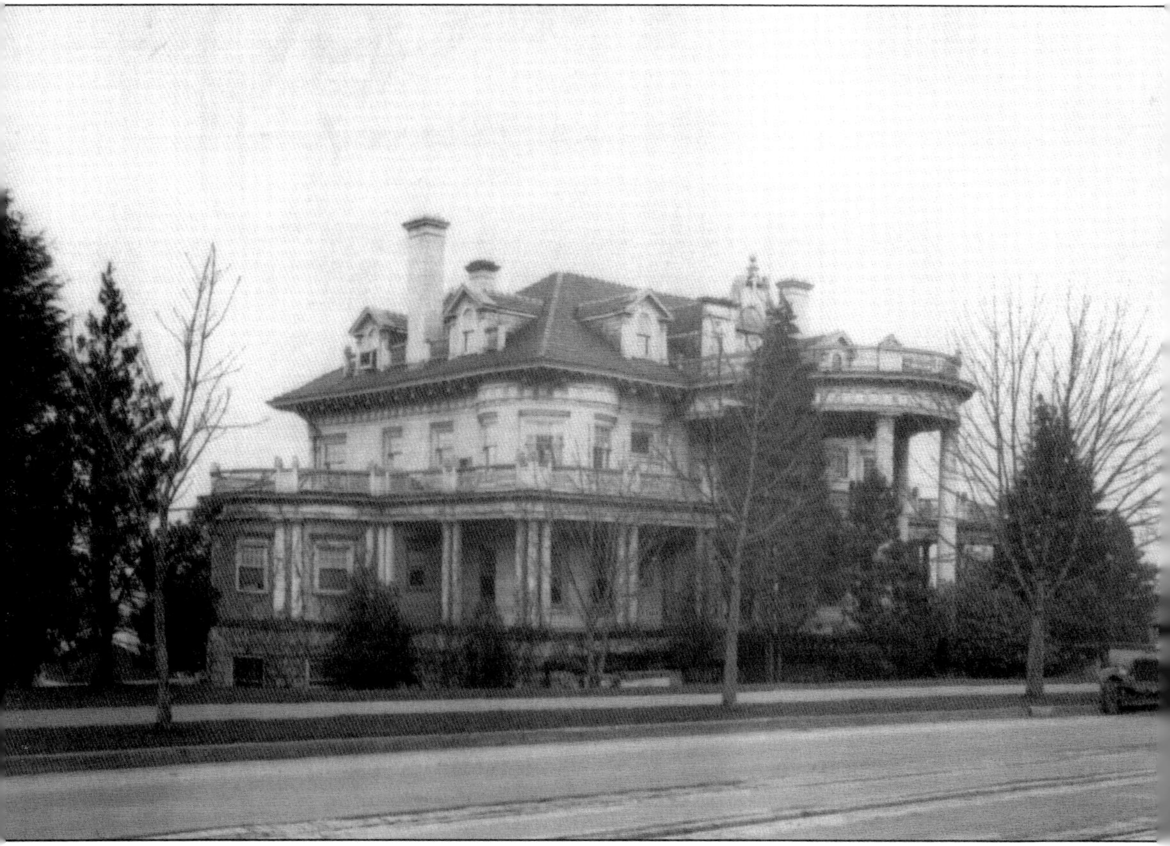

The mansion shown here was built for William Ross Rust in 1905 at North Tenth and I Streets with funds from his business. Rust bought a struggling mill and smelter from Dennis Ryan in 1889, shut it down, and completely rebuilt it, and according to historian Murray Morgan, "Tacoma was proud as the pollution plume of the new plant rose above the Indians' place of the maples and drifted north toward Seattle." By fall of 1890, processed bullion was being shipped to San Francisco, and Rust started his fortune. He had left college to learn a trade. After some years in Colorado gathering skills and some money, he had come to Tacoma. Rust's new business, the Tacoma Smelting and Refining Company, suffered during the hard times of 1893. As things improved, he received business from other companies under the powerful influence of financier Darius Ogden Mills. With the profits, Rust installed an electrolytic copper refinery, the first on the Pacific coast, in 1905. Soon after, he sold the company to the Guggenheims for about $5 million in cash.

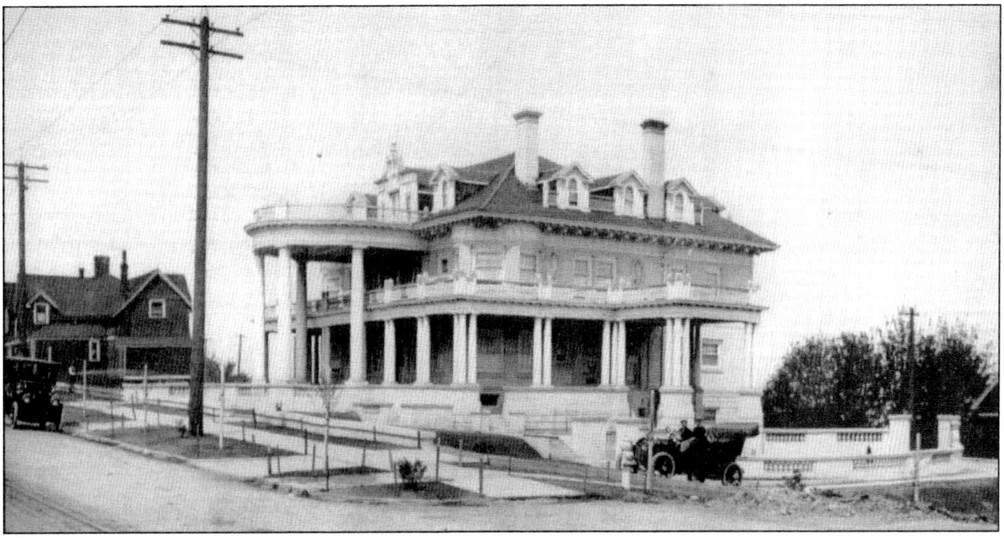

Upon the sale of his foundry, W.R. Rust was paid a bonus from Bernard Baruch, who had acted as intermediary, for helping to close the deal. Rust used this money to build and furnish the Rust mansion (pictured above and on page 76), made of hand-dressed Wilkeson sandstone. The 18-room Neoclassical home was designed by architects Russell and Babcock and modeled after the John A. McCall mansion in Long Branch, New Jersey. By 1920, work had begun on W.R. Rust's 12-story Rust Building at 950 Pacific Avenue, which is seen under construction in the photograph below. When he died in 1928, Rust left shares that later paid for both a men's club and a playfield in the town of Ruston.

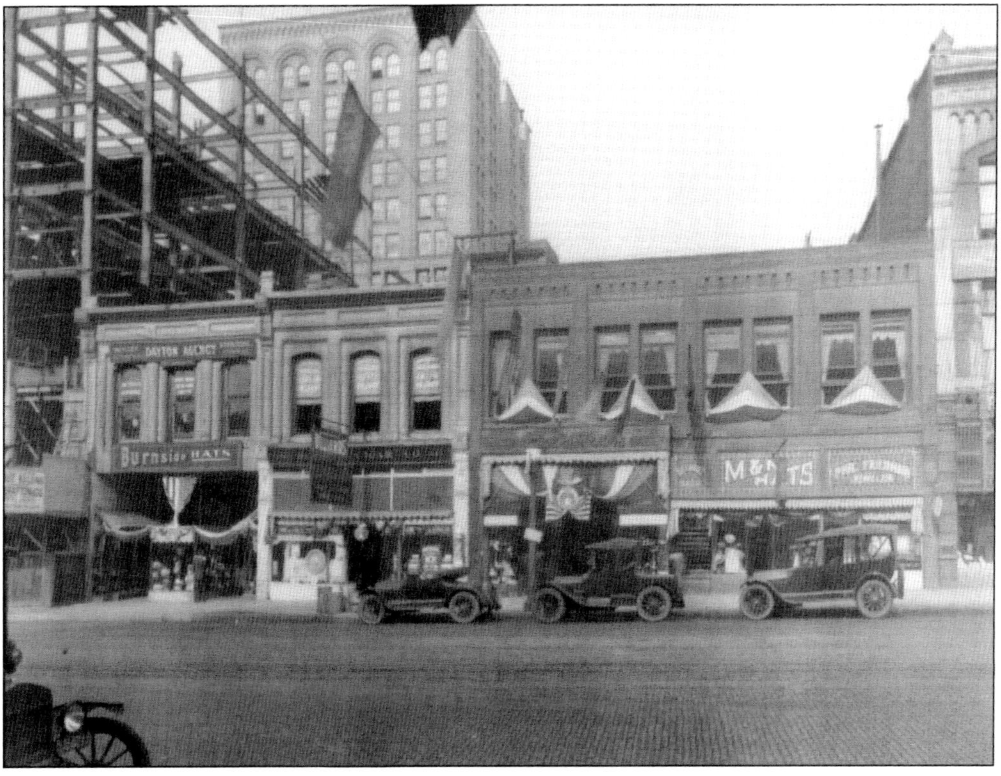

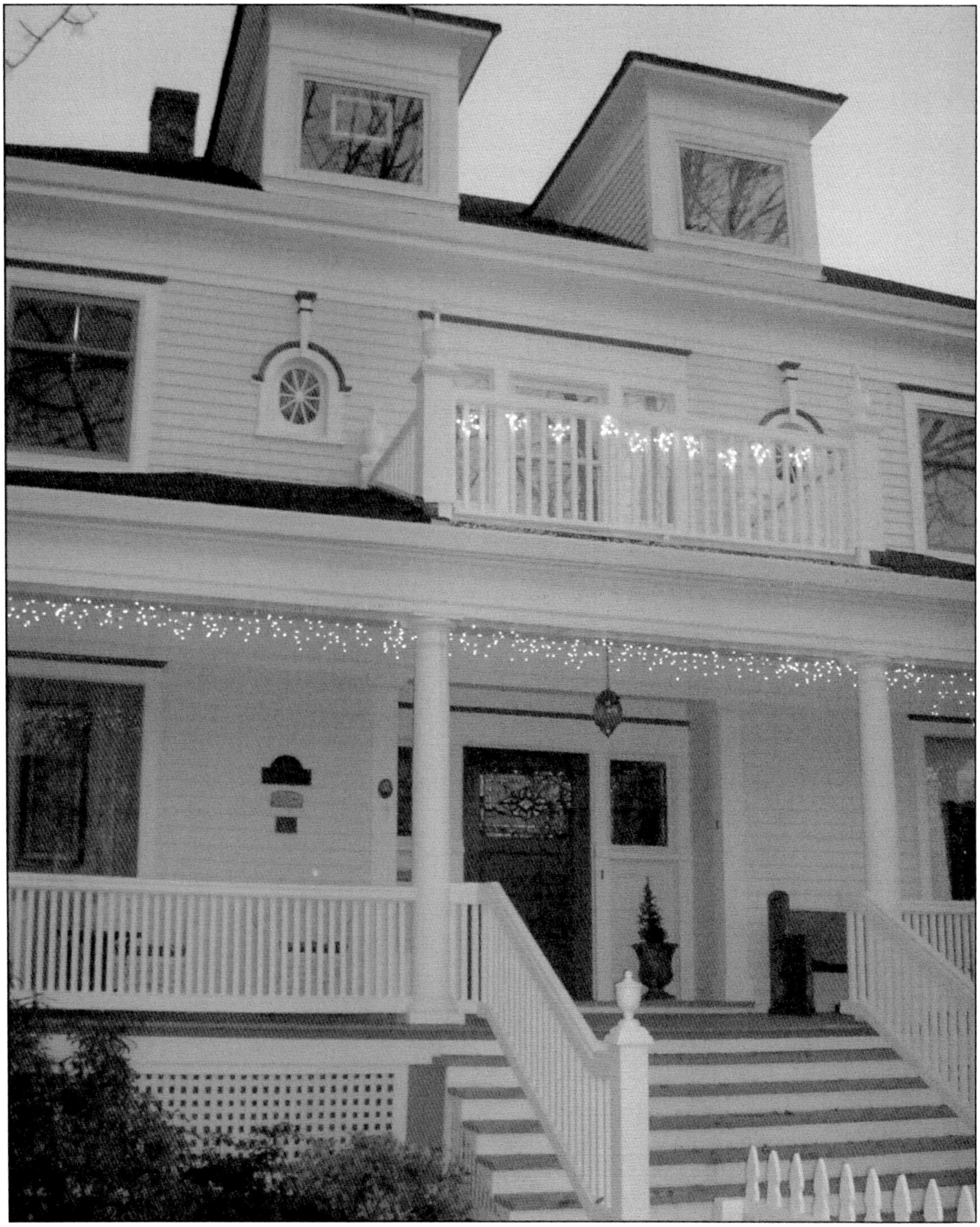

The Cornell brothers built this 1901 Neocolonial Foursquare for F.G. and Virginia Cushman Fisher. Fisher came to Tacoma in 1889 and started a shoe business with his brother. In 1895, he opened Tacoma Shoe on Pacific Avenue. By 1906, he joined with Stone to form Stone-Fisher Company, a clothing store that became the Bon Marché, later Macy's. It was one of the most popular department stores in Tacoma. Fisher's spent $500,000 in 1947 to remodel and modernize, including new fixtures in all departments. Ernest C. and Daniel Cornell, natives of Ohio, moved to Tacoma in the late 1880s. The brothers started working in the contracting business immediately and, for a while, partnered. By the 1920s, they helped create the firm of Albertson, Cornell Brothers, and Walsh, a large business that constructed roads, erected power stations, and built a large part of Fort Lewis during World War II. (Gyda May photograph.)

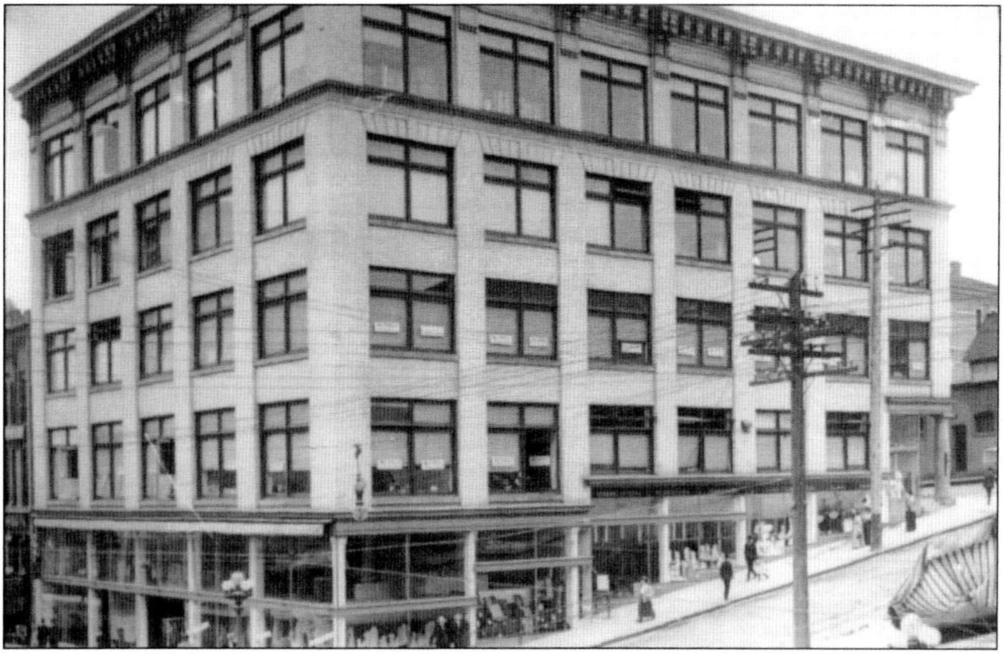

This photograph from around 1910 of the Stone-Fisher Department Store on Eleventh Street and Broadway shows the building's original facade, designed by Frederick Heath.

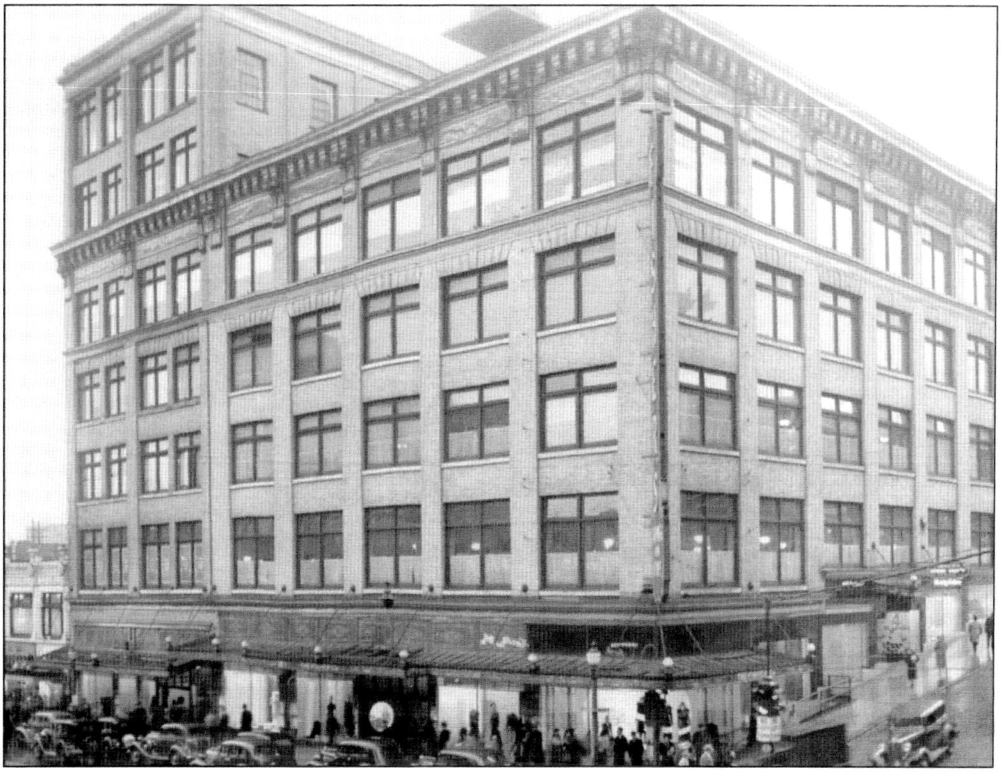

In the 1920s, a seven-story addition was added to the side of the building, and in 1925, the name was changed to Fisher Company.

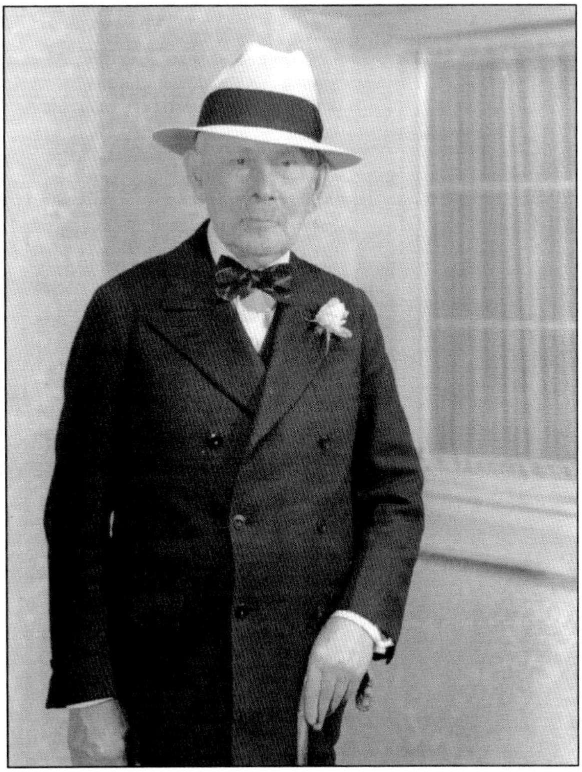

This photograph of John A. Rea shows him in a dashing suit with his white fedora at a rakish angle and a rose in his lapel. According to historian Ron Magden, for 50 years Rea strode daily from his North Slope home to his real estate office downtown. John Rea had a wide influence. US presidents from Grover Cleveland to Franklin D. Roosevelt called him "Mr. Tacoma." He was the first executive director of the Port of Tacoma in 1918. Born in Pennsylvania in 1848, John Rea graduated from Cornell University and led an exciting career as a journalist for 30 years. In 1873, he married Mary Terry. In the late 1890s, Rea and his family settled in Tacoma. John Rea lived in this American Foursquare–style house since it was constructed in 1907 until his death in 1941.

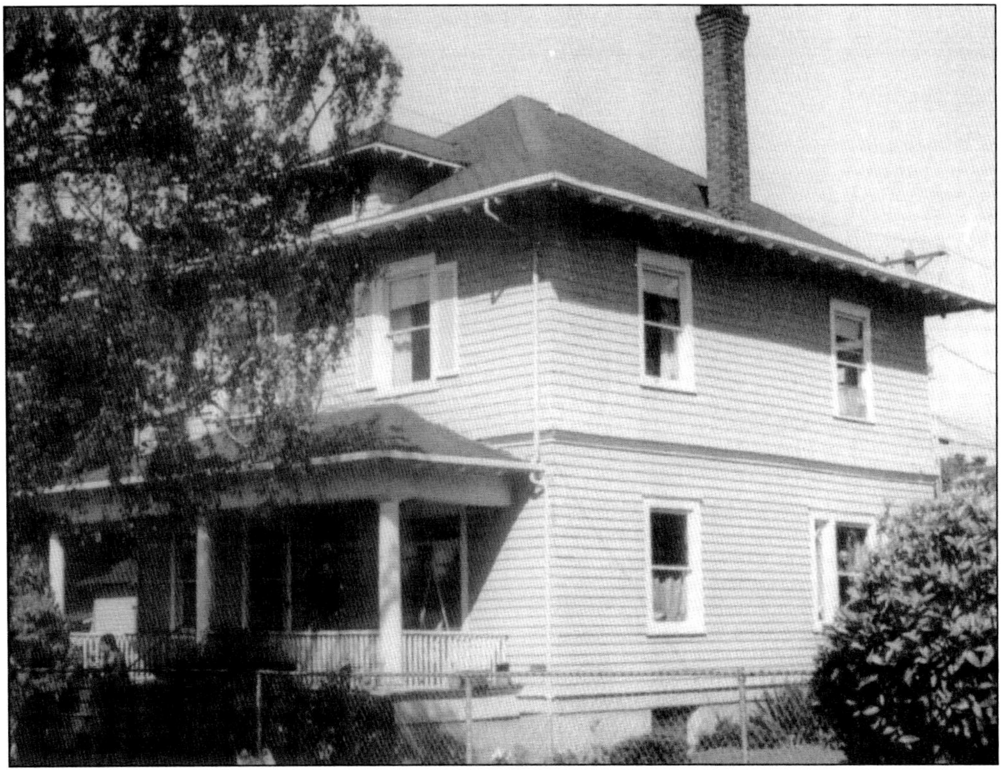

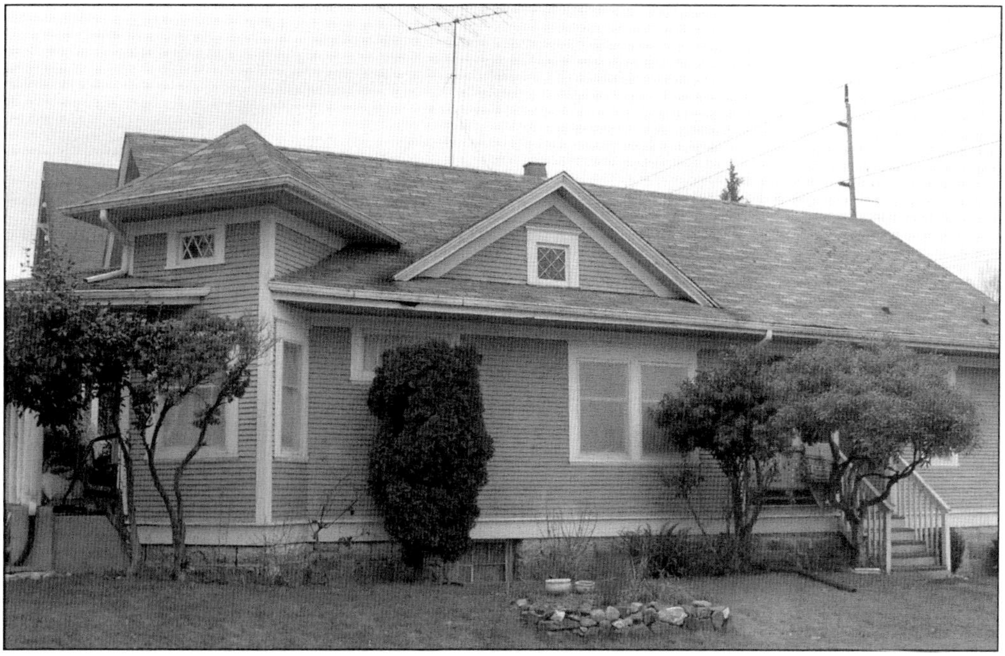

During 1914, Howard B. and Carolyn Davis lived at 601 North Cushman in this 1903 cottage. Their son John "Jack" Davis was born in 1914. Jackie (his stage name) later appeared in the *Our Gang* comedies. His older sister, Mildred Davis, became a silent film star. She was Harold Lloyd's leading lady. (Gyda May photograph.)

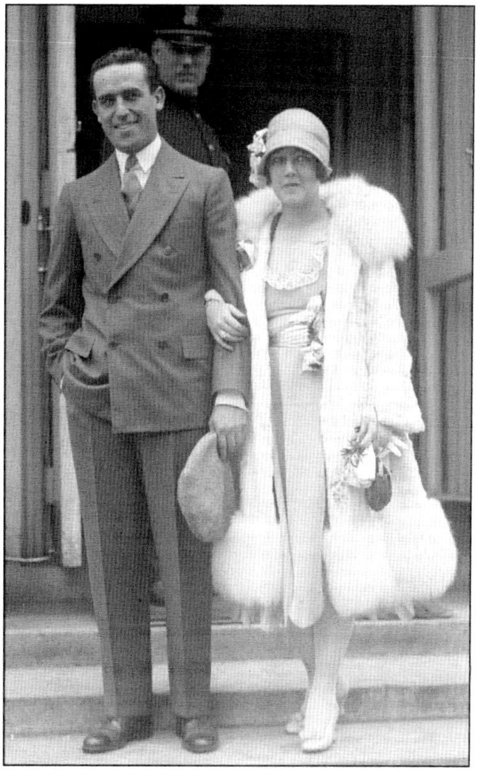

Mildred Davis starred in 15 films with Harold Lloyd from 1919 until their marriage in 1923. This photograph was taken a couple of years later, after Davis had retired. Harold arranged for Mildred's brother Jack to go to military school. Jack went on to practice medicine in Beverly Hills. Mildred and Harold had three children, including Harold Lloyd Jr. (Courtesy of Library of Congress.)

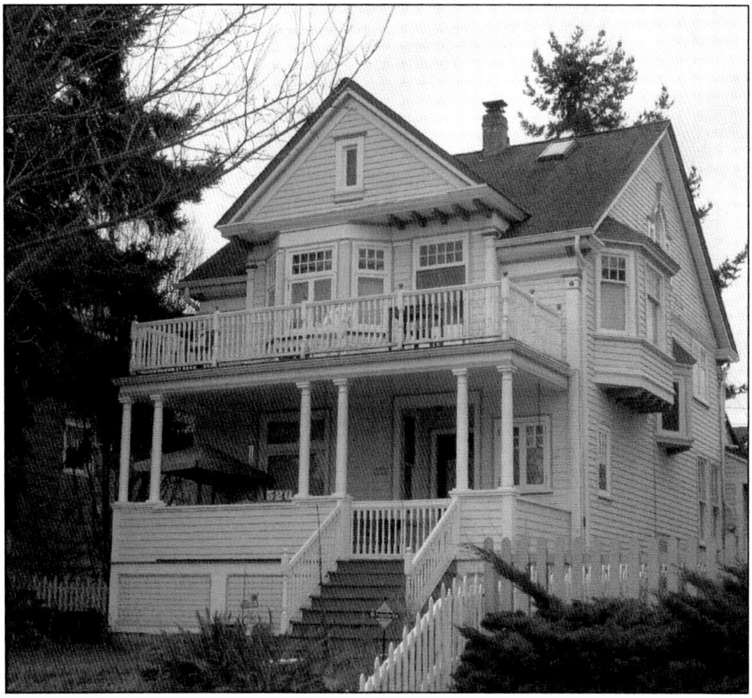

Carl August Darmer, born in Germany, arrived in Tacoma in 1884. In 1898, he designed this home at 520 North L Street for his family, including his wife, Sofia, and their three children. They lived here for more than 20 years. Darmer designed the Crystal Palace Market downtown, with building contractor William R. Nichols, manager of the Pacific Coast Gypsum Company. Nichols also built other concrete structures in Tacoma. (Gyda May photograph.)

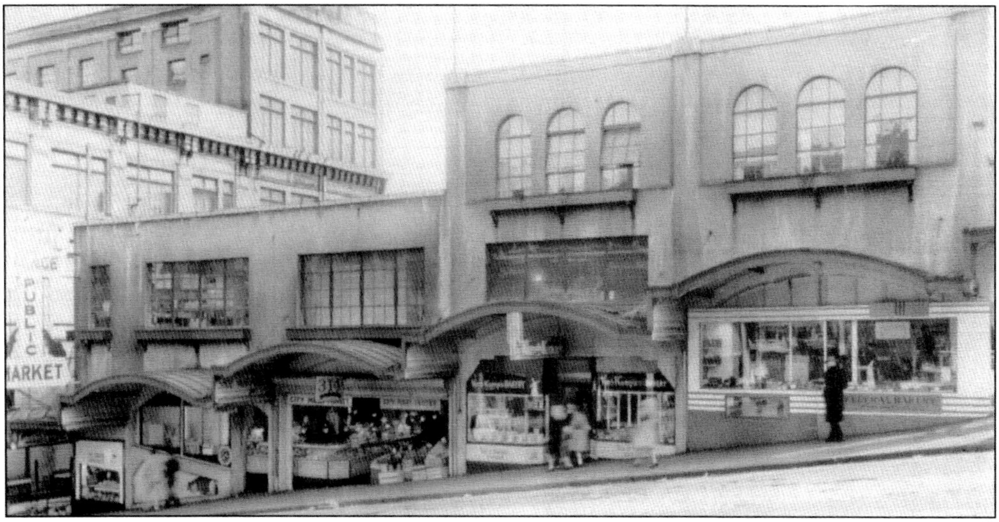

This photograph shows the Crystal Palace Market, at 1101–1113 Market Street, as it appeared in 1945. In 1926, Charles Hurley had paid $2 million for a 99-year lease on the 20,000 square feet of land at the corner of South Eleventh and Market Streets. In June 1927, the Crystal Market opened for trade. It was one of the largest and most unique businesses of its kind in the world. Similar to the Crystal Palace Market in New York City, it was a public market selling foods, clothing, and artisanal products.

This photograph shows the Peoples Department Store Building. Carl August Darmer was the architect and designed it in 1895. Shown in May 1938, the storefront has scaffolding, visible at upper left between top windows and the roof, and a steam cleaner. The sign reads, "This building is being steam-cleaned by Universal Cleaning Contractors." The structure was built for and occupied by the Peoples Department Store from 1895 to 1983, which was when the store closed its doors.

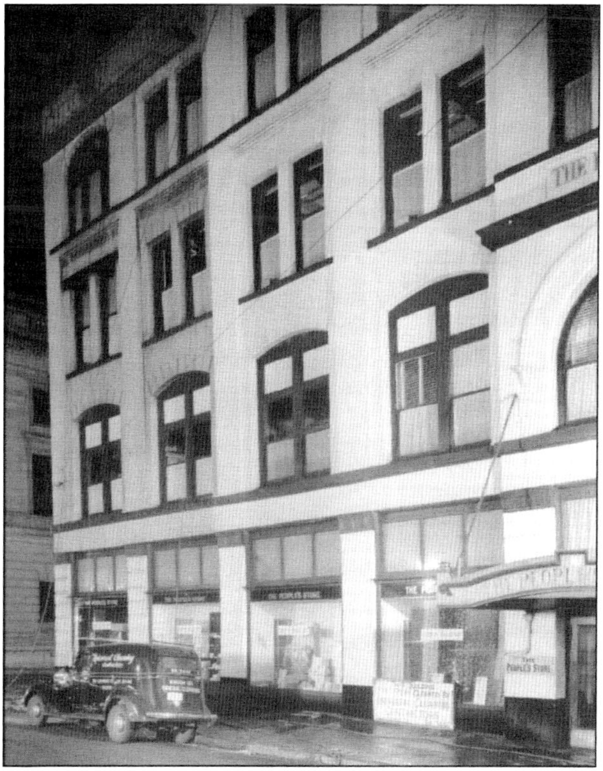

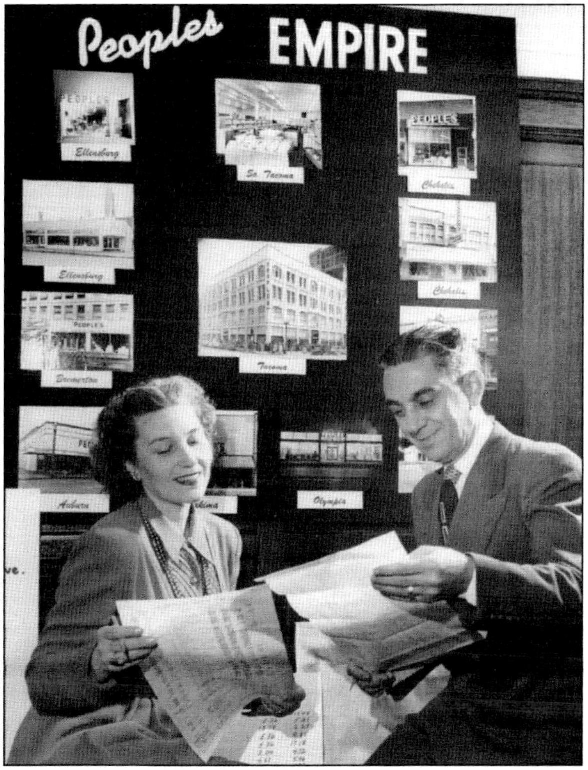

In 1948, the Peoples Department Store chain had an empire of 12 stores. For two days, starting on November 12, 1948, Mildred Davis (not the retired actress) became president of the Peoples Empire during the semiannual Women's Day. On these two days, women took over all executive positions. Davis, the switchboard operator, was elected by her coworkers to be president and general manager. On the right, president William P. Fitpold assists.

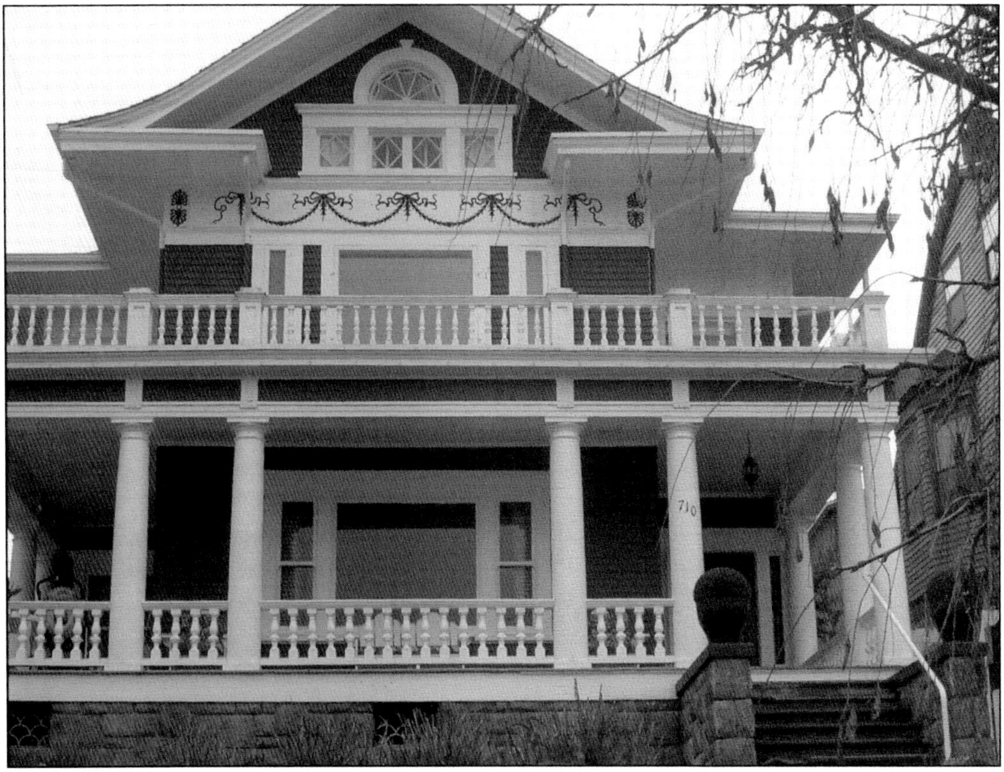

Russell designed this house in 1907 for William R. and Elzora Nichols. The lower floor was finished in oak, with a large reception hall, a wide staircase, a Colonial fireplace, a dining room with built-in buffet, and a living room extending across the entire front of the house. The upstairs included an open deck porch and a large attic with servants' quarters. (Gyda May photograph.)

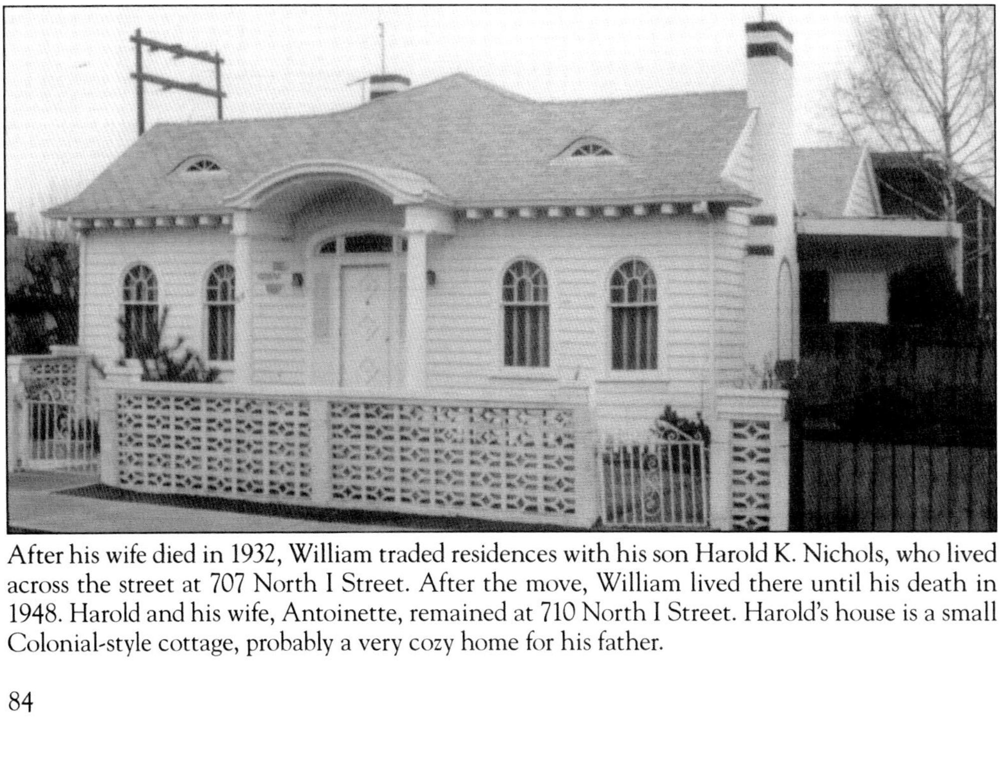

After his wife died in 1932, William traded residences with his son Harold K. Nichols, who lived across the street at 707 North I Street. After the move, William lived there until his death in 1948. Harold and his wife, Antoinette, remained at 710 North I Street. Harold's house is a small Colonial-style cottage, probably a very cozy home for his father.

The clipping at right shows the notice on page 1 in the *Tacoma News Tribune* of the death of Silas "Si" Weber on March 17, 1943. He had lived at 1213 North Seventh Street from 1907 until his death in 1943 at age 65. His wife, Mary Frances, had passed away that January after a long illness. Si was a well-known and respected African American who worked for 31 years as maitre d' hotel in the dining room at the old Tacoma Hotel until 1935. He was also the president of Weber Investment Company in 1921. The article continues on page 26, shown below, with a photograph of Silas Weber. Manager George Calvert declared that more people asked for "Si" than anyone else on the payroll. At his burial, the honor guards and pallbearers were members of the Tacoma Police Department.

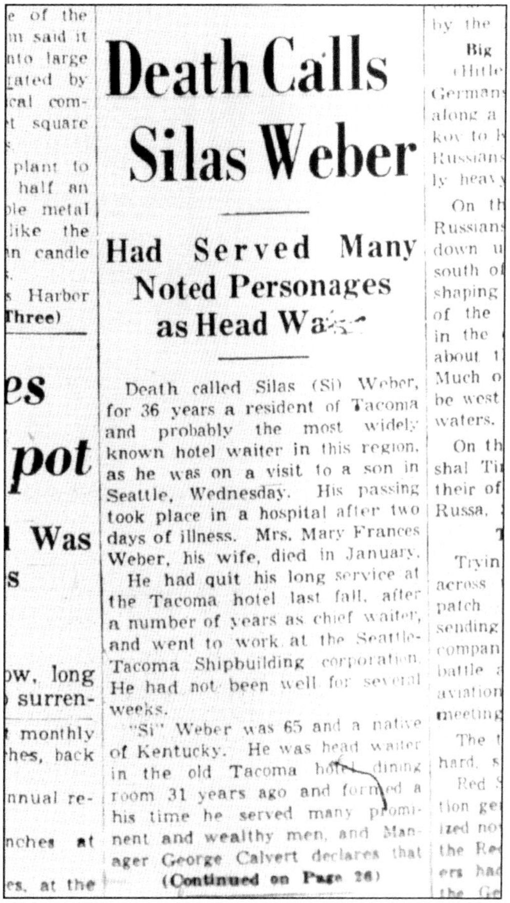

Death Calls Silas Weber

Had Served Many Noted Personages as Head Wa[illegible]

Death called Silas (Si) Weber, for 36 years a resident of Tacoma and probably the most widely known hotel waiter in this region, as he was on a visit to a son in Seattle, Wednesday. His passing took place in a hospital after two days of illness. Mrs. Mary Frances Weber, his wife, died in January.

He had quit his long service at the Tacoma hotel last fall, after a number of years as chief waiter, and went to work at the Seattle-Tacoma Shipbuilding corporation. He had not been well for several weeks.

"Si" Weber was 65 and a native of Kentucky. He was head waiter in the old Tacoma hotel dining room 31 years ago and formed a his time he served many prominent and wealthy men, and Manager George Calvert declares that

(Continued on Page 26)

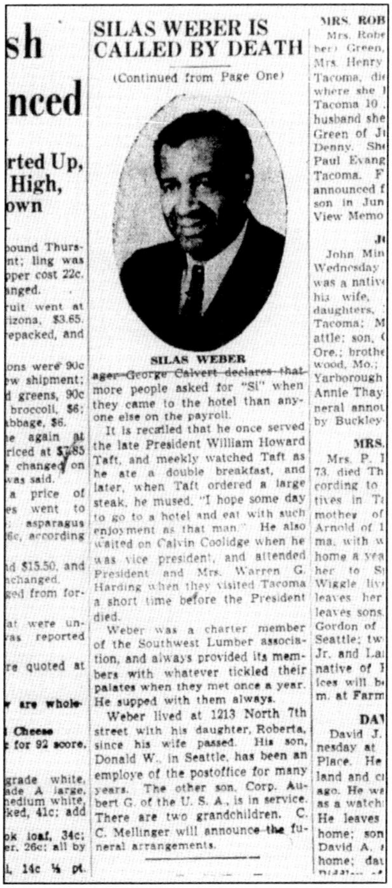

SILAS WEBER IS CALLED BY DEATH

(Continued from Page One)

SILAS WEBER

ager George Calvert declares that more people asked for "Si" when they came to the hotel than anyone else on the payroll.

It is recalled that he once served the late President William Howard Taft, and meekly watched Taft as he ate a double breakfast, and later, when Taft ordered a large steak, he mused, "I hope some day to go to a hotel and eat with such enjoyment as that man." He also waited on Calvin Coolidge when he was vice president, and attended President and Mrs. Warren G. Harding when they visited Tacoma a short time before the President died.

Weber was a charter member of the Southwest Lumber association, and always provided its members with whatever tickled their palates when they met once a year. He supped with them always.

Weber lived at 1213 North 7th street with his daughter, Roberta, since his wife passed. His son, Donald W., in Seattle, has been an employe of the postoffice for many years. The other son, Corp. Aubert G. of the U. S. A., is in service. There are two grandchildren. C. C. Mellinger will announce the funeral arrangements.

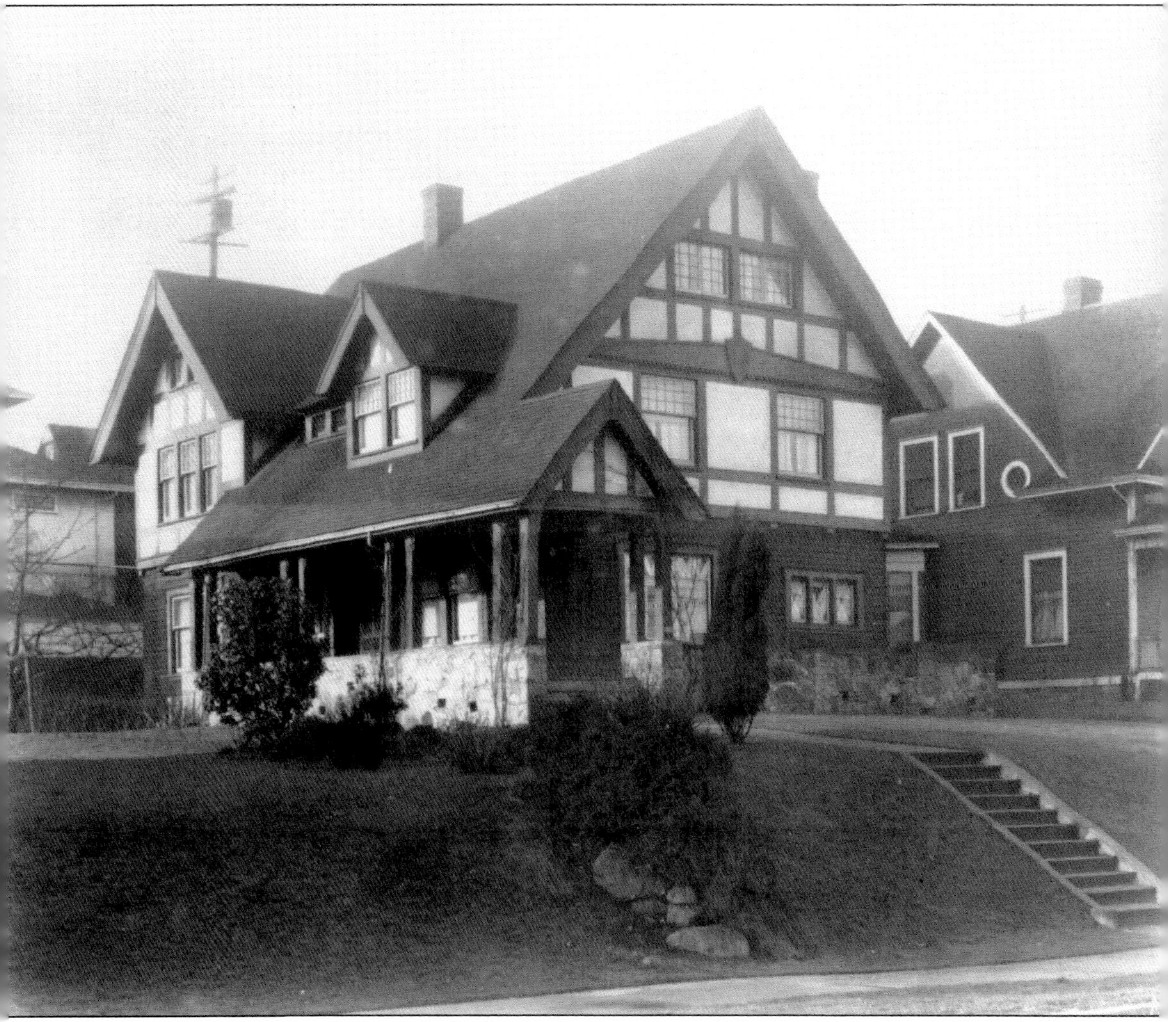

Architects Russell and Heath built this Tudor in 1902 for Albert and Harriet Williams Rhodes at 702 North I Street, on the high spot known as Job Carr's Mountain, between Seventh and Eighth Streets. Garfield Gulch, later filled in, ran along what would be Seventh Street at I Street, located on the left in the photograph. Albert was the secretary of Rhodes Brothers, Inc., in the early 1900s and left in 1907 to found his own store in Seattle. For the next few years, owners were merchant Dave Gross (1907–1909), hotel businessman Jack Donnelly (1910), and Capt. O.G. Olson (1911–1914) until the house was purchased in 1915 by Sarah J. Wingate, widow of Robert Wingate, well-known mining engineer and a director of the Tacoma National Bank. In 1920, the *Tacoma Daily Ledger* touted the home as one of the most beautiful in the city. Sarah passed away in 1921. Isabelle Wingate and her sisters, Grace and Sadie, lived in the house three more years after their mother's death. The original owner, Albert Rhodes, died of influenza in 1921. (Courtesy of Marilyn Torgerson.)

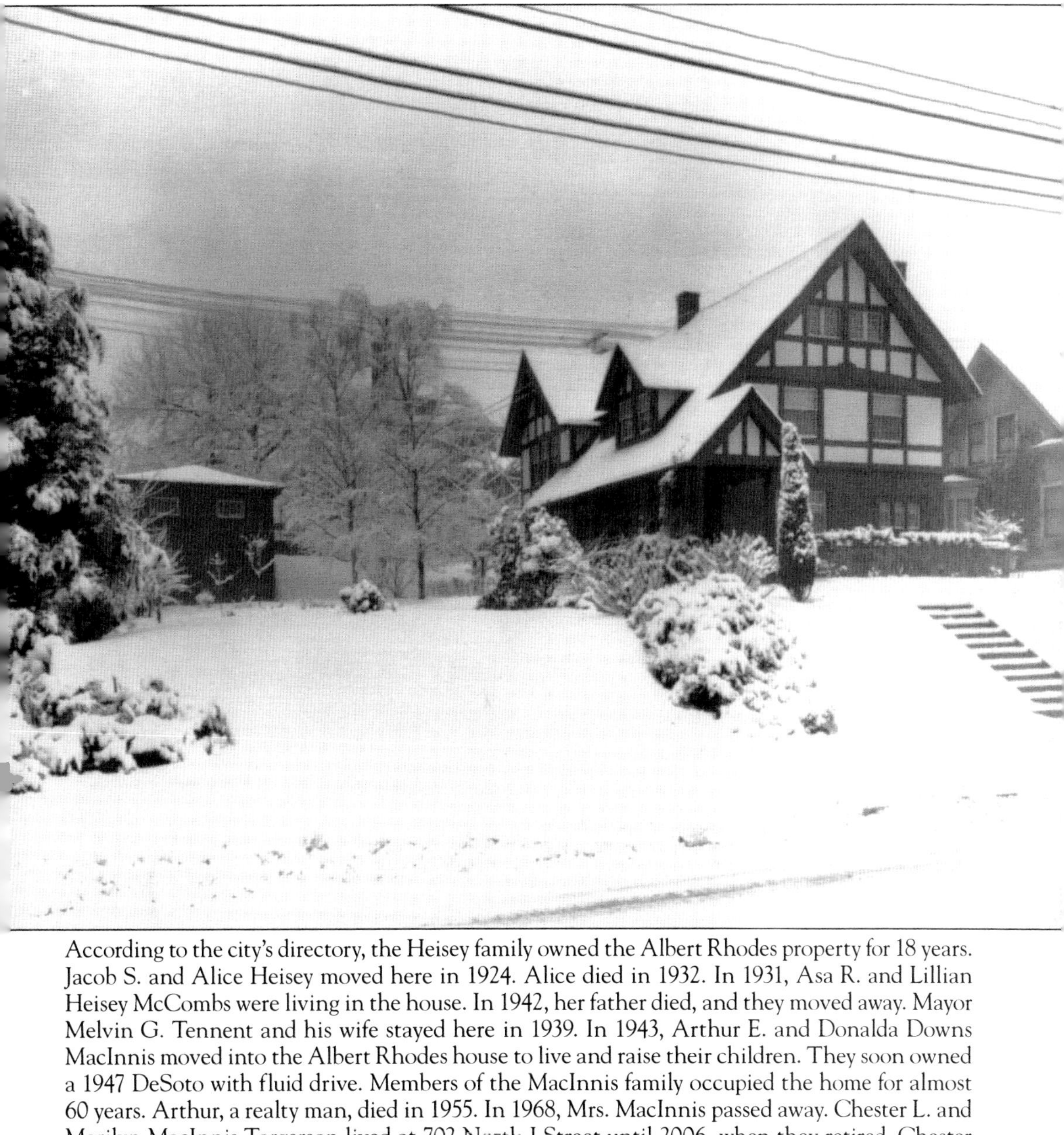

According to the city's directory, the Heisey family owned the Albert Rhodes property for 18 years. Jacob S. and Alice Heisey moved here in 1924. Alice died in 1932. In 1931, Asa R. and Lillian Heisey McCombs were living in the house. In 1942, her father died, and they moved away. Mayor Melvin G. Tennent and his wife stayed here in 1939. In 1943, Arthur E. and Donalda Downs MacInnis moved into the Albert Rhodes house to live and raise their children. They soon owned a 1947 DeSoto with fluid drive. Members of the MacInnis family occupied the home for almost 60 years. Arthur, a realty man, died in 1955. In 1968, Mrs. MacInnis passed away. Chester L. and Marilyn MacInnis Torgerson lived at 702 North I Street until 2006, when they retired. Chester was a teacher in Tacoma. (Courtesy of Marilyn Torgerson.)

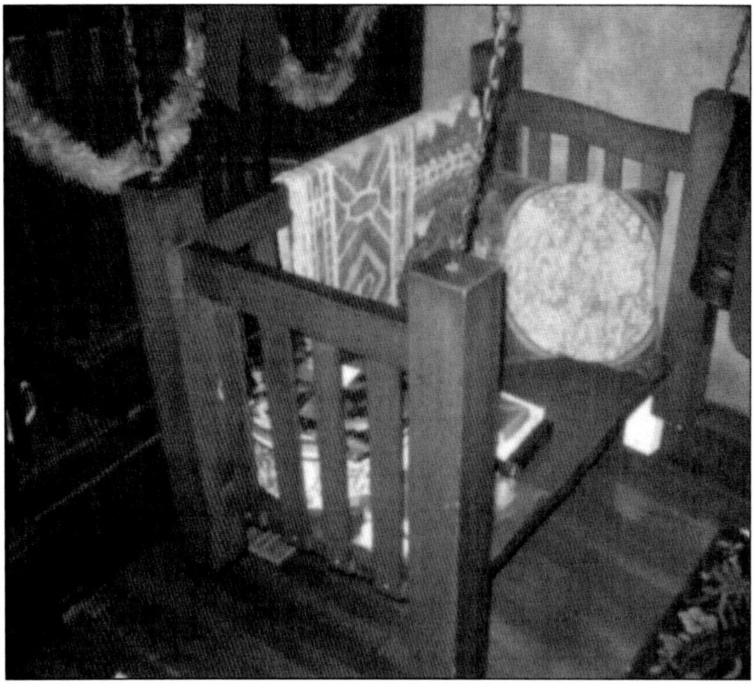

The house is entered from a porch, which runs along the full left side. To the right of the porch is a large picture window with a leaded-glass upper transom. This wooden Craftsman-style swing chair with chains bolted to the ceiling is located opposite the door in the entry near the stairs. (Courtesy of Marilyn Torgerson.)

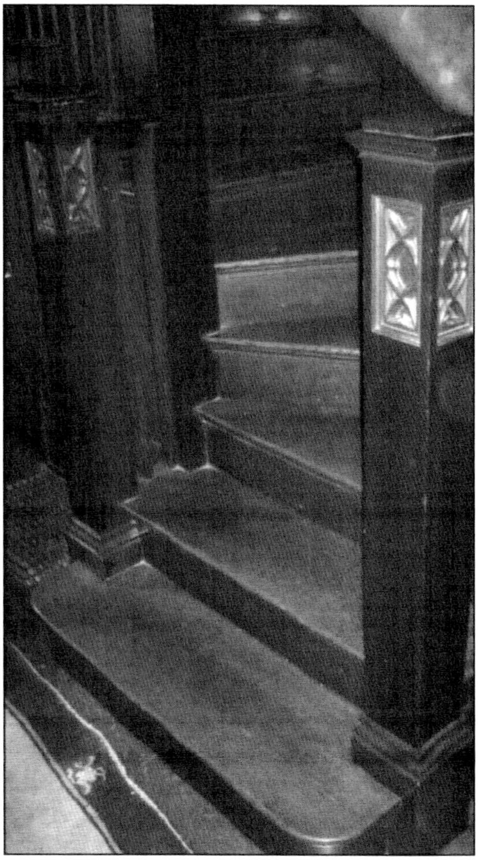

The main stairway is of oak, with wooden newel posts with decorative inlays. For the MacInnis Christmas, festive garlands would decorate the banisters and posts. The stairs curve upward, with three landings. There is a small closet under the steps, big enough to fit a vacuum cleaner, and a cool-air register is located in the floor next to the stairs. (Courtesy of Marilyn Torgerson.)

The attic windows on the front of the house are shown facing I Street. There is a chimney in the center, dividing the attic. A maid's room is located in the back half and has windows facing the backyard. The unfinished attic is covered with old-growth panels and beams. The bare lightbulb had a string long enough to reach from the stairwell. (Courtesy of Marilyn Torgerson.)

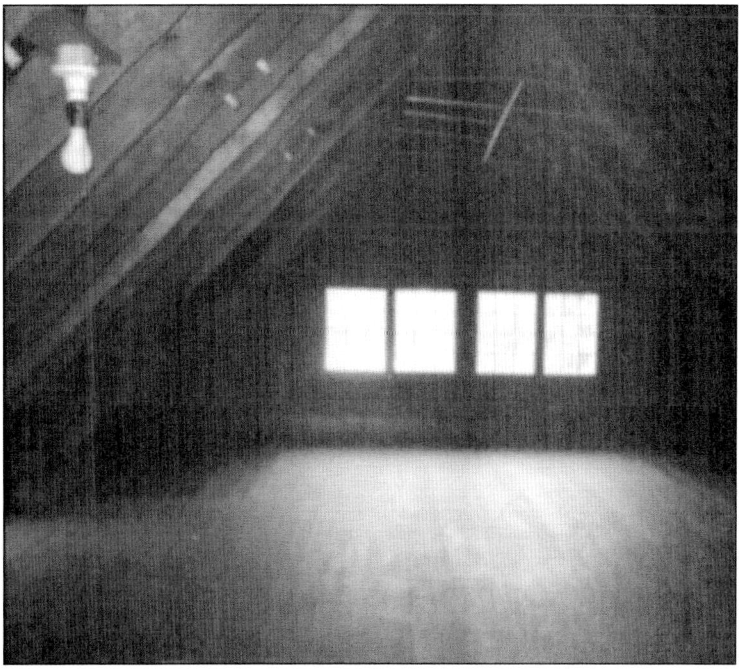

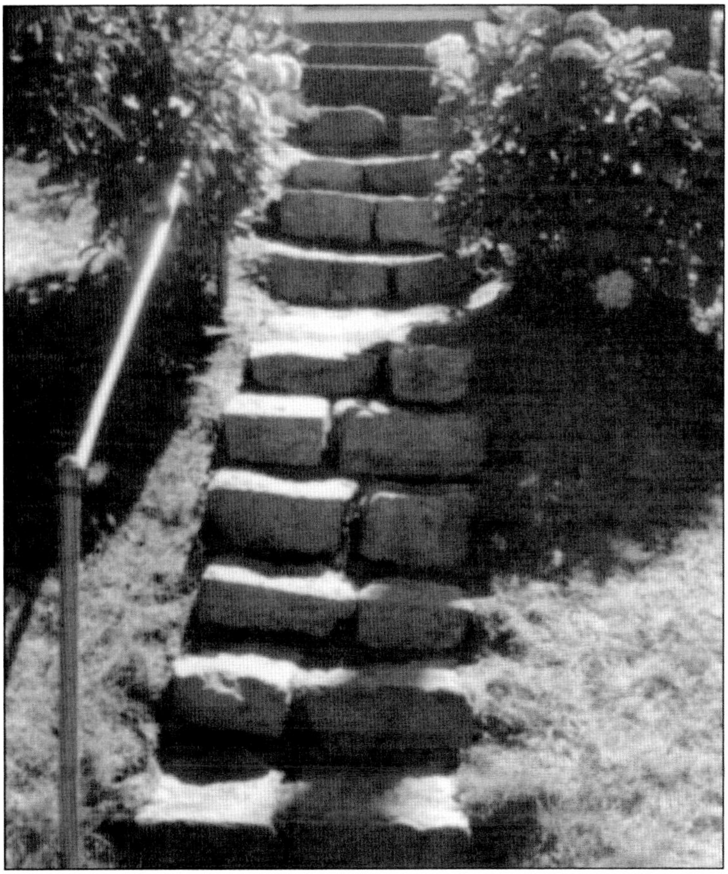

Uneven granite stairs climb up to the alley behind the house to access the garage. Railings were added for safety. As a child, Marilyn MacInnis used to pull the trash container up the steps to the alley, which is shared with the Henry Rhodes house at 701 North J Street. (Courtesy of Marilyn Torgerson.)

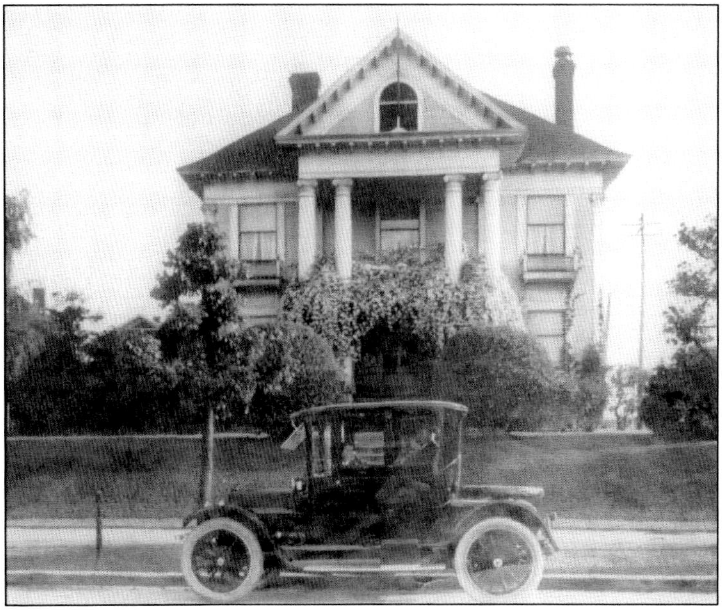

Samuel R. and Anna Corbett Balkwill are shown in their 1913 Cadillac coupe, purchased from the St. Helens garage. Samuel Balkwill was the owner and architect of the 1901 Neoclassical home in the background. It was built by the Cornell brothers at 1022 North K Street. The Balkwills were married in 1886 and in 1888 came to Tacoma, where he dealt in real estate, loans, and investments.

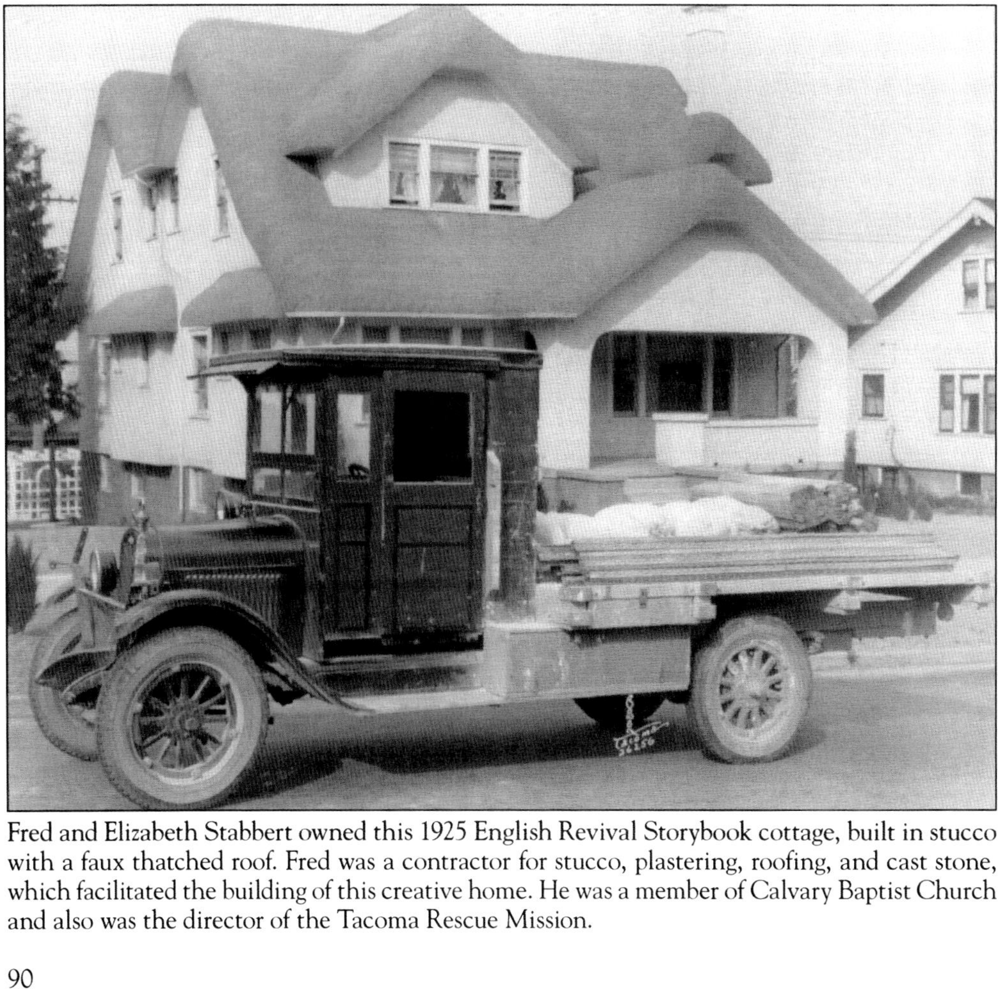

Fred and Elizabeth Stabbert owned this 1925 English Revival Storybook cottage, built in stucco with a faux thatched roof. Fred was a contractor for stucco, plastering, roofing, and cast stone, which facilitated the building of this creative home. He was a member of Calvary Baptist Church and also was the director of the Tacoma Rescue Mission.

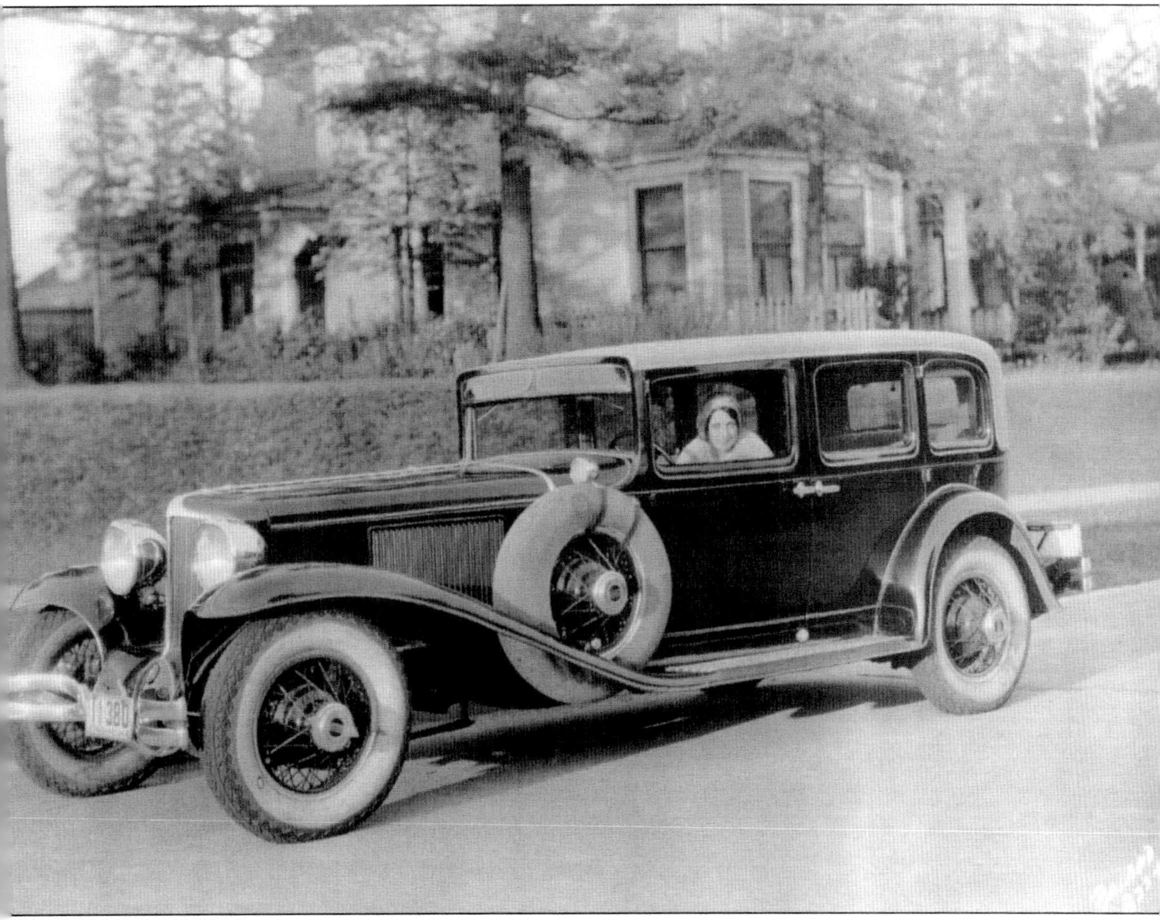

A notice in the *Tacoma Sunday Ledger* on May 4, 1930, states: "Parked outside the John Gallucci residence of 516 North M Street on April 29, 1930, was a new L29 model Cord courtesy of Remmert Motor Company. Miss Florence Gallucci is the daughter of John Gallucci, local contractor. This is the second car purchased by Mr. Gallucci from Remmert Motors, distributors of Auburns and Cords." Automobiles were the new rage in the 1920s—and the sportier the better. The Depression had not yet hit, and the building boom had peaked, so contractors were prospering. As for women, they had just gotten the vote, and they were enjoying their new freedom after the "war to end all wars," World War I, was over and the Roaring Twenties were strutting their stuff. Auburns, Cords, and Duesenbergs were the top of the line for touring cars.

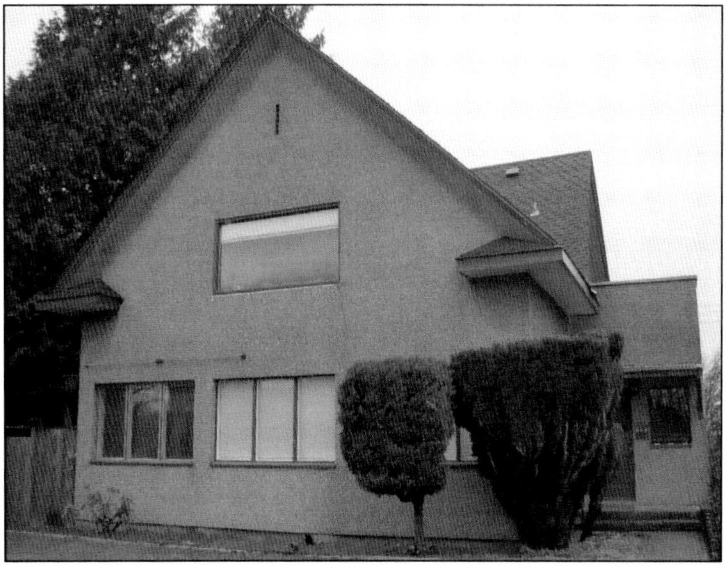

A 1912 brochure from the Southern Pacific Railroad mentions Mrs. Overton Ellis, who resided at 613 North K Street with her family. Her campaign for pure food was the subject of an article by Alfred Jeffreys. Judge Overton G. Ellis had recently been appointed to the state supreme court and had proudly taken his wife, Jennie, and family to Olympia. (Gyda May photograph.)

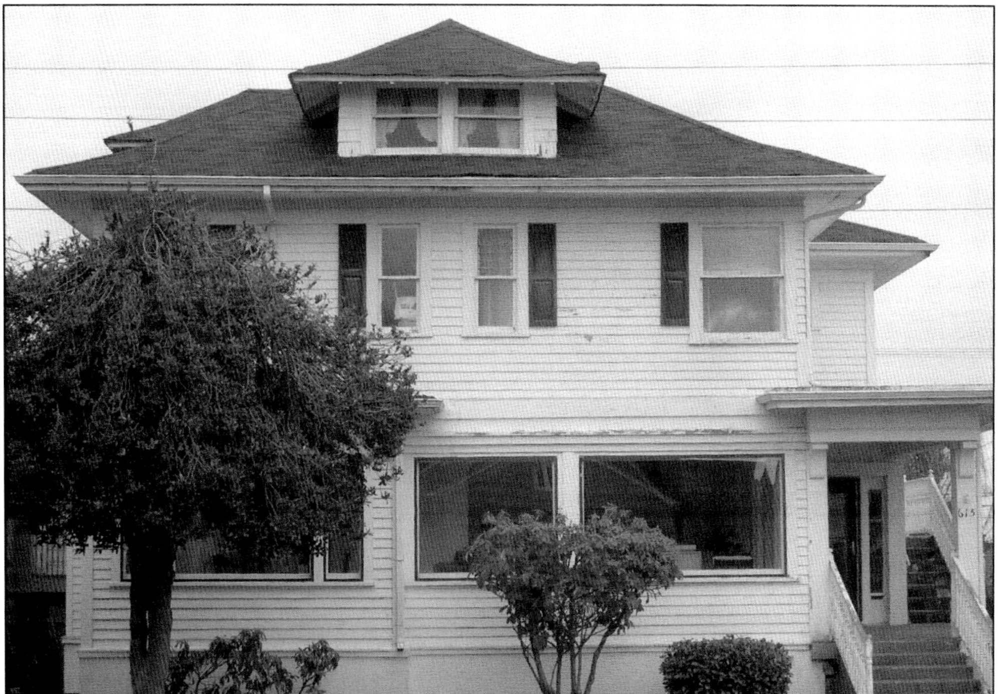

Dr. Burton E. Lemley was the owner and architect of this home at 615 North Cushman, built in 1910. He and his wife, Margaret Hughes Lemley, had two children, Lyle and Margaret. Dr. Lemley was a dentist who practiced very advanced techniques, such as prevention of gum tissue disease, in his downtown office. He also was in finance and real estate. (Gyda May photograph.)

This Foursquare house at 1112 North J Street was built by the father of Harry Lillis "Bing" Crosby. In 1906, Crosby's family moved to Spokane, Washington. He was the fourth of seven children. His parents, Harry Lincoln Crosby, a bookkeeper, and Catherine Helen "Kate" Harrigan, were English American and Irish American, respectively. The plaque placed on the steps in front of the Crosby house (below) in 1979 shows Bing Crosby's birth date as May 2, 1904, as stated by his mother and marked on his grave. There is a debate however, since baptismal records from the St. Patrick Catholic Church in Old Tacoma show a date of May 3, 1903. Whatever the actual date, he was born in Tacoma's North Slope. (Both, Gyda May photographs.)

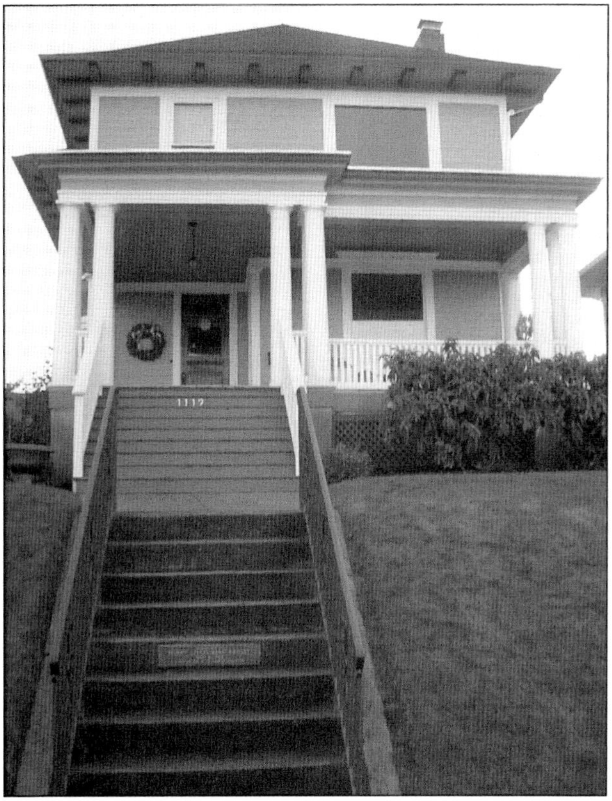

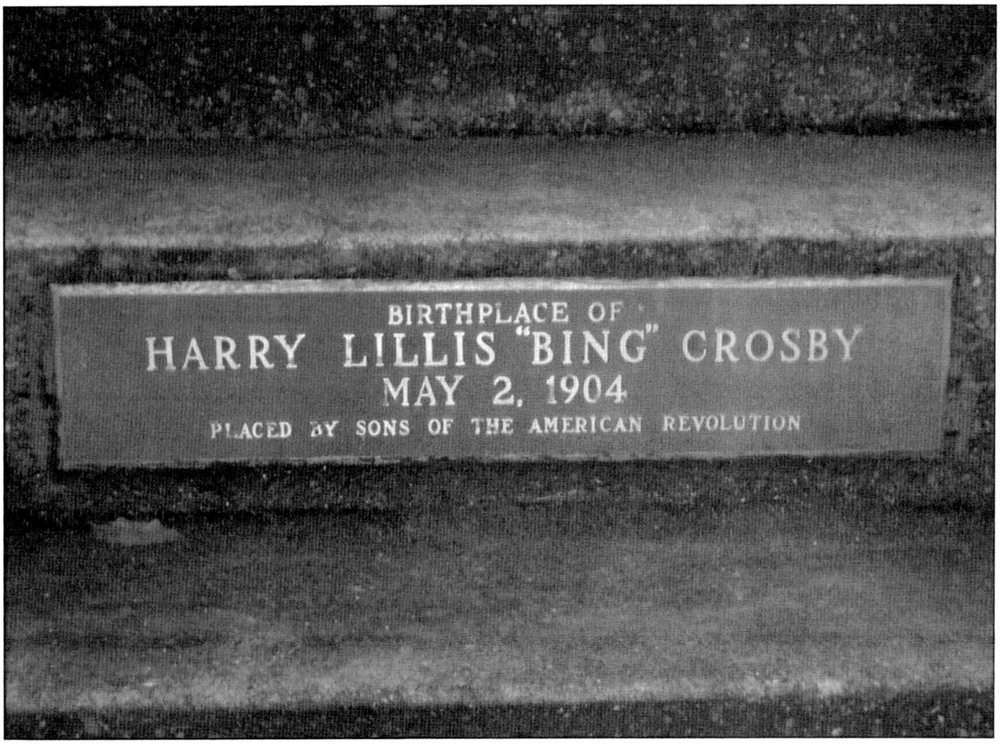

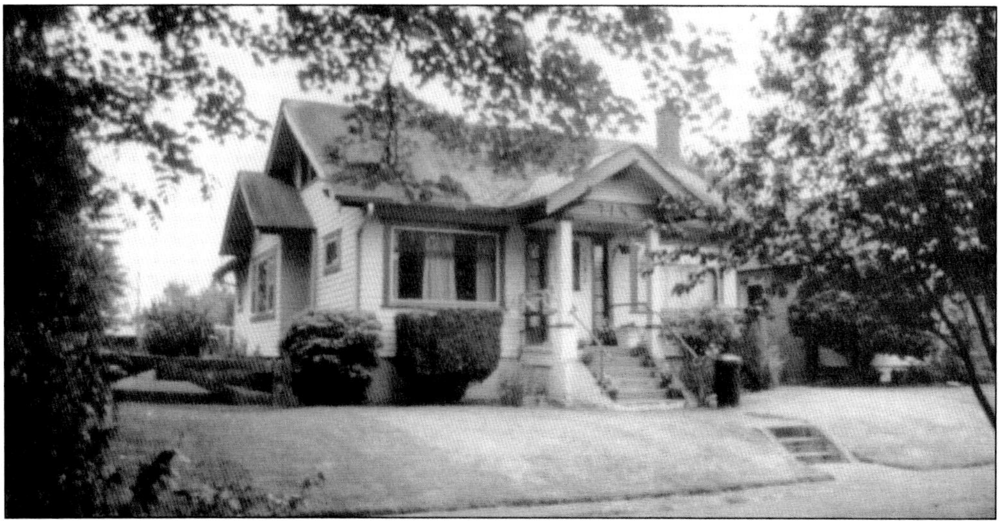

In the 1920s, Marcus and Elizabeth Nalley lived in this Craftsman bungalow at 714 North Ainsworth Avenue, with their sons, Robert Marcus Nalley (born in 1914) and George Nalley (born about 1923). In this small residence, an office was located off the living room, which was where sales and accounting were conducted by Mr. Nalley. This home office was separate from the factory, which produced the Nalley products.

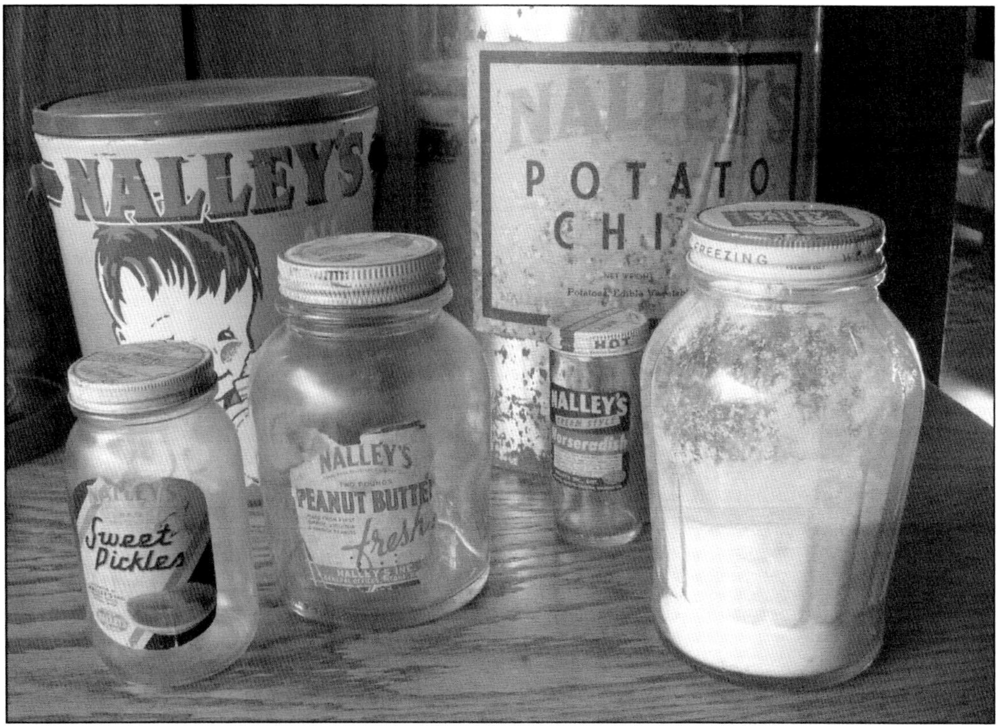

Nalley's, Inc., was founded in Tacoma in 1918. Marko Narancik (Marcus Nalley) had come from Croatia and found work in a hotel kitchen in New York. Later, he became a chef on the first *Olympian* train of the Milwaukee Railroad between Chicago and Tacoma. Marcus Nalley learned to make special potato chips at the Bonneville Hotel in Tacoma. Nalley's began with chips and expanded to more products, such as pickles and salad dressing. (Gyda May photograph.)

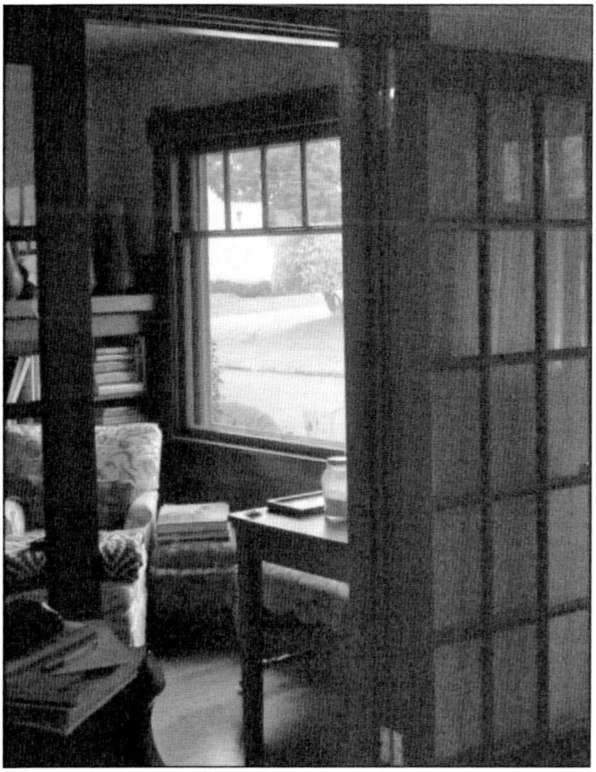

The front door to the house opens to the living room. The residence is built in true bungalow style, without an entry hall. To the right is a small room, which had been made into a business office, with a pocket door added. There is a window facing the front of the house. (Gyda May photograph.)

Inside the Nalley business office was a desk, upon which the accounting book was placed. This was the room where business was conducted. An outside door led to the side of the house, where salesmen and customers could come and go without disturbing the family in the rest of the home. (Gyda May photograph.)

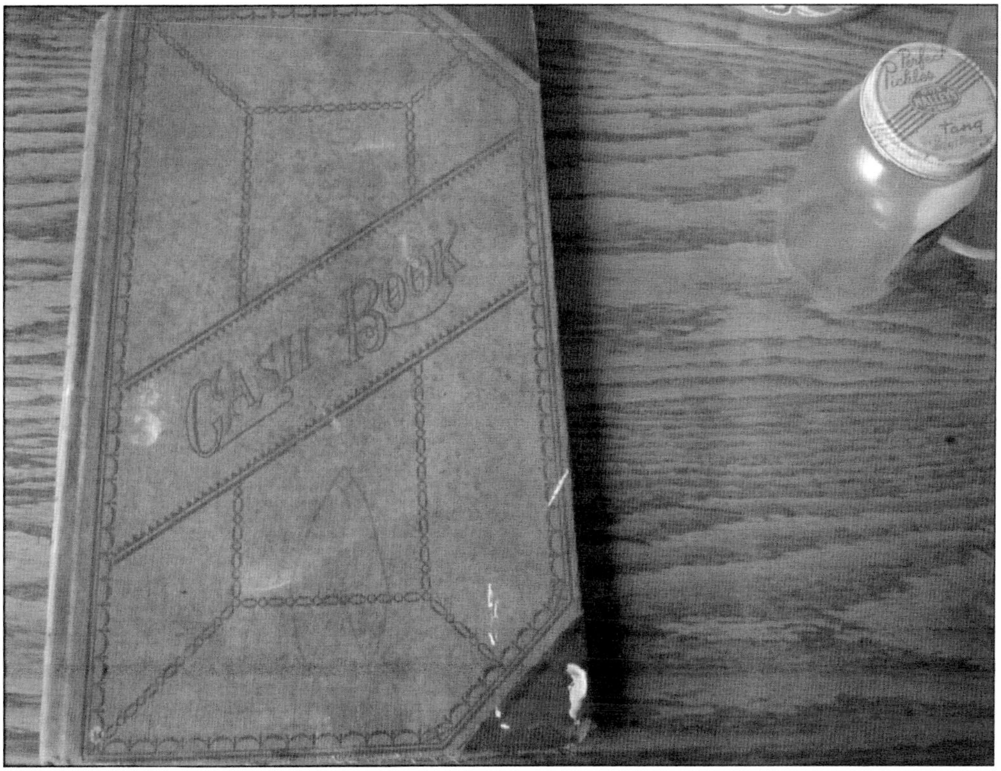

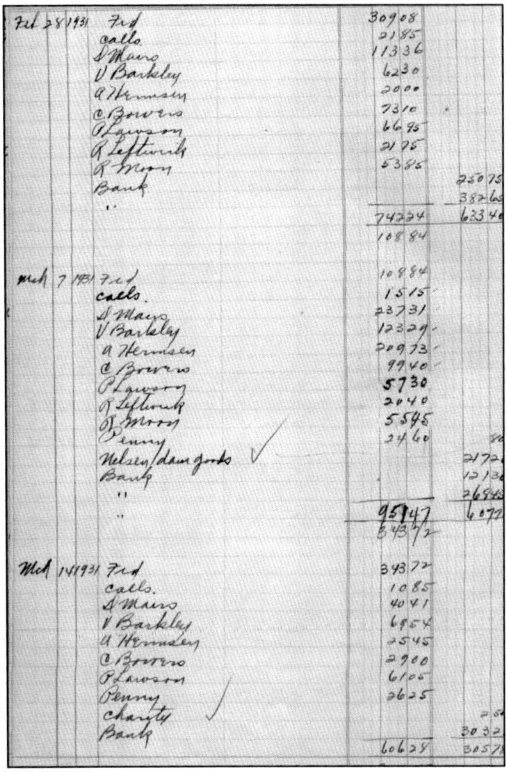

Feb 28 1931 Fred 30908
calls 2185
S Mairs 11336
V Barkley 6230
A Hermsen 2000
C Bowers 7310
P Lawson 6695
R Leftwich 2175
R Moon 5385
Bank
"
74224
10884

Mch 7 1931 Fred 10884
calls 1515
S Mairs 23731
V Barkley 12329
A Hermsen 20973
C Bowers 9940
P Lawson 5730
R Leftwich 2040
R Moon 5545
Penny 2460
Nelsen/dam goods
Bank
"
"
95147
34372

Mch 14 1931 Fred 34372
calls 1085
S Mairs 4041
V Barkley 6854
A Hermsen 2545
C Bowers 2900
P Lawson 6105
Penny 2625
Charity
Bank
60628

Pages in the accounting book are neatly filled out with columns for credit, cash, and deposits, with withdrawals duly noted. Most of the entries deal with office supplies, such as tablets and ink. Names of customers and sales staff are written with money amounts in the right column. (Gyda May photograph.)

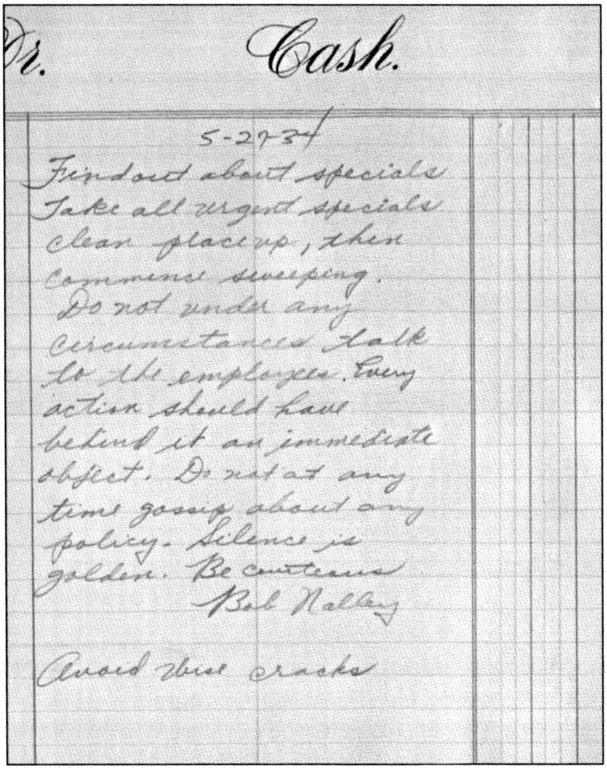

Cash.

5-27-34

Find out about specials
Take all urgent specials
clean place up, then
commence sweeping.
Do not under any
circumstances talk
to the employees. Every
action should have
behind it an immediate
object. Do not at any
time gossip about any
policy. Silence is
golden. Be courteus
Bob Nalley

Avoid these cracks

By 1934, when Robert Marcus Nalley was 20, he was helping with the business. The following are some lines from a note from "Bob" Nalley to the salesmen: "Find out about specials, clean place up, then commence sweeping. Do not under any circumstances talk to the employees, Do not at any time gossip. Be courteous." (Gyda May photograph.)

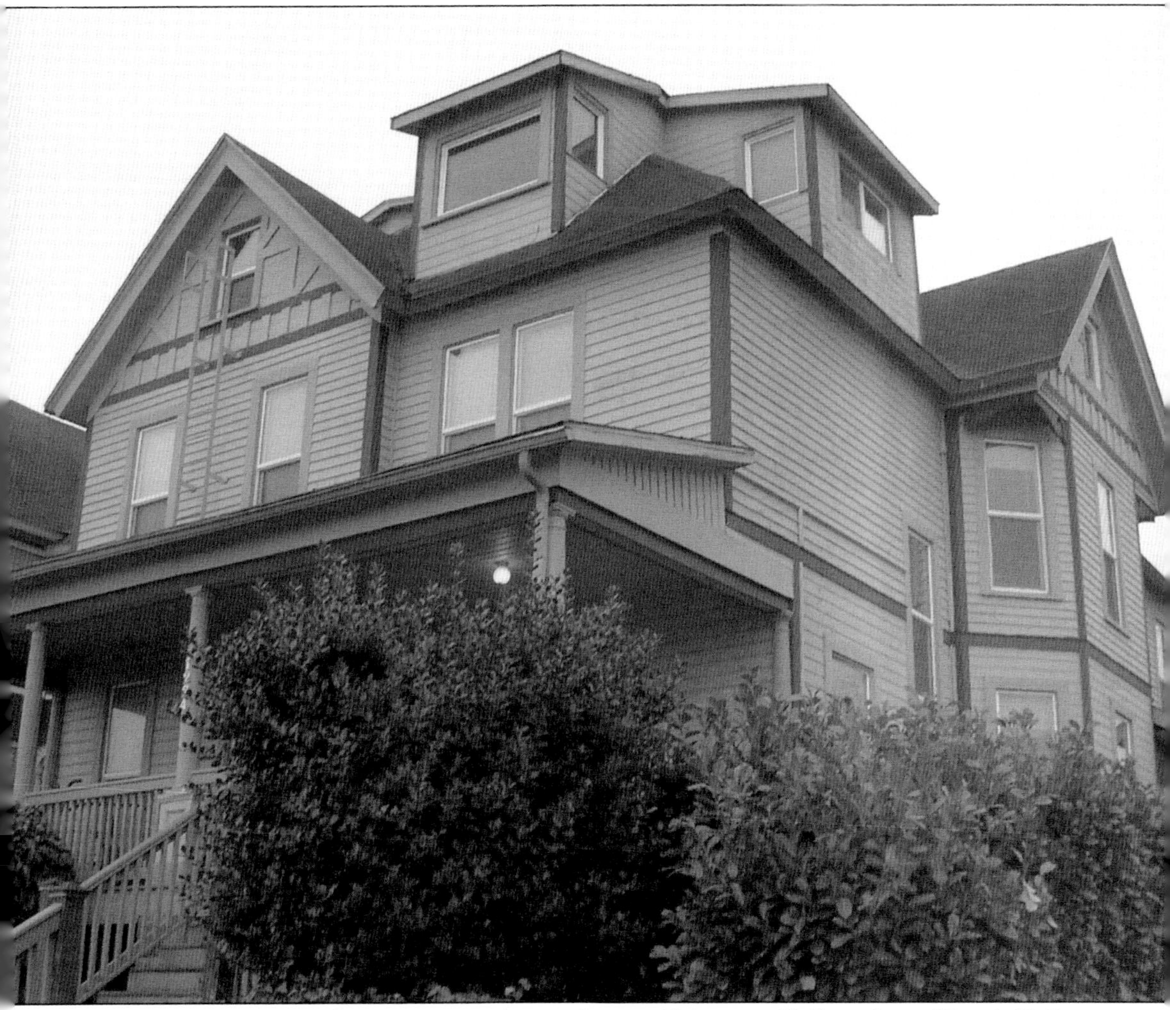

The house at 1224 North I Street was the residence of Margaret Hall, widow of Frank Hall. The following story was told by the *Times Daily Ledger* of March 6, 1904. Built in Gig Harbor on Harborview Drive, it was considered that city's "largest and most pretentious dwelling." But Margaret Hall, desiring to be closer to her daughter Mrs. W.W. Powell, who lived at 1118 North I Street, decided to move her house by barge from Gig Harbor to Tacoma in 1904. As the structure was being shifted onto two scows for transportation, "a portion of the building dropped off into the water, and the house was badly wrecked." The portion lost was a woodshed and upper apartment, and James M. Nichols, "a member of the contracting firm, stated last night that while the house was seriously injured, he thought he could repair it and set it together so that it would be all right." After the accident, it was decided to send all the furnishings over by steamer. The transportation of the home was completed successfully. (Gyda May photograph.)

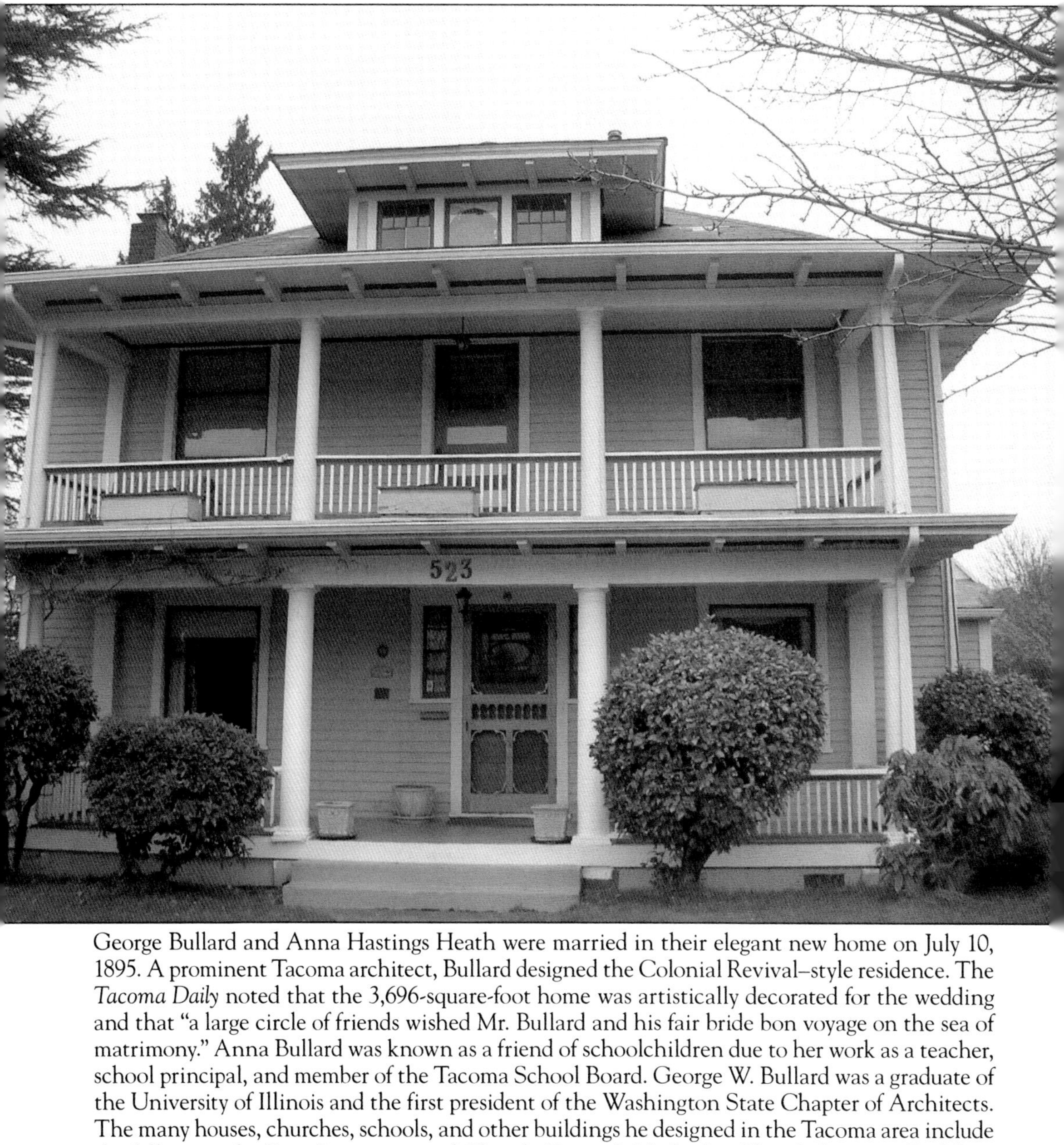

George Bullard and Anna Hastings Heath were married in their elegant new home on July 10, 1895. A prominent Tacoma architect, Bullard designed the Colonial Revival–style residence. The *Tacoma Daily* noted that the 3,696-square-foot home was artistically decorated for the wedding and that "a large circle of friends wished Mr. Bullard and his fair bride bon voyage on the sea of matrimony." Anna Bullard was known as a friend of schoolchildren due to her work as a teacher, school principal, and member of the Tacoma School Board. George W. Bullard was a graduate of the University of Illinois and the first president of the Washington State Chapter of Architects. The many houses, churches, schools, and other buildings he designed in the Tacoma area include the following: the First Congregational Church, Epworth Methodist Church, Japanese Buddhist Church, Washington State Historical Society Building, and the first permanent University of Puget Sound campus at Sixth and Sprague Avenues. (Gyda May photograph.)

Born in Rochester, Minnesota, George Gove arrived in 1908 in Tacoma, where his brother Herbert had lived since 1889. George lived at 311 North L Street, two blocks from architect Carl Darmer's house. As part of the Heath, Gove, and Bell architect firm from 1914 to 1953, George designed Lincoln High School in Tacoma and Paradise Inn at Mount Rainier National Park. (Gyda May photograph.)

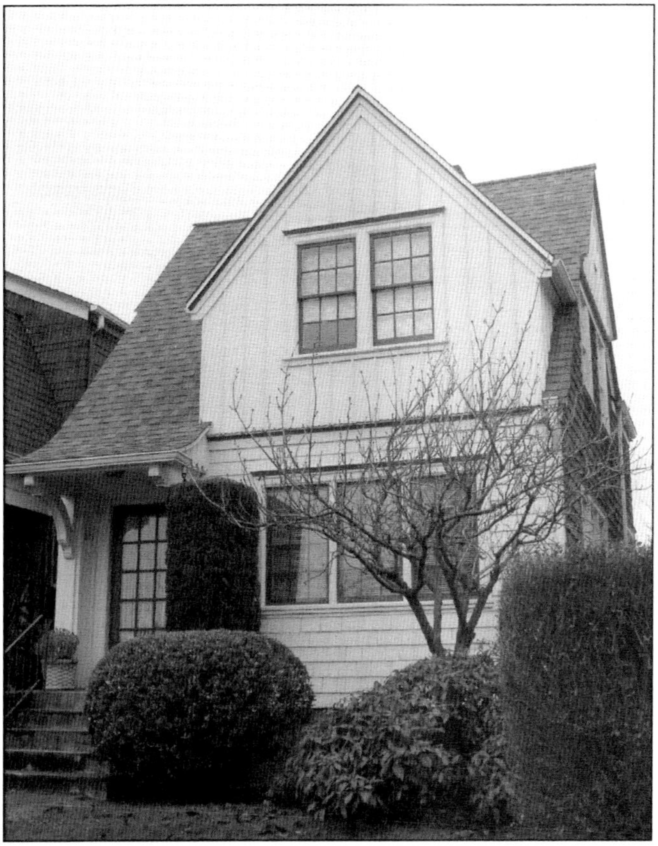

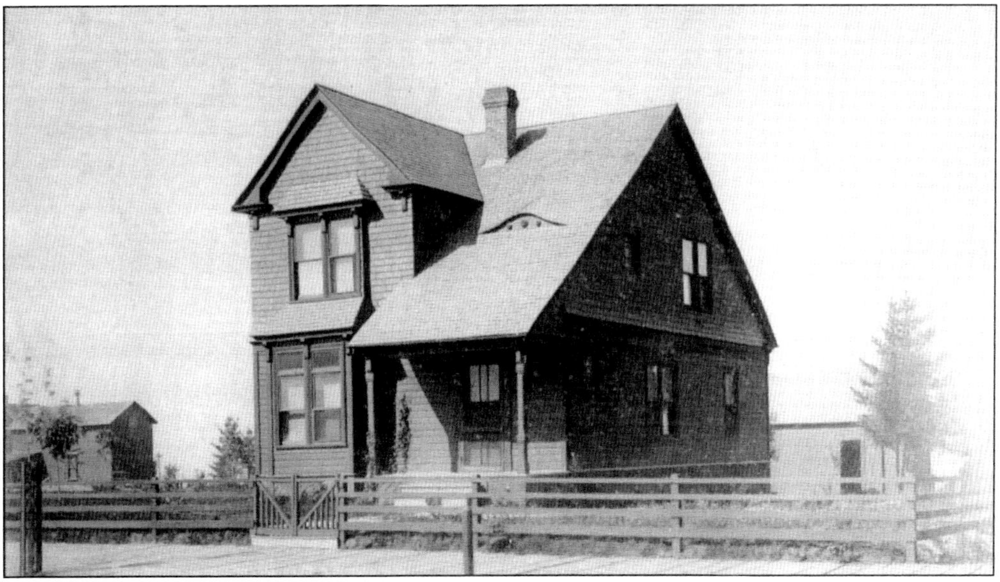

This was the residence of W.B. Allen at 419 North J. Street, Tacoma, around 1890. William B. Allen, his wife, Florence (Long) Allen, and their children lived at this address for many years. It was the couple's first home in Tacoma following their marriage in Chehalis in 1888. W.B. Allen was a prominent banker and later a lumberman. In 1890, he was mayor of Tacoma.

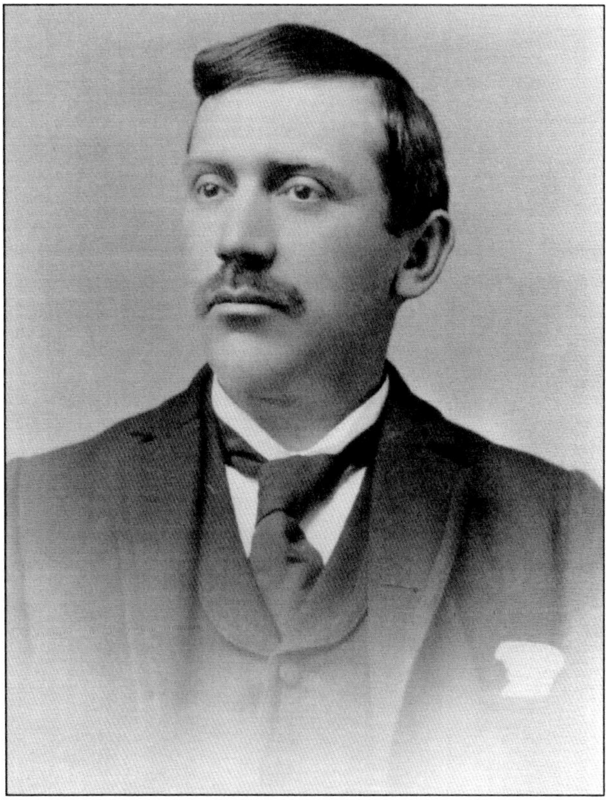

Aaron R. Titlow was elected on the Democratic ticket to the office of prosecuting attorney for Pierce County from 1897 to 1898. Born in Ohio, he journeyed west and arrived in Tacoma shortly before Washington achieved statehood. He is perhaps best known as the owner of the luxury Hotel Hesperides, named in honor of his three young daughters and built on Titlow Beach in the city's west end.

Architect O.P. Dennis and builders Sawyer and Brockenbrough built the Dutch Colonial house at 1605 Division Avenue in 1893 for Aaron R. Titlow. He lived there with his wife, Stella, and their daughters: Ione, Constance, and Marcelle. When he died in 1923, Aaron had disposed of all of his holdings on the beach, which were later acquired by the Metropolitan Park District. (Gyda May photograph.)

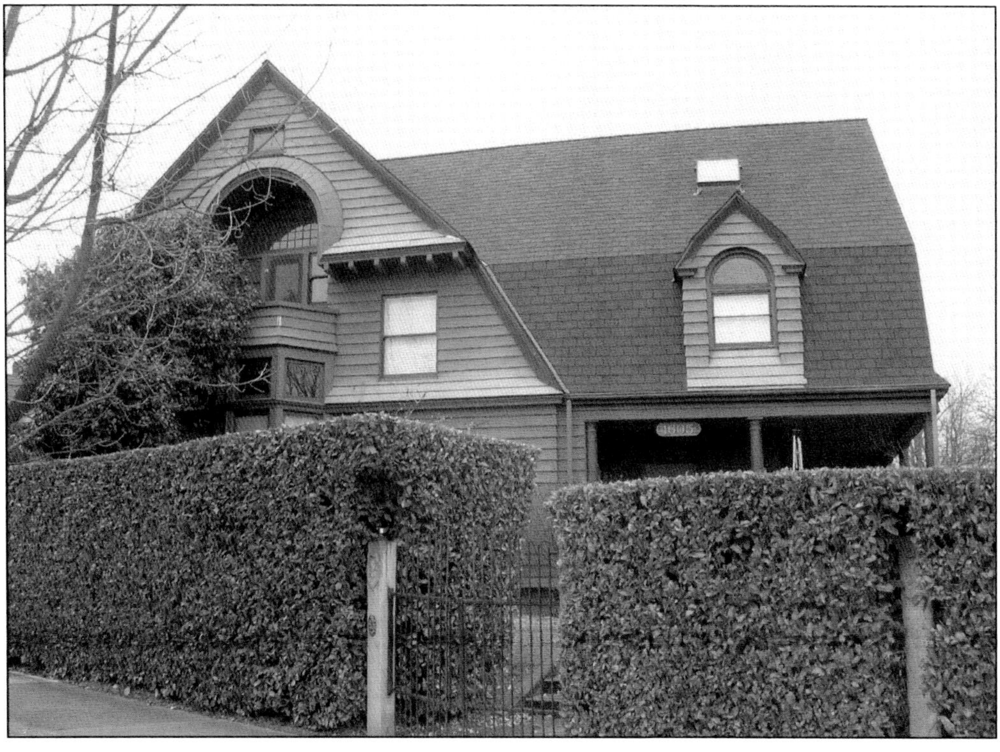

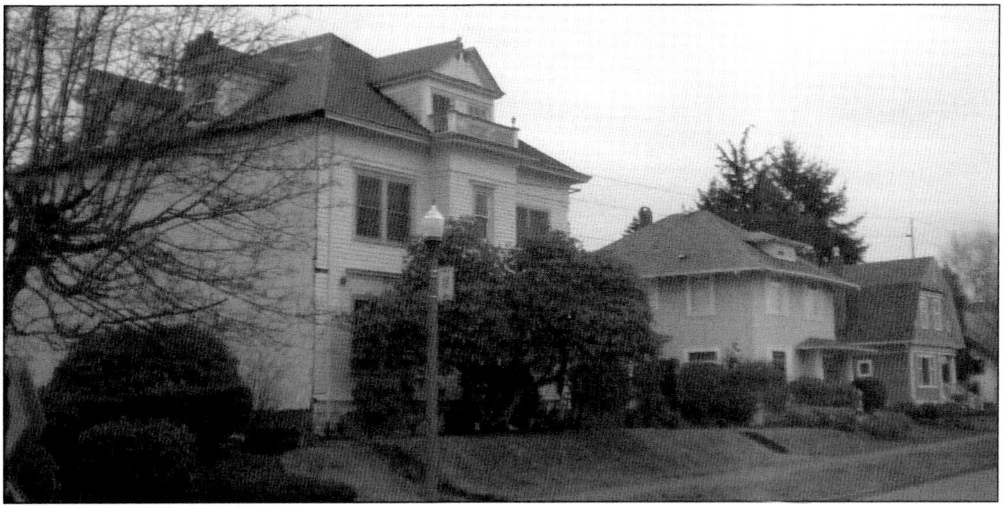

The Neocolonial at 1401 North Fifth Street and the one at 1415 were designed and built by the Cornell brothers in 1895 for two business partners, William Ferguson (1401) and William Gardener (1415). Ferguson was considered one of the founders of the First Presbyterian Church, and his wife and son donated the chapel there in his memory. On the right, the Louis Stewart house (below) is just visible. (Ben Cody photograph.)

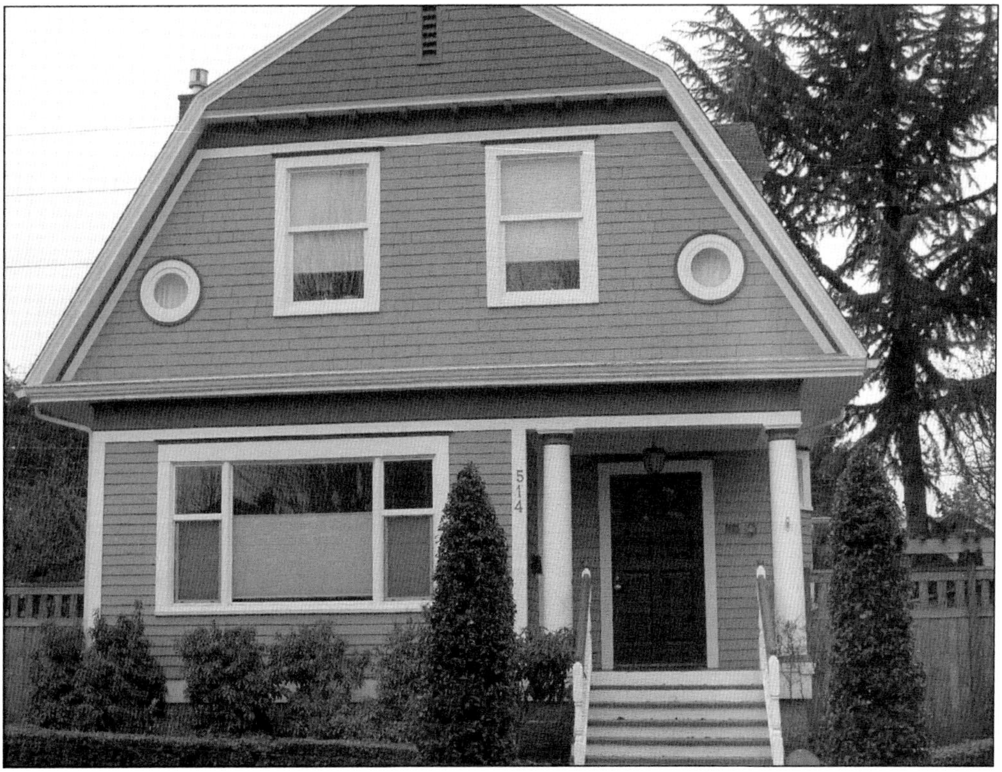

The 1902 Dutch Colonial at 514 North Sheridan Avenue, designed by George Bullard, was the home of Louis Stewart, who came to Tacoma in 1888 from West Virginia. He and his brother formed Kona Koffee in 1905, with Louis serving as president. During a North Slope tour of homes in 2008, coffee cans were prominently displayed in the kitchen. (Gyda May photograph.)

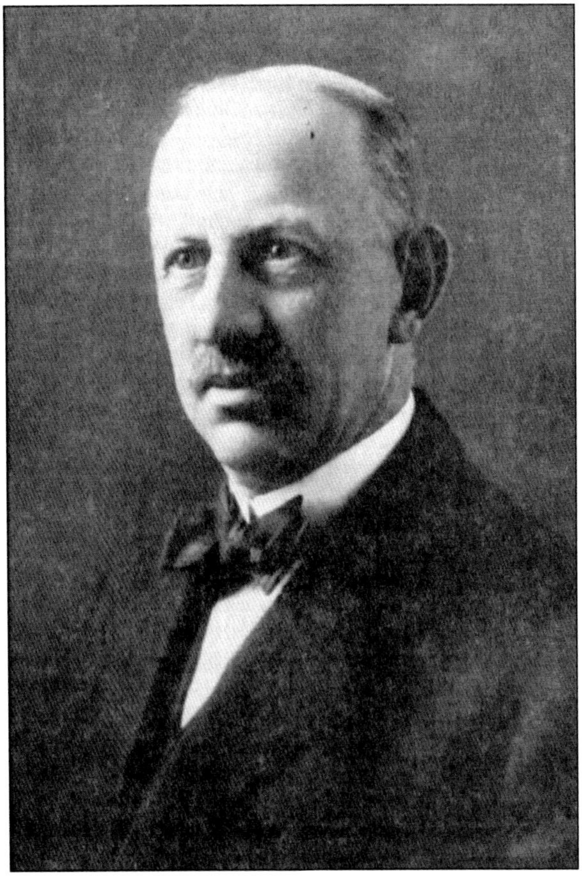

Arthur Freeman Albertson was originally from Michigan but developed his banking and manufacturing career here. He married Martha Lloyd Voorhees in 1890 in Tacoma. The Albertsons also lived at 619, 805, and 823 North I Street. They had a daughter, also named Martha Lloyd, and were very prominent socialites in Tacoma and members of the Episcopal church. He was on the board of trustees of the chamber of commerce for many years. The house built at 808 North I Street for the Albertsons in 1892 is an example of mirror-image construction. The home at 806 is the mirror of this residence. The house is located on 1.5 lots. It has eight rooms that were originally papered and varnished in the style of the time. It also had the latest porcelain plumbing fixtures in 1892.

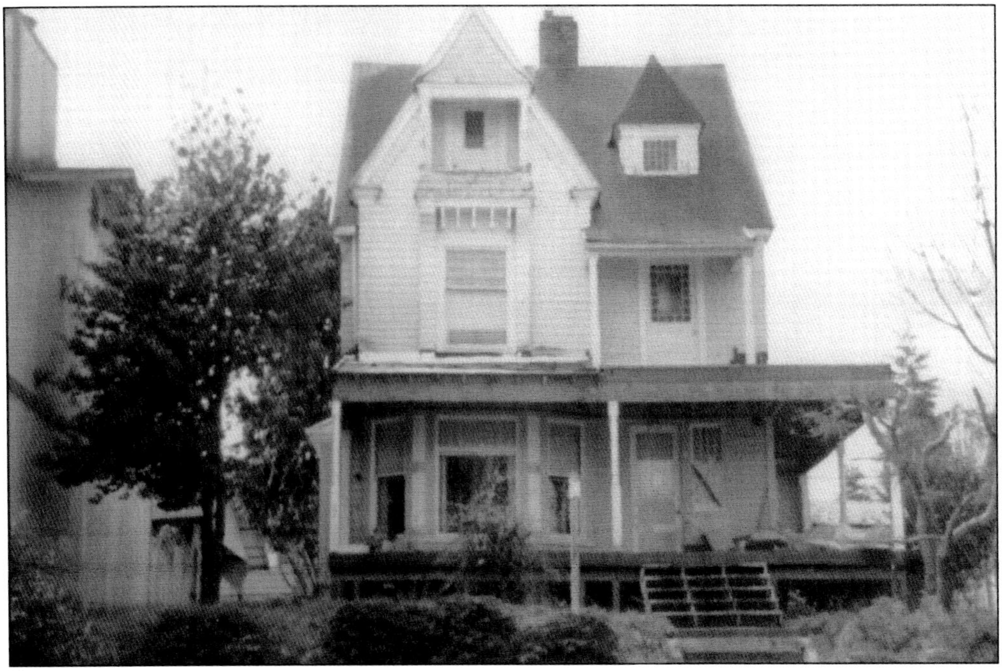

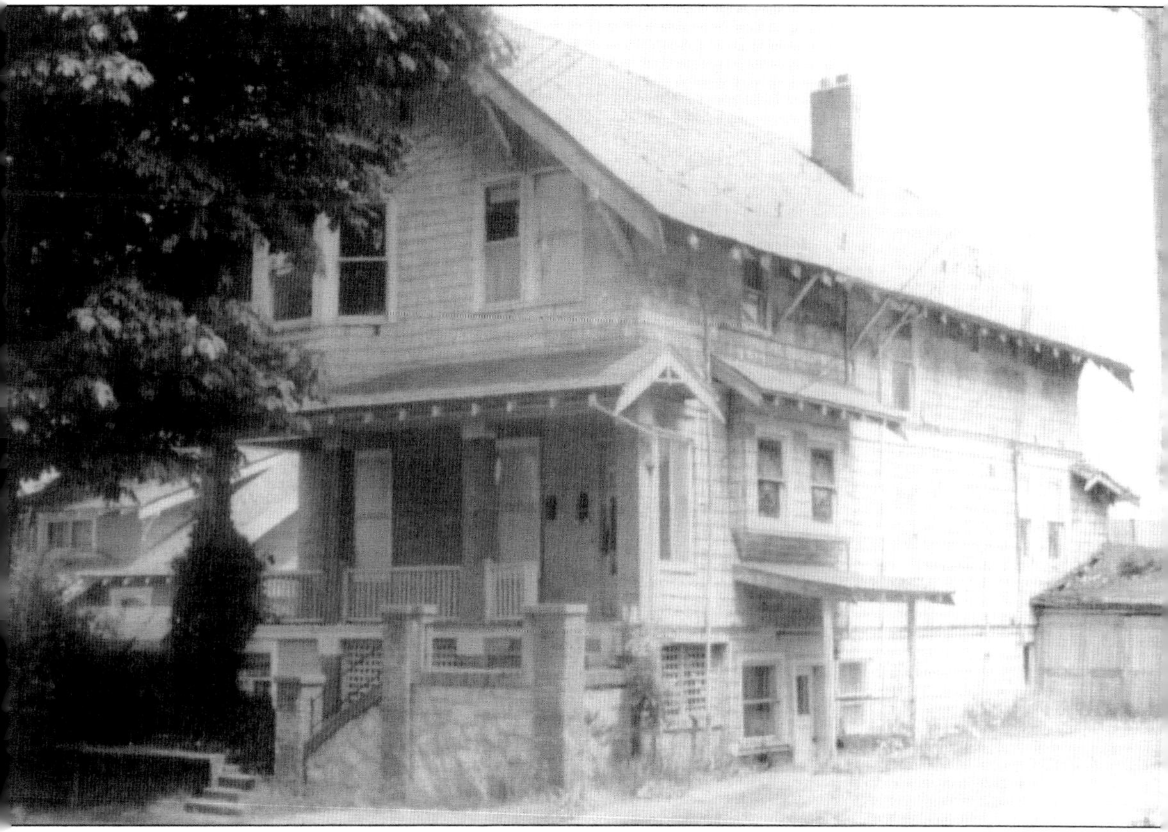

This Craftsman-style home was built in 1892 for architect Edward A. Hatherton at 1210 North Ninth Street. Hatherton came to Tacoma from San Francisco, where he had been that city's official architect. A porch extends across the front, supported on heavy, square columns of brick. Decorative granite blocks cover the base under the porch. In 1892, the Hatherton home had a large, landscaped lawn on two extra lots, which extended to the corner of North Ninth and L Streets. Mrs. Hatherton was a member of the Aloha Club, the first women's club in Tacoma. According to historian Herbert Hunt, the new chamber of commerce in 1893 offered prizes for the best set of plans for the erection of a beautiful chamber building. The first prize of $500 went to Hatherton and McIntosh, of Tacoma. The new chamber building was then traded to the City of Tacoma to be used as a new city hall. In May 1894, amid fanfare, the cornerstone was laid. This later photograph shows a smaller house on the property, at 1206 North Ninth Street.

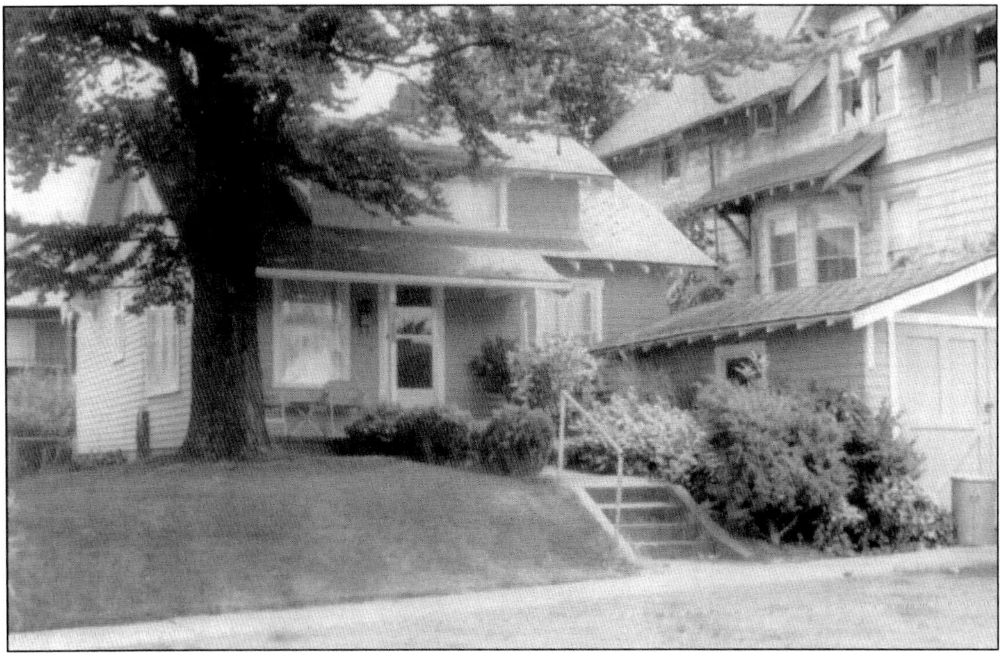

In 1919, J. Vaughn and Son was issued permits to construct bungalows with garages at 1202 and 1206 North Ninth Street. Shown is the bungalow at 1206, next to the large Craftsman built by E.A. Hatherton. Some owners in the neighborhood sold their spacious lawns, and smaller houses were built in the area.

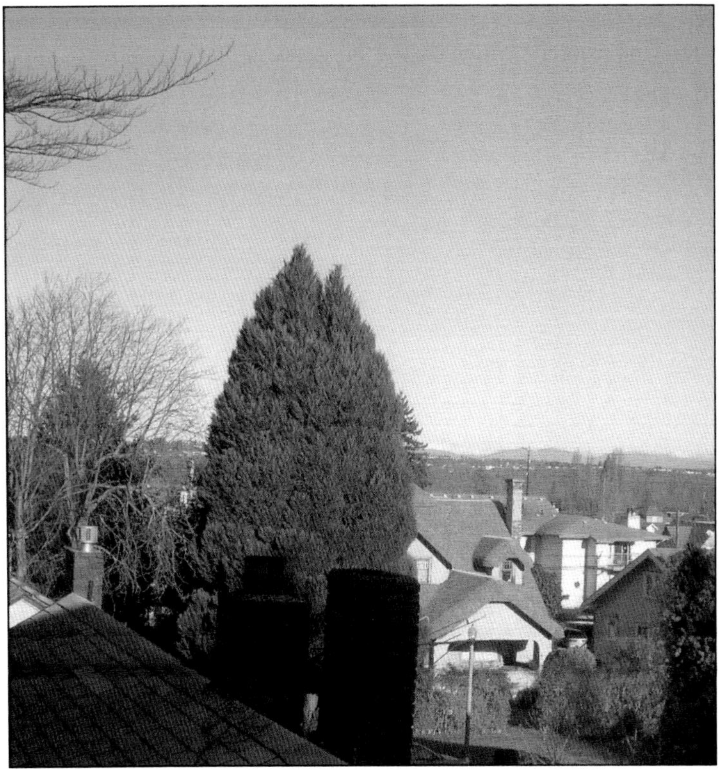

This is the view from an upstairs room in the Hatherton house. To the left of the evergreen tree are two roofs. The first one is at 1206 North Ninth Street (foreground), and the second belongs to 1202. To the right of the tree is the 815 North L Street Storybook cottage. Farther away is the Cascade Range. (Gyda May photograph.)

Five

North Slope Historic District

The North Slope Historic District (NSHD) is a designated area bounded by North I Street, Division Avenue, North Grant Avenue, and North Steele Street in which the majority of homes are of comparable ages and styles. Residents unite to preserve the integrity of the structures. It is also a neighborhood where people greet one another as they stroll along the tree-lined streets.

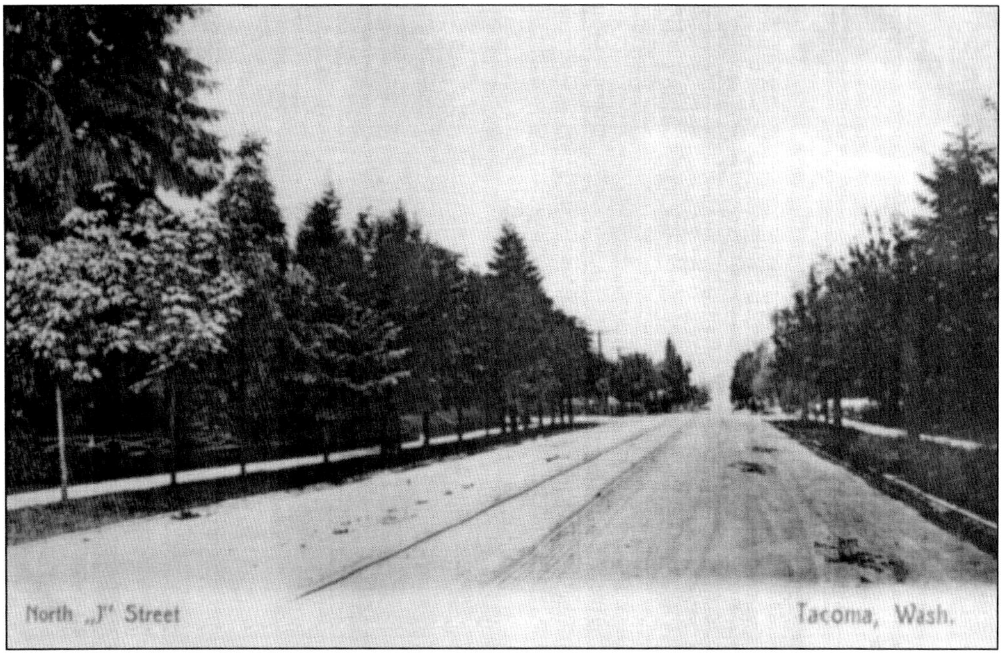

This 1905 postcard shows trees along North I Street. The company erroneously printed J Street, but someone wrote "North Eye Street" (instead of Jay Street) on the back to correct it. Streetcar tracks can be seen in the center of the roadway. North I Street has always been a major thoroughfare and is the northernmost street in the North Slope Historic District.

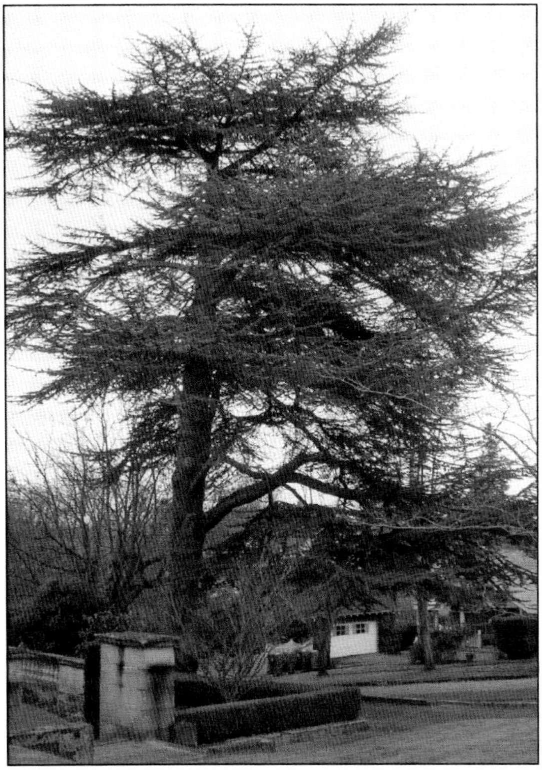

On North I Street at North Tenth Avenue, on the property of the Rust Mansion, is a cedar of Lebanon that was probably planted back when the house was built in the early 1900s. Its singular appearance makes it stand out among the trees in the neighborhood. It has been well preserved and shares the history of the neighborhood. (Gyda May photograph.)

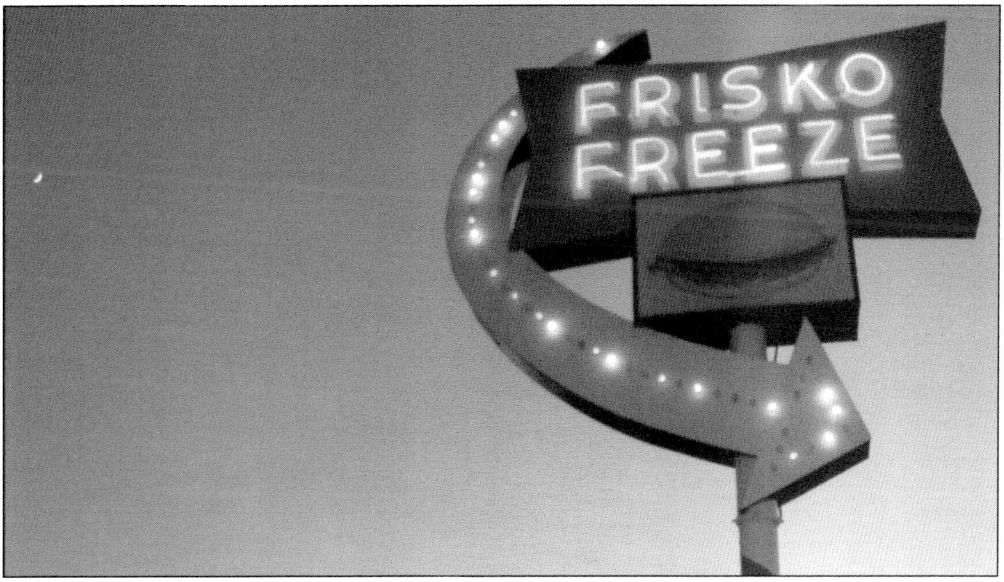

In the summer of 1950, the year the new Tacoma Narrows Bridge opened (10 years after Galloping Gertie had collapsed), a gas-company driver named Perry Smith wanted to start an ice cream stand on the corner of North L Street and Division Avenue. He used a bold, new, uniquely American building style called Googie that was influenced by the car culture and the fascination people had at the time for space-age themes. One famous example of Googie architecture is the Space Needle in Seattle. A big, bright sign points the way to the stand, designed to be seen from blocks away. Frisko Freeze is now a pop-culture icon and has recently been declared a historic landmark and listed on the city's historic register. Thousands of fans soak in its "warm and fuzzies," as preservation consultant Michael Sullivan calls it. (Both, Gyda May photographs.)

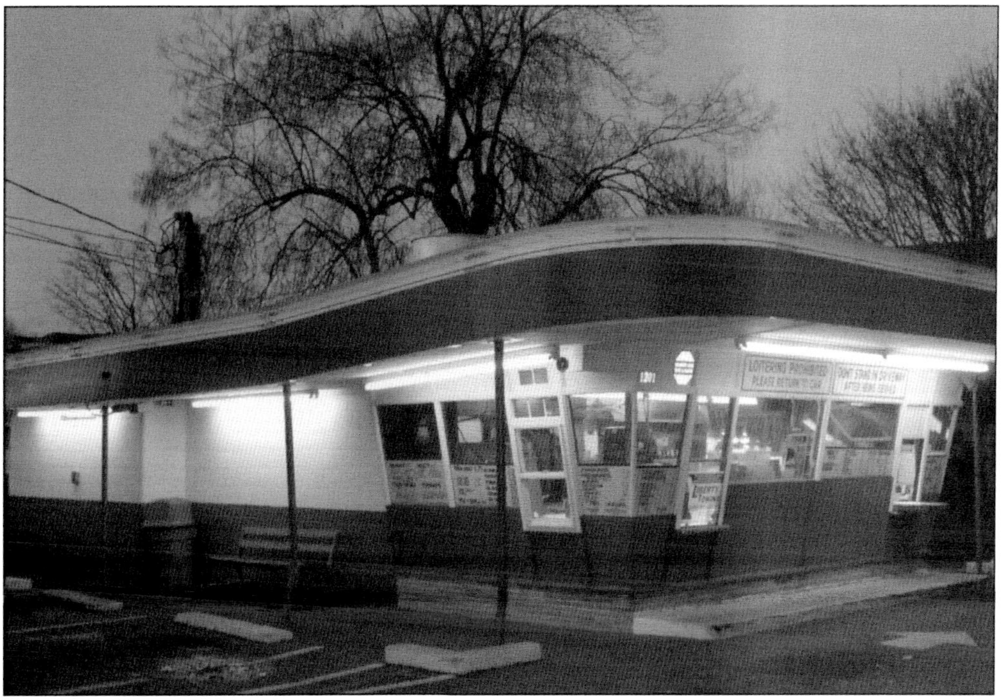

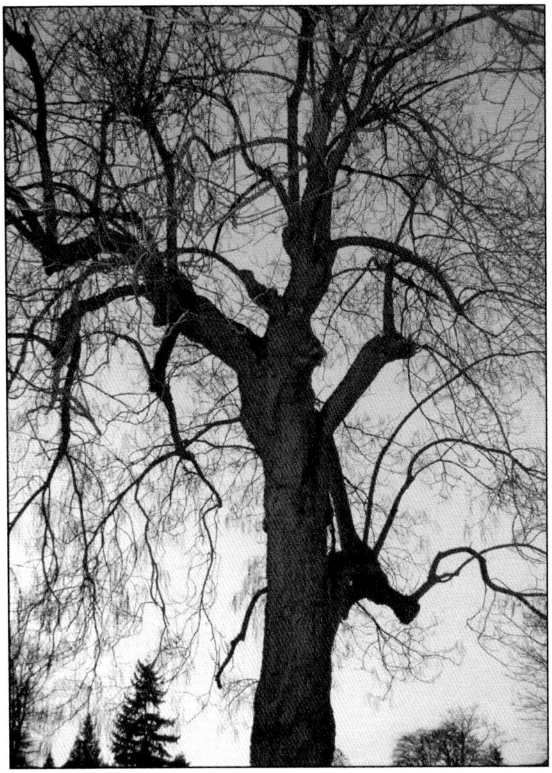

Trees such as this catalpa located behind Frisko Freeze are very old and well liked by neighborhood residents and visitors. They increase the value of the neighborhood and add to the experience of walking down its streets. There is currently a movement to create a register of historic trees, such as this one, to save them from being removed by developers. (Gyda May photograph.)

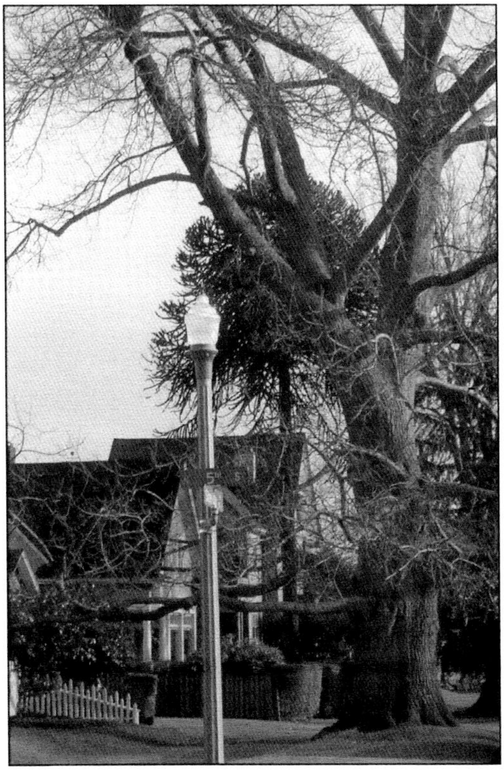

Probably one of the best-known trees in the neighborhood is the Spanish chestnut tree located on a parking strip near North Sheridan Avenue and North Fifth Street. It is known as "the big chestnut tree" and is much loved by residents. People say that it has a lot of personality. (Gyda May photograph.)

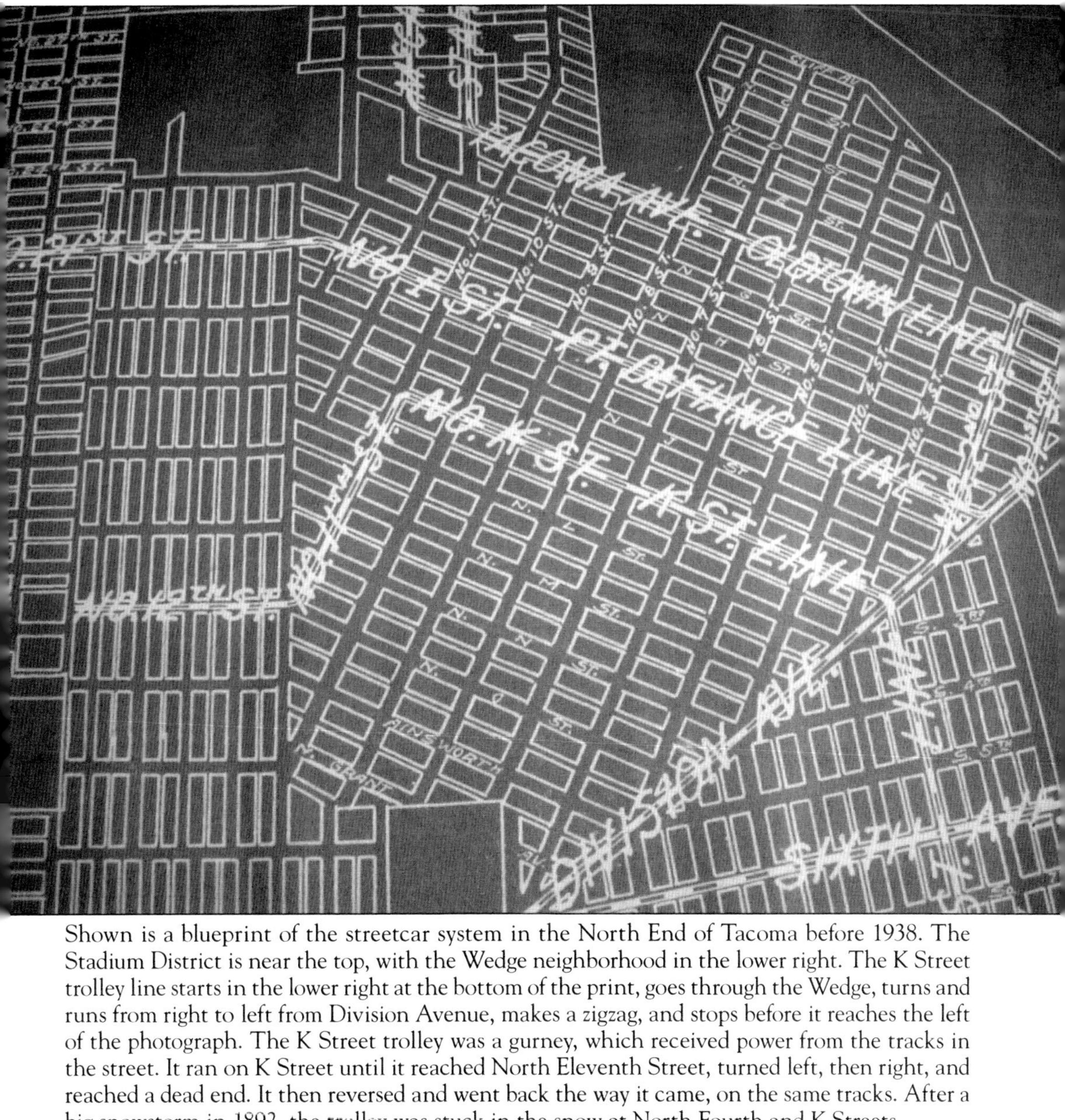

Shown is a blueprint of the streetcar system in the North End of Tacoma before 1938. The Stadium District is near the top, with the Wedge neighborhood in the lower right. The K Street trolley line starts in the lower right at the bottom of the print, goes through the Wedge, turns and runs from right to left from Division Avenue, makes a zigzag, and stops before it reaches the left of the photograph. The K Street trolley was a gurney, which received power from the tracks in the street. It ran on K Street until it reached North Eleventh Street, turned left, then right, and reached a dead end. It then reversed and went back the way it came, on the same tracks. After a big snowstorm in 1892, the trolley was stuck in the snow at North Fourth and K Streets.

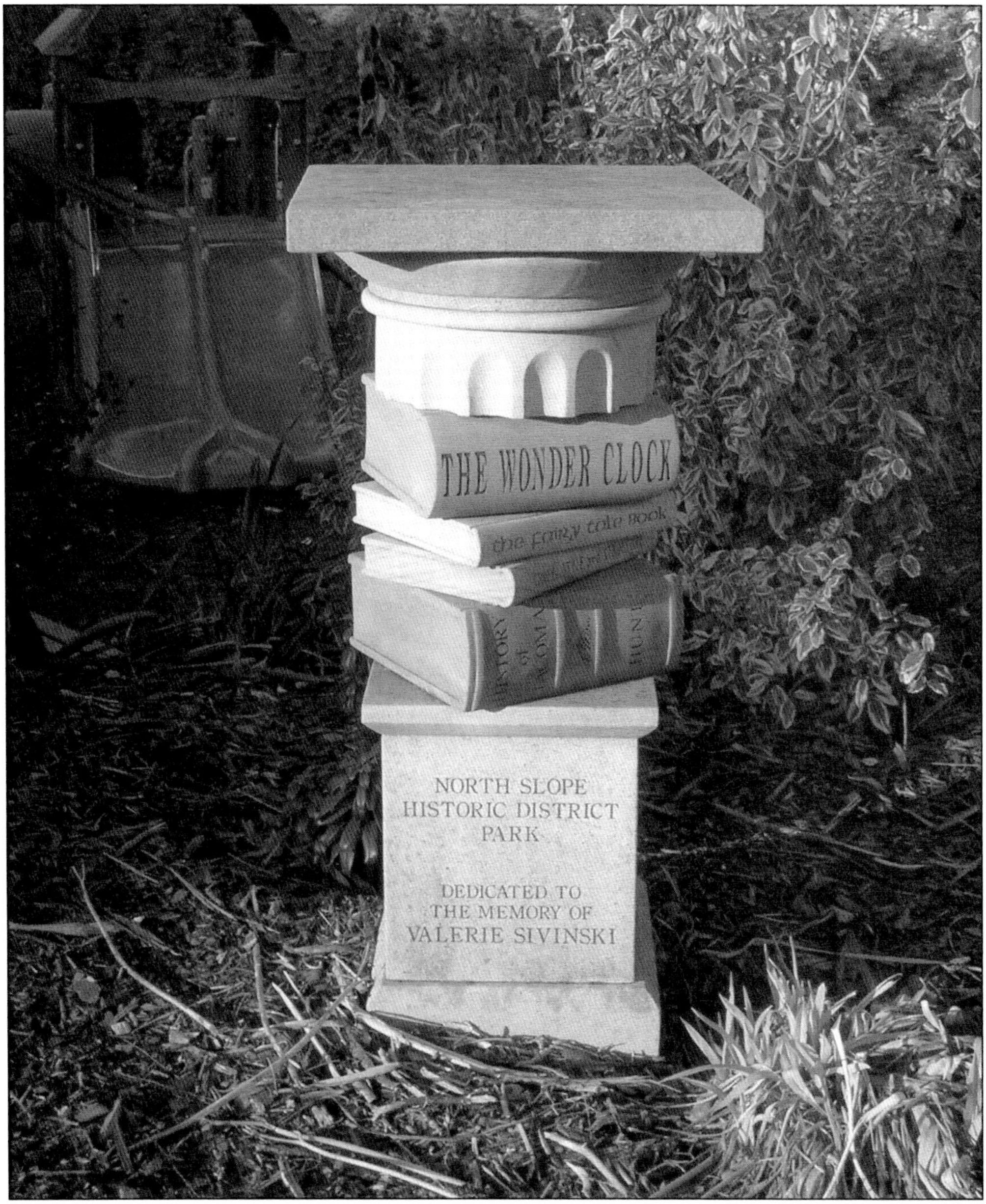

This statue is located in the North Slope Historic District Park. The park and this monument are dedicated to Valerie Sivinski, former historic preservation officer, who provided practical advice to the group of residents who wanted to preserve the historic homes and the distinctive character of Job Carr's Hill, which became the North Slope Historic District. For 13 years, residents had tried to change the zoning to protect elegant houses from deterioration or being demolished and replaced by multiplexes, which were not compatible with the character of the North Slope, where 80 percent of the homes had been constructed before 1930. With the national and local historic designation, neighbors can feel pride and confidence that their valuable buildings will survive another 100 years. During the process of becoming a historic district, the original homeowners who struggled to make this dream a reality were joined by new residents eager to preserve the ambience that makes the North Slope special. (Gyda May photograph.)

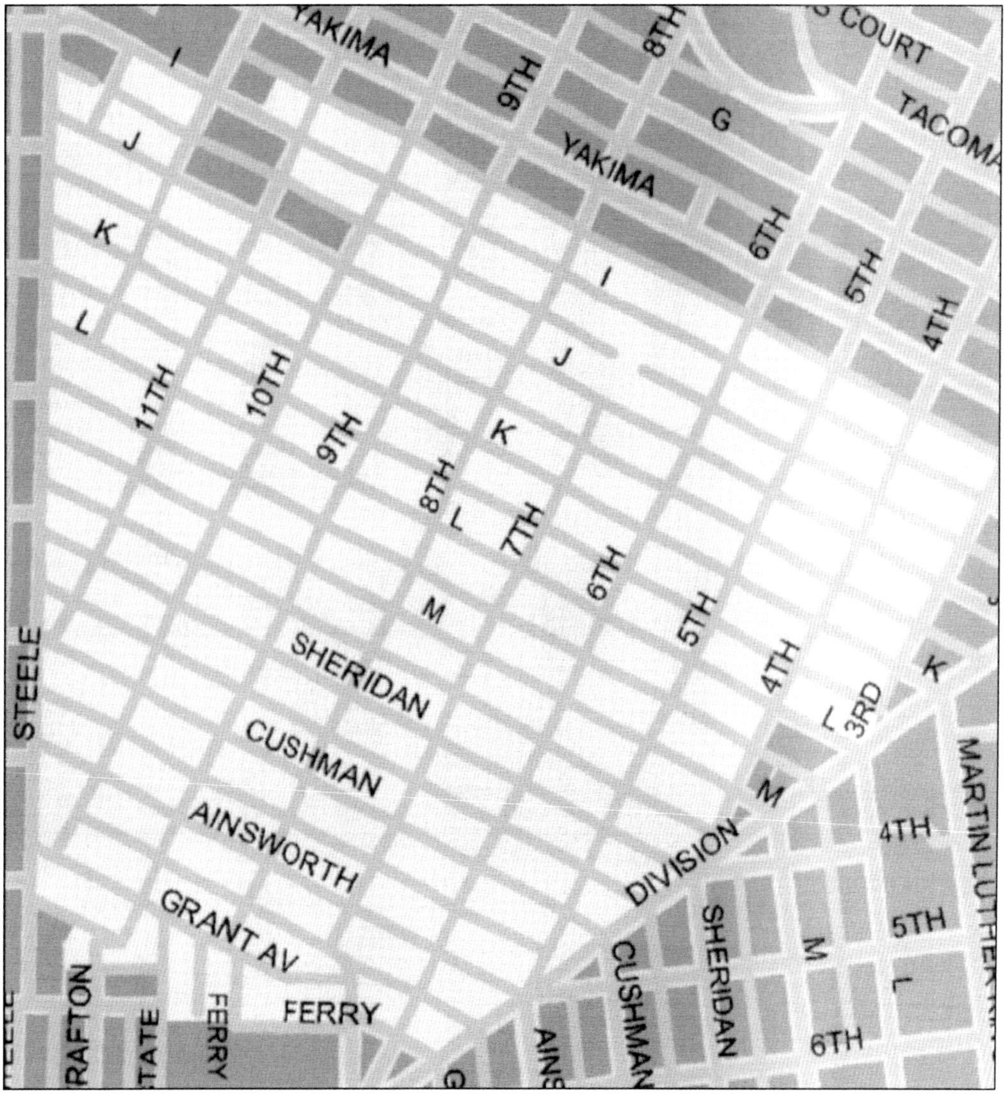

The map of the NSHD shows the designated boundaries of the neighborhood. It is at a 45-degree angle to the north-south orientation of surrounding streets. North I, North J, North K, North L, North M (Sheridan), North O (Cushman), North P (Ainsworth), and Q (Grant) Streets face Commencement Bay. Numbered roadways run from North Third to North Thirteenth between Division Avenue and Steele Street. After the neighborhood became a historic district, these maps were distributed to residents and made available to community and government agencies to inform everyone that the district had definite boundaries and to notify residents that they were part of an area recognized for its historic as well as its residential natures. The history of the NSHD was that it grew to encompass most of the Job Carr farm area on Job Carr's Hill. Although Prospect Street and Sprague Avenue are not on the map, they were historically part of the area. (Courtesy of Tacoma Historical Society.)

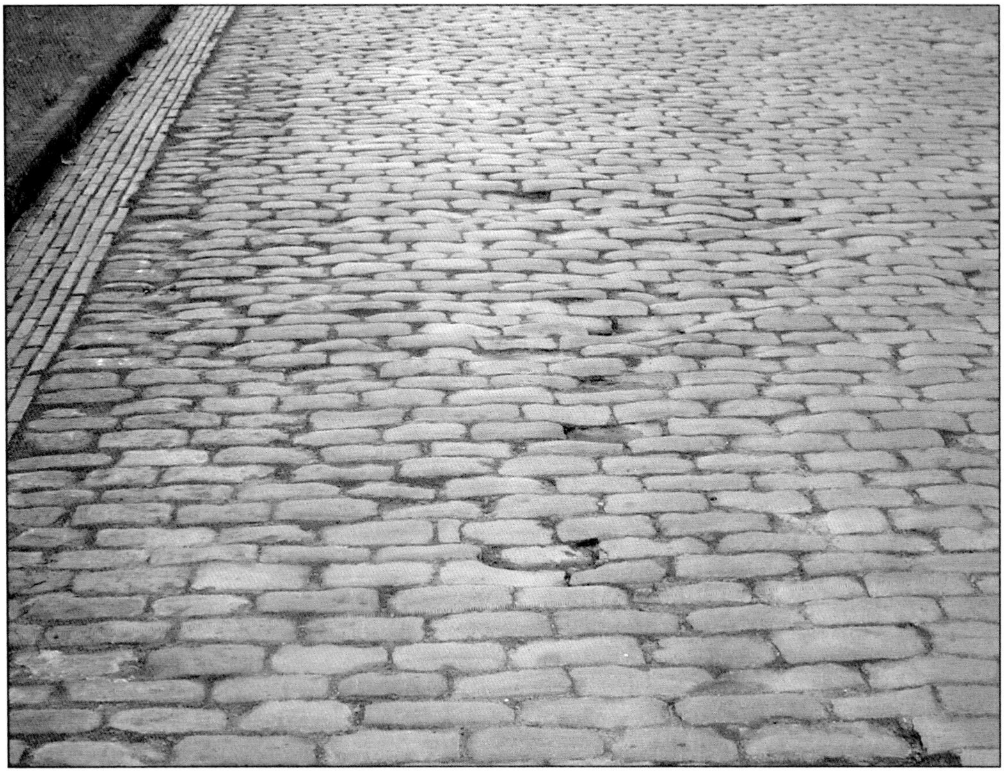

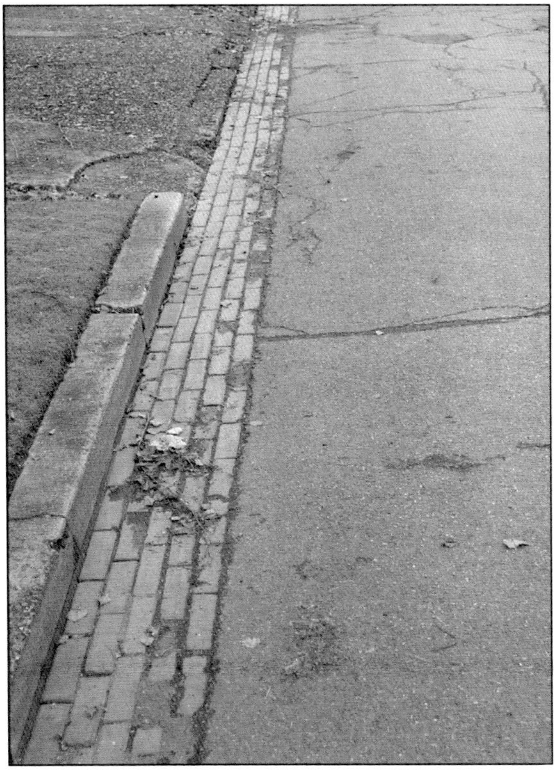

As Tacoma entered a new century, the search for durable street pavement material was on. Brick-shaped formed blocks, or setts (known locally as cobblestones), were used mainly on hilly streets because of the traction they provided for horses, and if they were sandstone, they worked even better. When they were cut, the blocks were uneven in size. Each required its own sand foundation so that the resulting surface would be smooth. There are places around the North Slope where setts are still visible. (Gyda May photograph.)

In 1905, city officials bought bricks produced along the Duwamish Waterway and sold by the Denny Clay Company. Although the high cost of material and labor limited their use for streets, the bricks were used for gutters in both the central business area and the North End. (Gyda May photograph.)

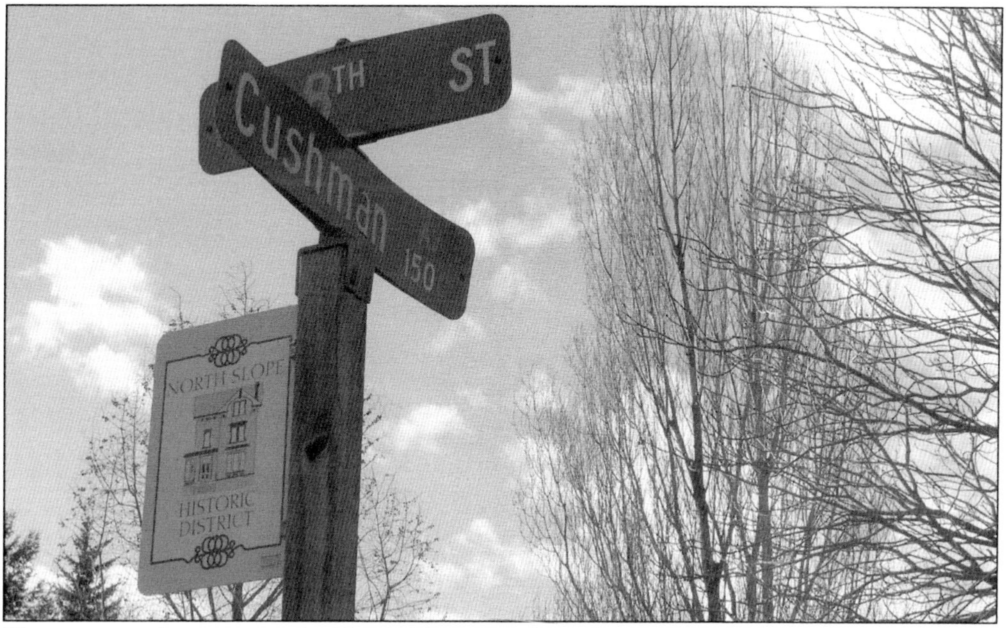

The street markers next to the North Slope sign show the intersection of North Eighth Street and North Cushman Avenue, which is the highest point in the historic district. North Cushman Avenue was formerly North O Street, Ainsworth was P, and Grant was Q Street. North Sheridan Avenue started as North N Street. Street names were changed between 1893 and 1915. (Gyda May photograph.)

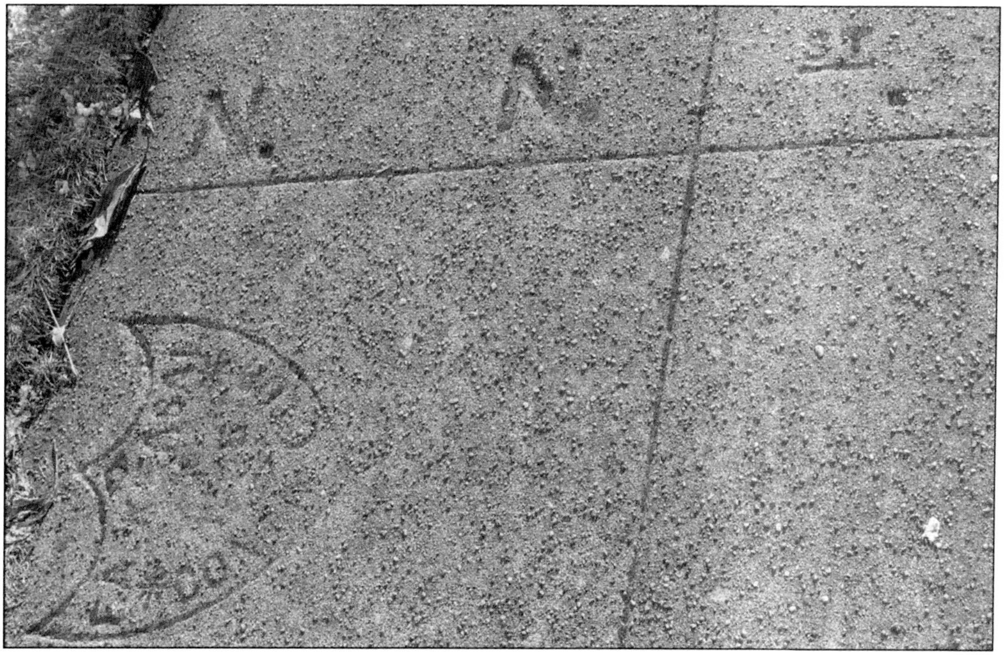

Street names were engraved into the sidewalks for people who strolled. The photograph is of North N Street. In an attempt to organize the chaotic street naming resulting from rapid growth between 1887 and 1889, Tacoma was sectioned, with Division and Sixth Avenues dividing north from south and A Street dividing east from west. (Gyda May photograph.)

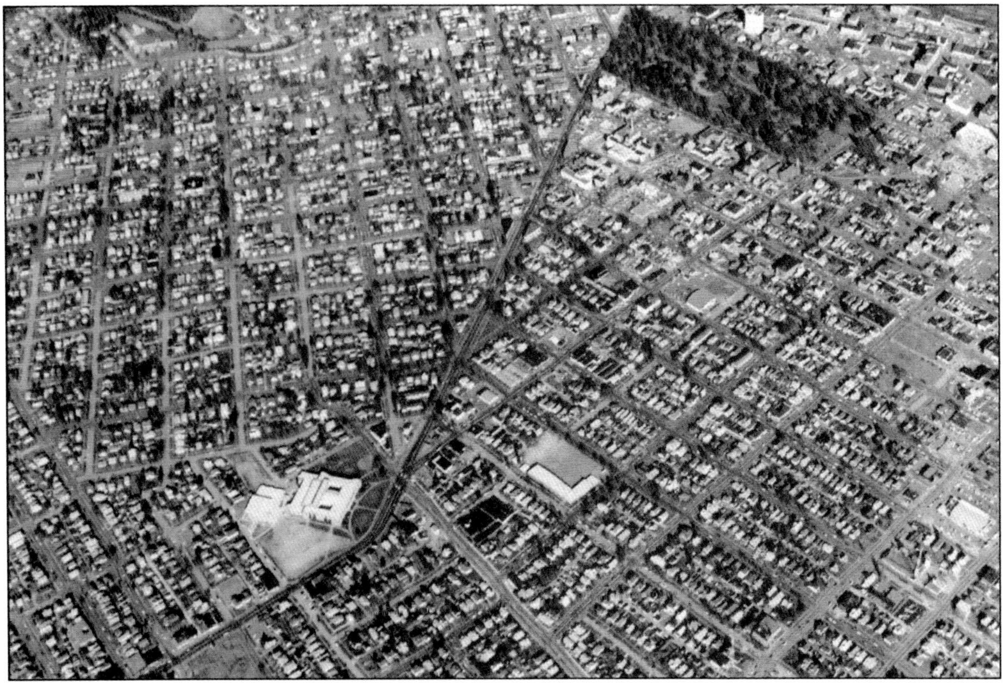

In the early years, Garfield Gulch divided the North Slope in half. In this aerial view of the area, the bending street is Sixth Avenue as it turns into Division Avenue, with Jason Lee Jr. High School in the bend. The large wooded area at Division Avenue and I Street is Wright Park. To the left of Division is the North End, including the North Slope. Garfield Gulch begins at the smaller wooded area in the upper left of the photograph. In the close-up, a wedge of Commencement Bay is in the top right corner of the picture. Stadium Bowl, formerly Old Woman's Gulch, is close to the right edge. Garfield Park, next to the Annie Wright Seminary, is the wooded area near the top of the photograph, marking the beginning of Garfield Gulch. Note how Tacoma Avenue curves as it clears the gulch area.

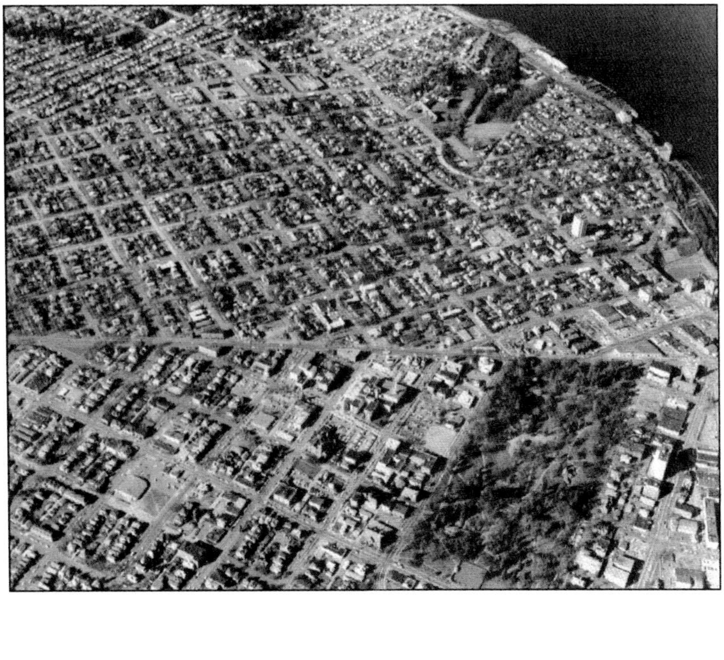

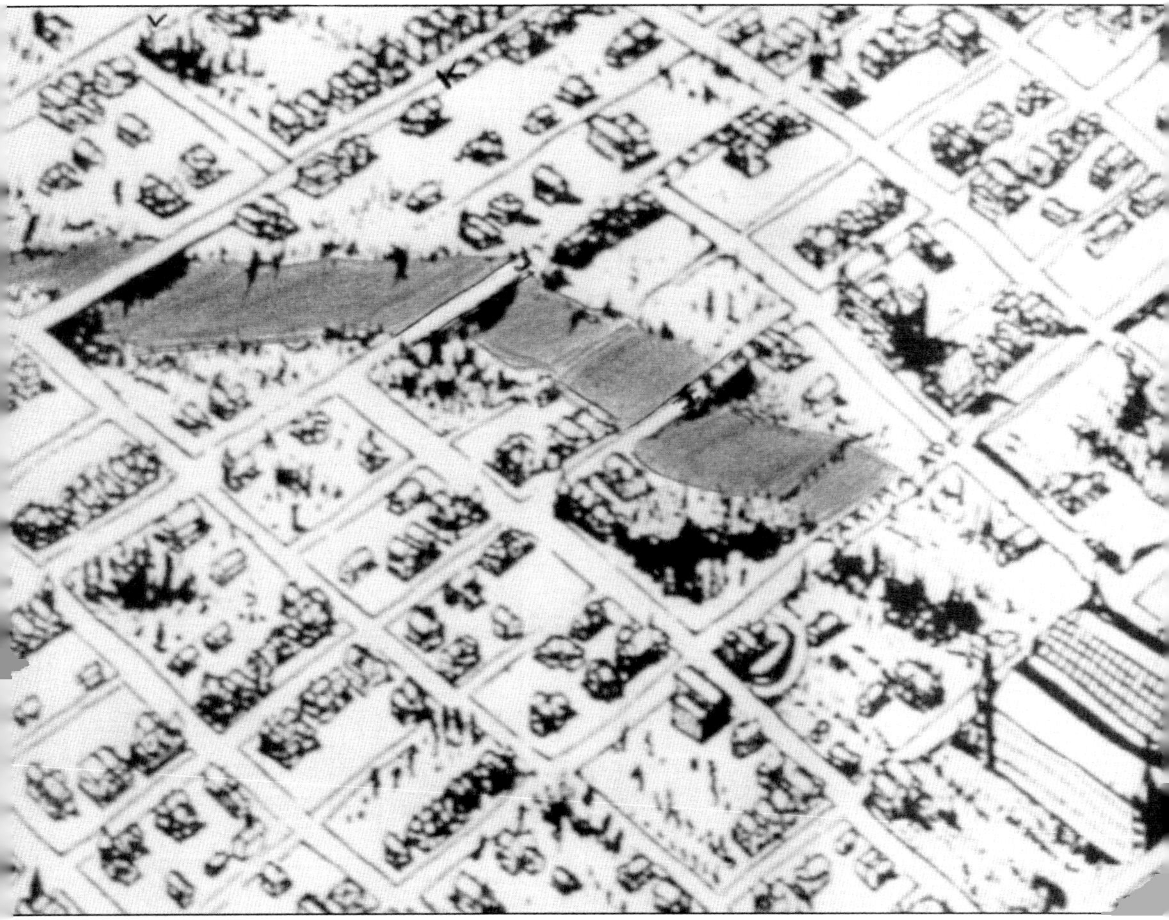

In this sketch, the shaded area indicates the Garfield Gulch from North Yakima Avenue to North I, J, and K Streets as it meanders toward the left of the photograph and ends at the intersection of North K and North Sixth Streets. This was a very deep gulch that was filled with bushes and brush and in which farm animals mingled with wild animals in the woods. An Exposition Building (shown in the lower right) is deep in the gully near Garfield Park. In 1912, the gulch was filled with dirt from nearby Ashton Hill. The bridge over Tacoma Avenue was removed, and the road made a curve over the filled gulch to continue on its way. The Exposition Building was torn down, and a filled-in Garfield Gulch was soon to be covered with new houses.

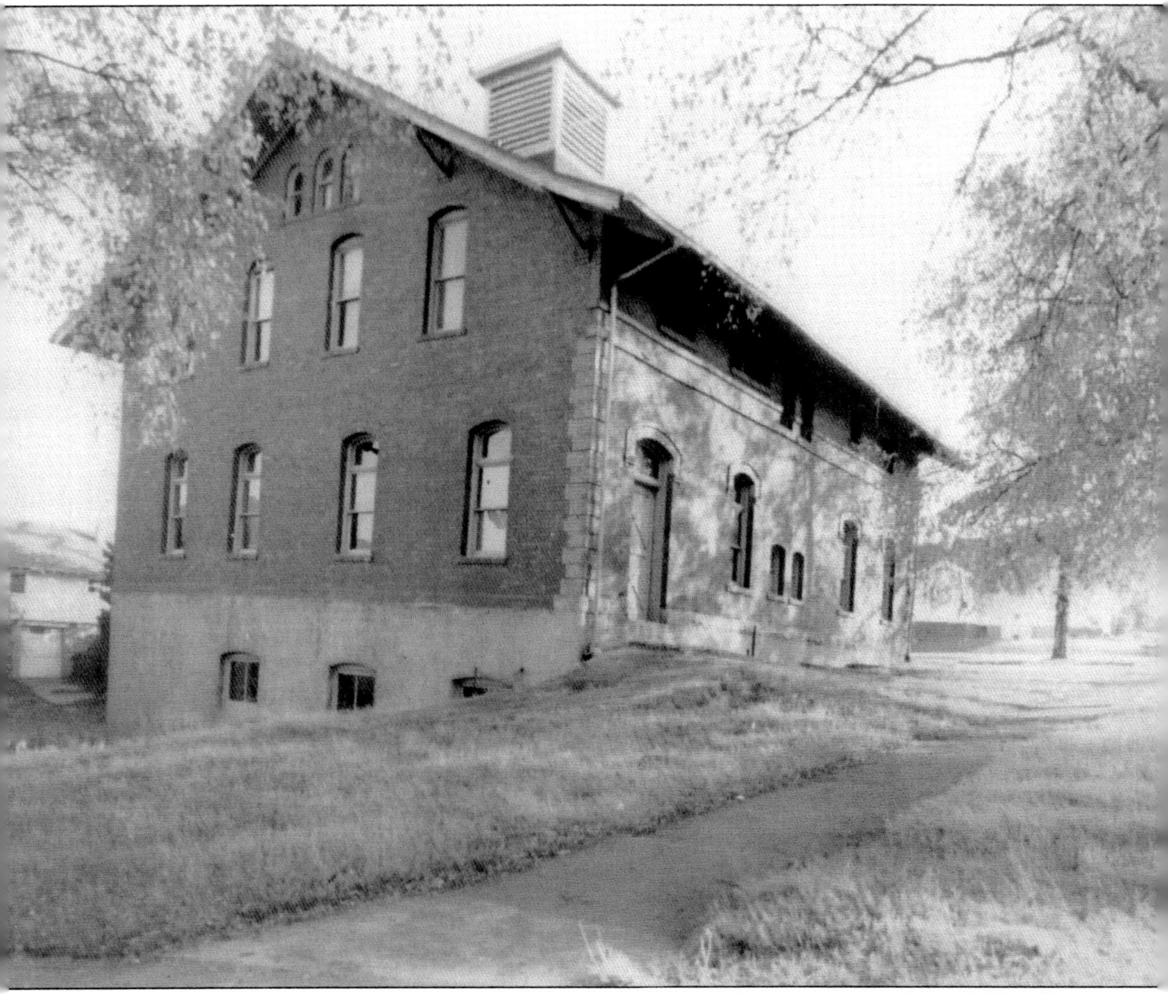

Serving the North Slope area, Engine House No. 3 was designed by architect Paul Bergfeld and built by J.H. Trude in 1907. The majority of buildings at that time were made of wood, and firefighting was in great demand. The station was in use until the 1950s, at which time it was converted into a youth club center and later into a senior center. In 1980, it had been made into apartments. It is a large brick building with a square bell tower. It is difficult to follow the history of firehouses in Tacoma, since numbers were used for more than one location and not necessarily in chronological order. At least one other station has been named No. 3, in Old Tacoma. In recent years, the old fire station has been refurbished again, and the condominiums have been sold.

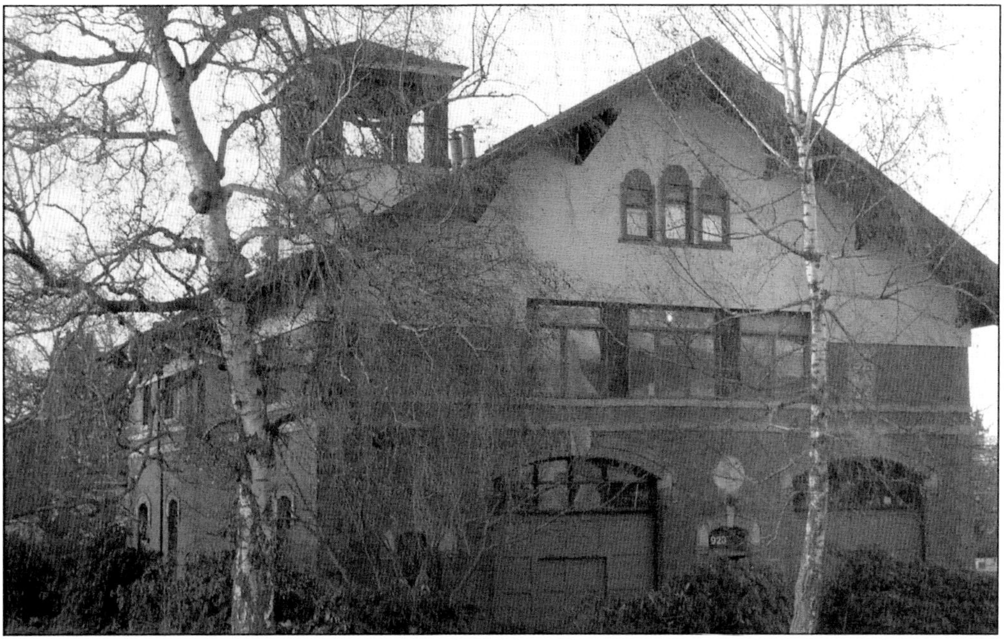

This is Engine House No. 3 with its new face-lift and mature trees and shrubs. Its landscaped yard has tall shrubs concealing it from view, and condo owners can relax in the privacy of the sheltered lawn. There is often a large dog lounging on the stairs, but it is a golden retriever, not a dalmatian. (Gyda May photograph.)

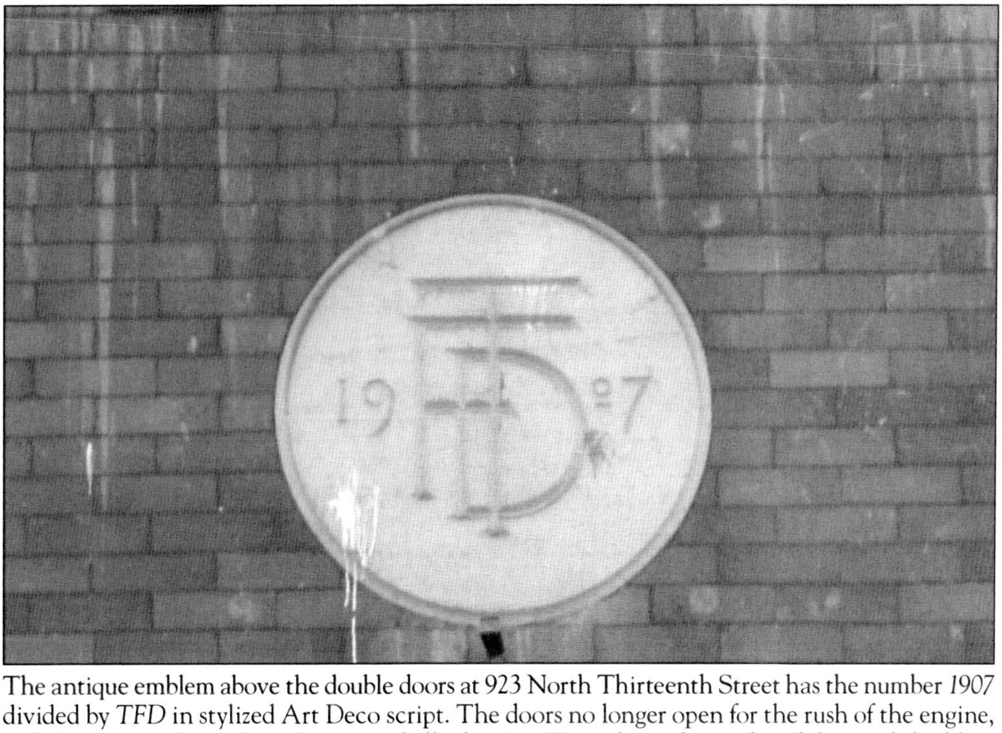

The antique emblem above the double doors at 923 North Thirteenth Street has the number *1907* divided by *TFD* in stylized Art Deco script. The doors no longer open for the rush of the engine, and there are no shouts from firemen or bells clanging. Times have changed, and the sturdy building is serving a different purpose, but the exterior has not changed. (Gyda May photograph.)

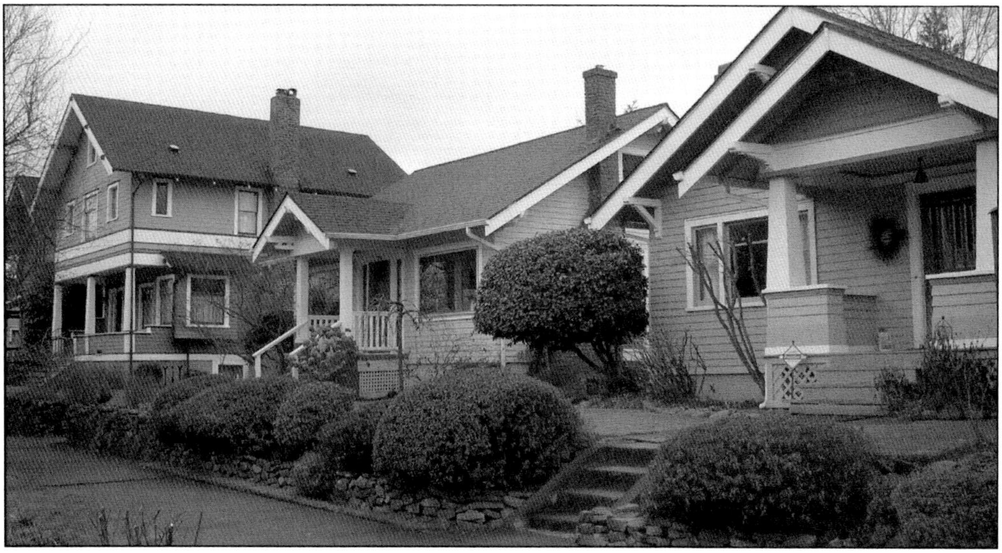

These bungalows include, from left to right, 710, 714, and 718 North Ainsworth. Builder George W. Cooper lived in the large Craftsman at 710, and Marcus Nalley lived in 714. Built in 1921, the house at 718 was home to Campbell relatives until 1984. Frederick Campbell's daughter Eva married Dr. Veith, who died in 1958. She then married Russell Wilson. Eva died in 1973 and was followed by Russell in 1984. (Gyda May photograph.)

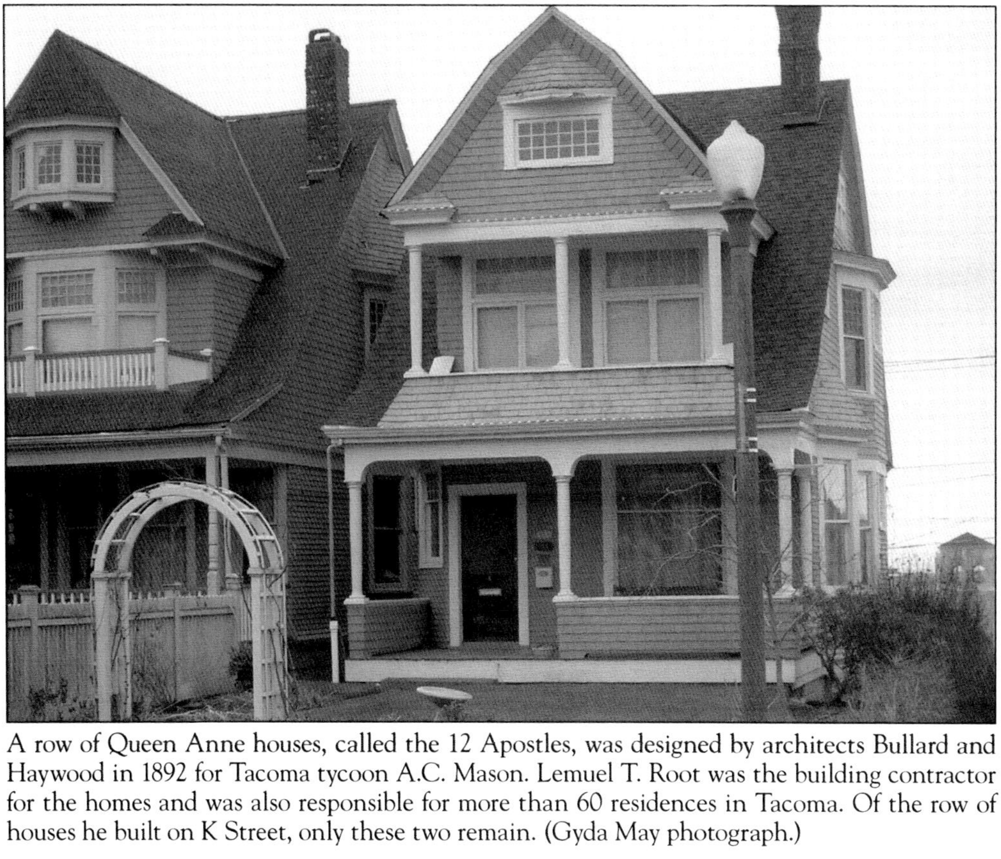

A row of Queen Anne houses, called the 12 Apostles, was designed by architects Bullard and Haywood in 1892 for Tacoma tycoon A.C. Mason. Lemuel T. Root was the building contractor for the homes and was also responsible for more than 60 residences in Tacoma. Of the row of houses he built on K Street, only these two remain. (Gyda May photograph.)

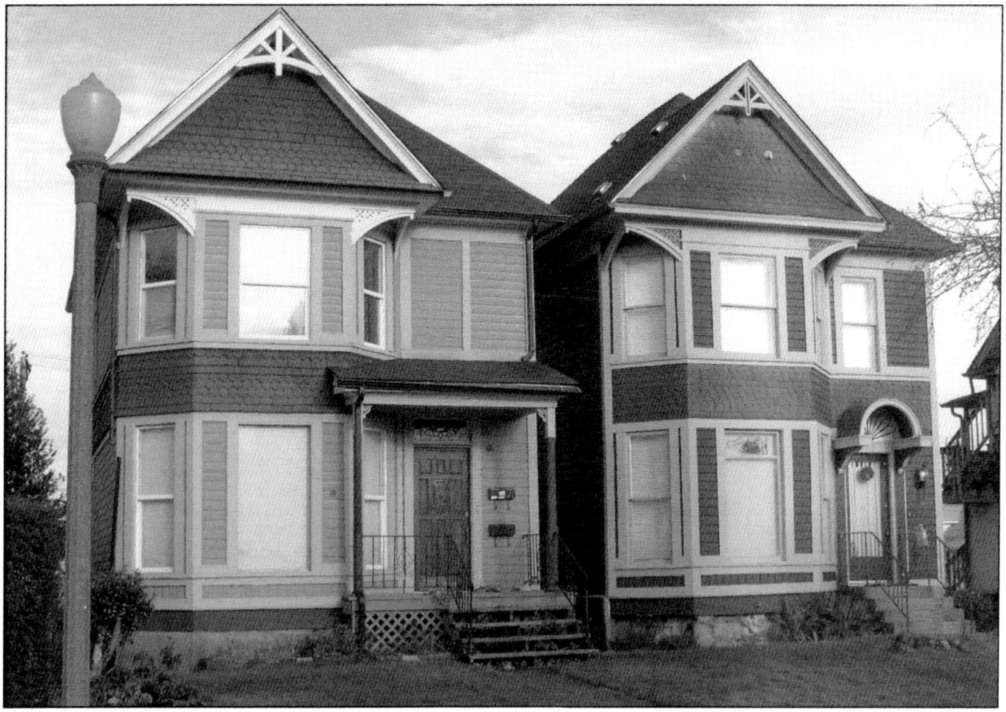

These "painted ladies" at 605 and 607 North K Street (above) are examples of row houses built at the turn of the century. The two homes were constructed by builders Blair and Ramsey. Number 607, on the right, was built in 1889 and number 605 two years later, in 1891. A group of three similar houses (below) was constructed about the same time, from 1891 to 1893. They are located, from left to right, at 902, 904, and 906 Sheridan Avenue. It is remarkable that these structures are still in excellent shape after more than a century. (Both, Gyda May photographs.)

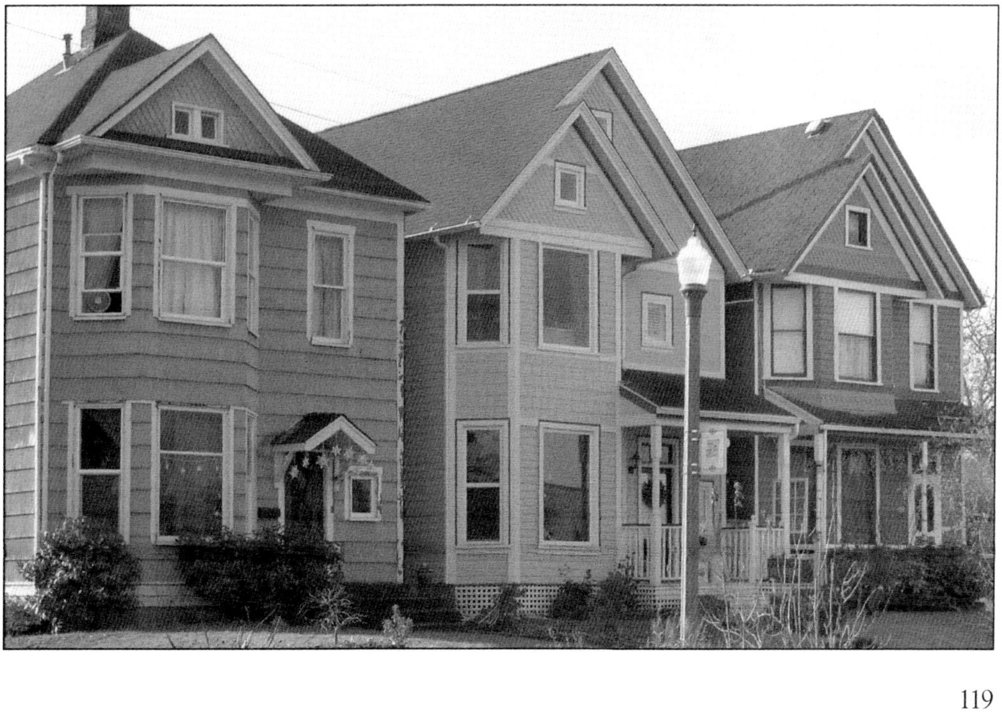

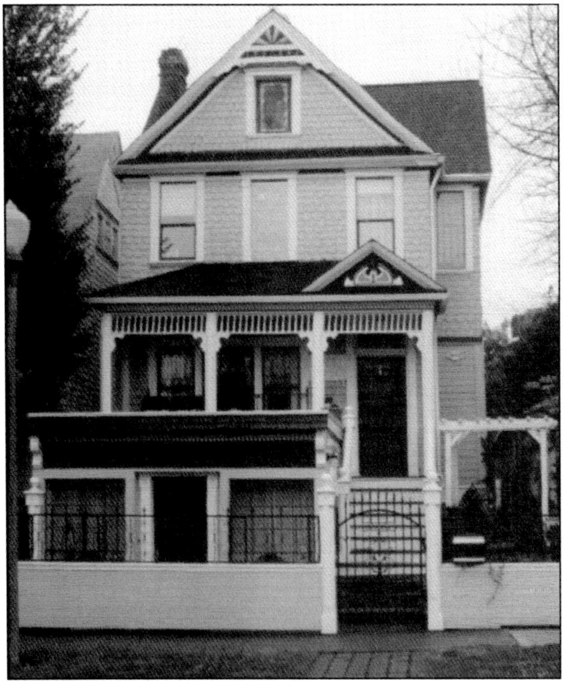

Built in 1890 by Sherman Schroeder, this house at 407 North K Street (left) was one of 11 homes in the first wave of construction on the North Slope. Stephen Ryder, president of Ryder and Company, owned the house from 1891 to 1895. Numerous residents came later. Joseph and Louise Jensen lived here from 1919 to 1947 and operated Jensen's Bakery in the front and Jensen Sheet Metal Works behind the house. Some homes in the North Slope are now bed-and-breakfasts. One is the Victorian Stick-style house (below), built in 1889 for Henry and Jeanette Geiger, who were prominent in early Tacoma. John Q. and Virginia Mason lived there from 1900 to 1905. A picture of the house was included in the book *Painted Ladies*, featuring Victorian homes across the country. (Left, courtesy Charlotte Medlock; below, Gyda May photograph.)

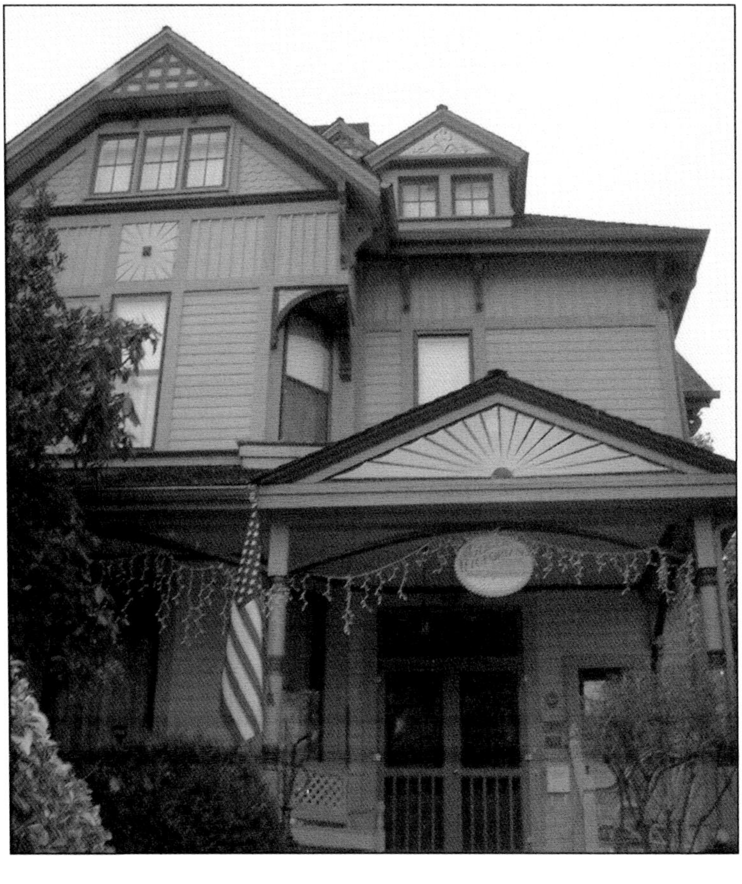

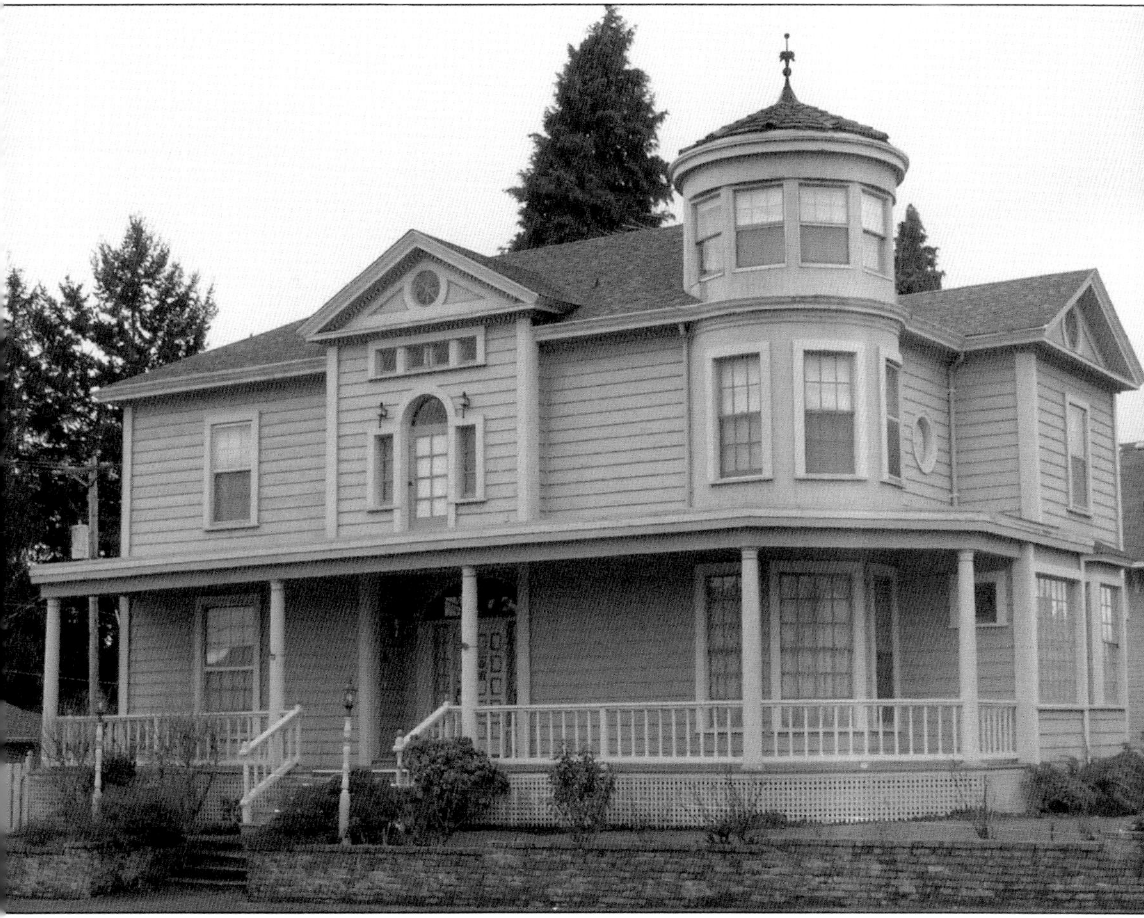

The Dutch Embassy Bed and Breakfast is at 1601 North Eighth Street. The house was built in 1894 for John R.A. Cort van der Linden. The architect was C.A. Darmer, G.L. Fries was the contractor, and H.E. Knatvold was the builder. Cort van der Linden's brother Pieter would become the prime minister of the Netherlands from 1913 to 1918. Rumor has it that the house received the title Dutch Embassy when it "entertained the community" during the brother's visit as a Dutch diplomat. John R.A. Cort van der Linden lived in it for about six years while working as a bookkeeper for the Puget Sound Brewing Company. He left the Tacoma area around 1900. The next person to own the house was John Donahue. He was president of the Donahue-Caithness Lumber Company and president of Mineral Lake Lumber Company. He also served on the city council at one point. (Gyda May photograph.)

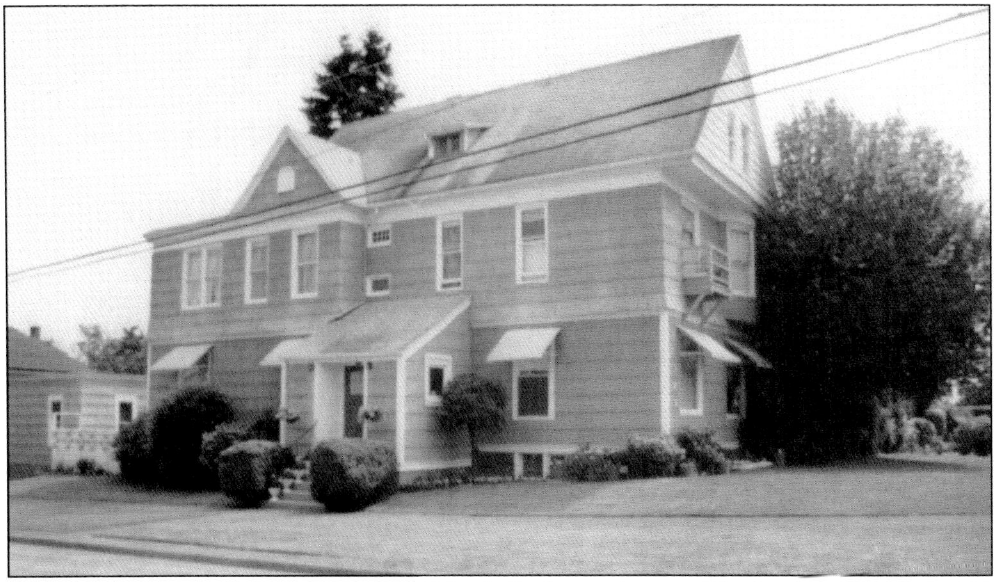

The Austrian Bed and Breakfast is at 723 North Cushman Avenue. This house was built in 1892 for Col. Clinton A. Snowden, who became editor of the *Tacoma Daily Ledger*. He had previously been the editor of the *Chicago Sun*. Current owner Eveline Smith explained in the January 2004 *Trolley Times* her decision to convert the house into a bed-and-breakfast. Eveline had one of the first bed-and-breakfasts in the North Slope.

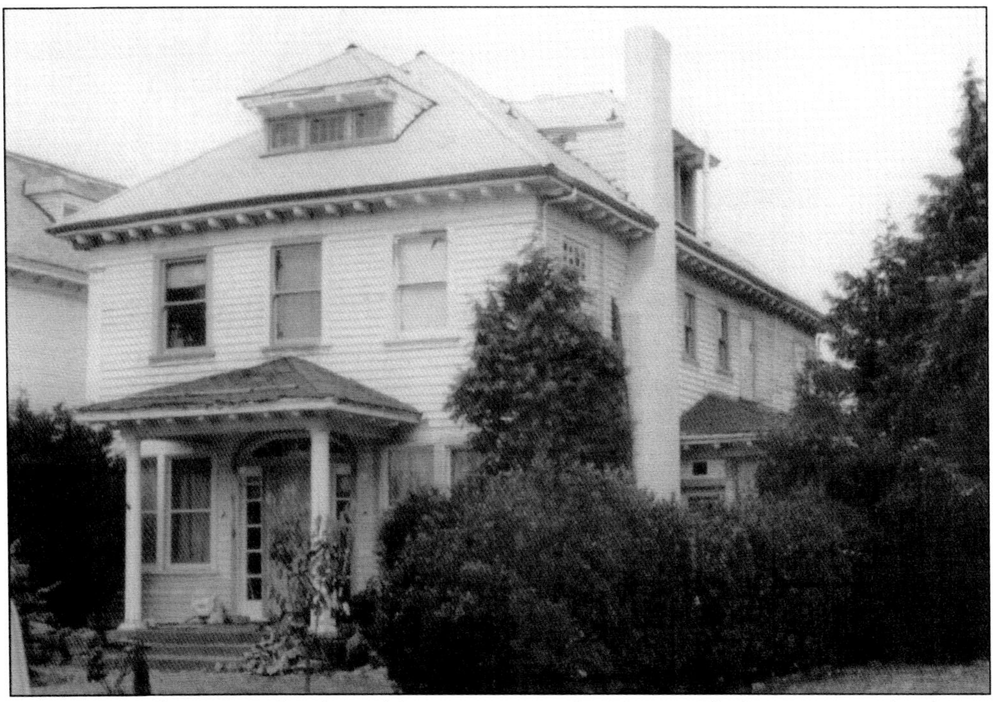

The Plum Duff House Bed and Breakfast is at 619 North K Street. The home is one of architect C.A. Darmer's many structures in Tacoma. It was built for Col. William S. Shank, the cashier for the St. Paul and Tacoma Lumber Company and a notary public. Kip Duff was the person who developed the house for its bed-and-breakfast role.

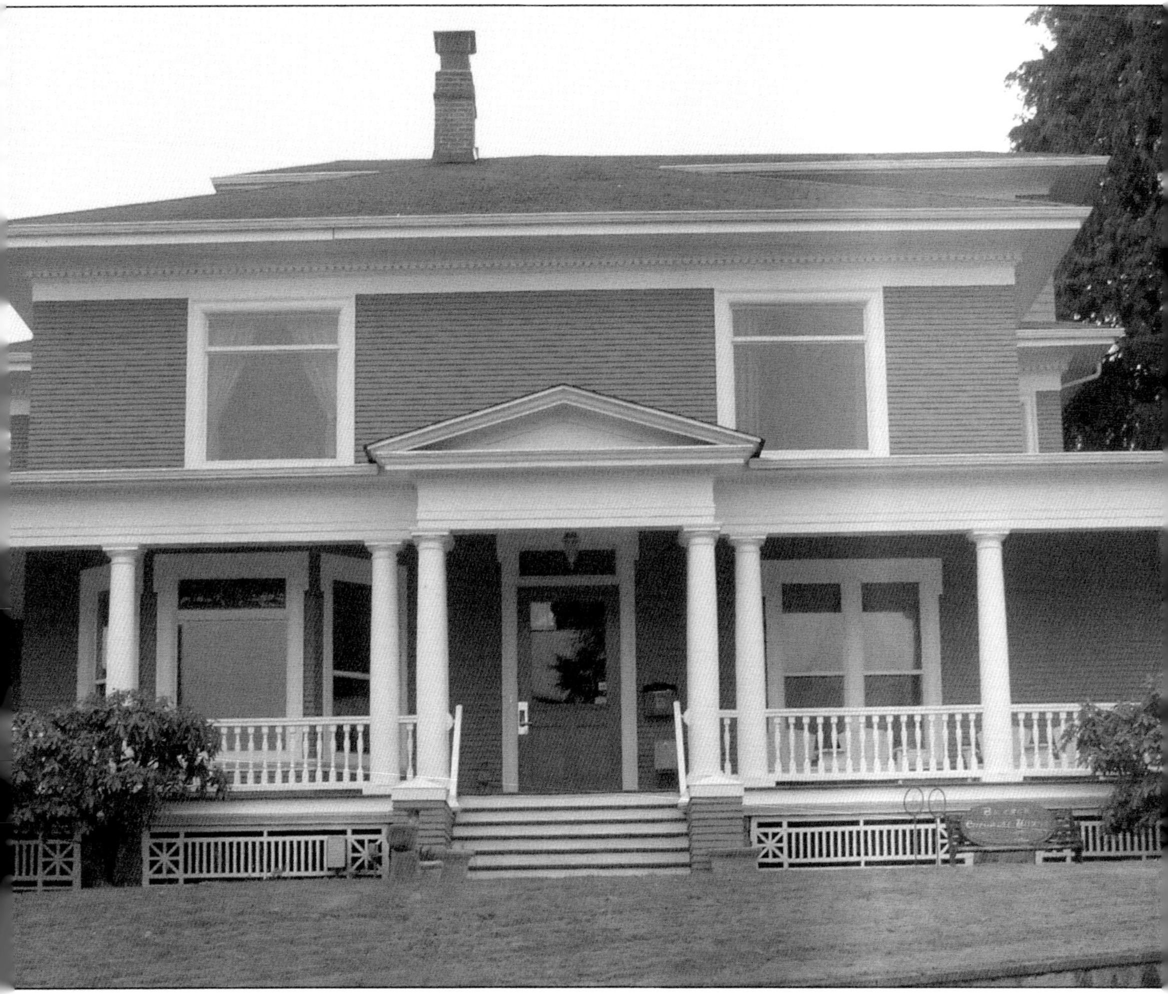

William T. Branch commissioned the architect George W. Bullard to design a house for him at the corner of North Twenty-first and Prospect Streets in 1904. According to an August 28, 1904, article in the *Tacoma Daily Ledger*, the 14-room residence contained "every convenience modern ideas can supply," including 14 closets, some as large as ordinary rooms. Branch also sought to protect his view of Commencement Bay by purchasing the surrounding lots. No expense was spared in the construction of this house. It had a modern laundry, hot-air furnace, bathrooms on every floor, a solid stone foundation and retaining wall, and sidewalks. William moved out four years later in 1908 and sold it to John Bagley. Bagley had come to Tacoma in 1896 after years of working in the forests of Maine, Wisconsin, and Michigan. He established lumber mills throughout the Puget Sound region. In 1900, he was instrumental in the construction of the Tacoma Eastern Railroad, which extended from Tacoma to Ashford, thus opening the region to logging, lumber mills, and tourist excursions to Mount Rainier. (Gyda May photograph.)

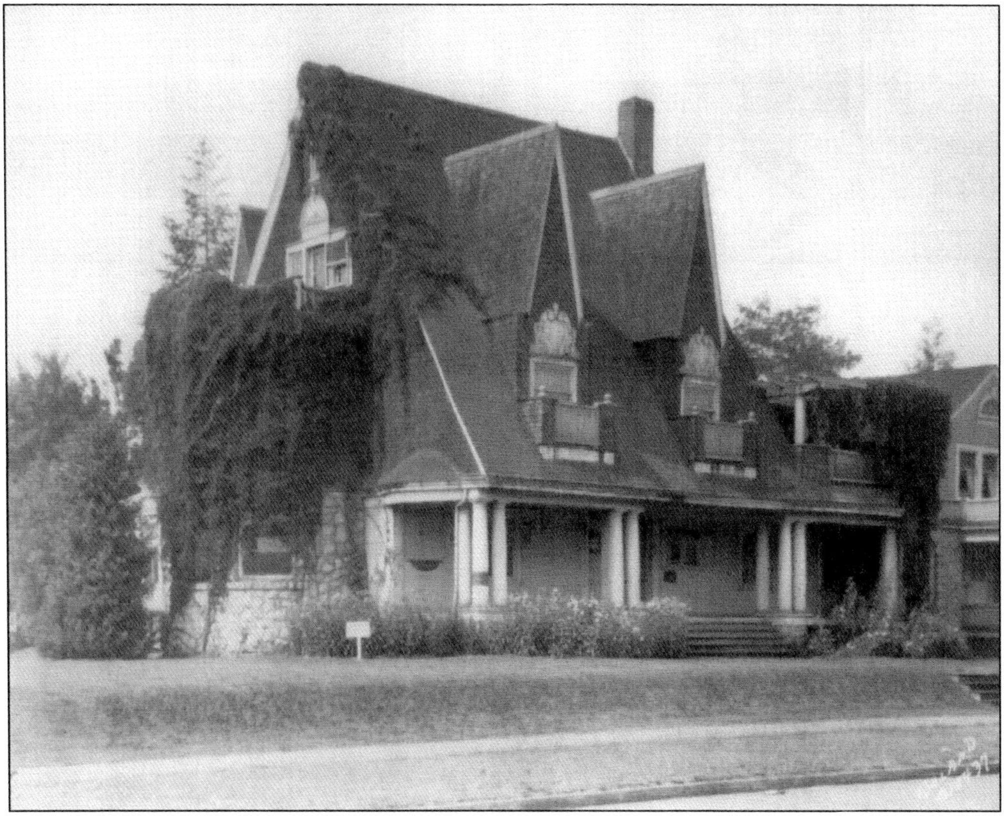

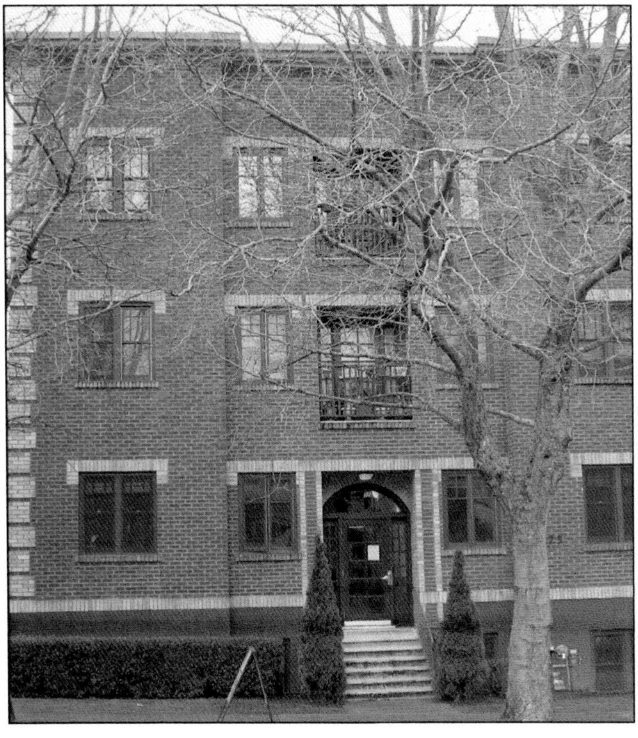

Ambrose Russell designed this unusual Shingle Style house (above) in 1901 for attorney Frederick H. Murray. Its extremely high-pitched roof and dormers faced with Art Nouveau panels are unique. Murray came to Tacoma as part of the Northern Pacific Railway Law Office and later started his own practice. The house was later converted to apartments. The Annobee Apartment Building (left), constructed in 1925, was designed in the Italianate style. Other apartment buildings built in the North Slope during the early years included the following: Biltmore (1889), McKeller (1917), Kellogg (1908), Orville (1910), Chelsea (1922), Elliot Hall (1913), Bain (1890), and Drury (1909). (Left, Gyda May photograph.)

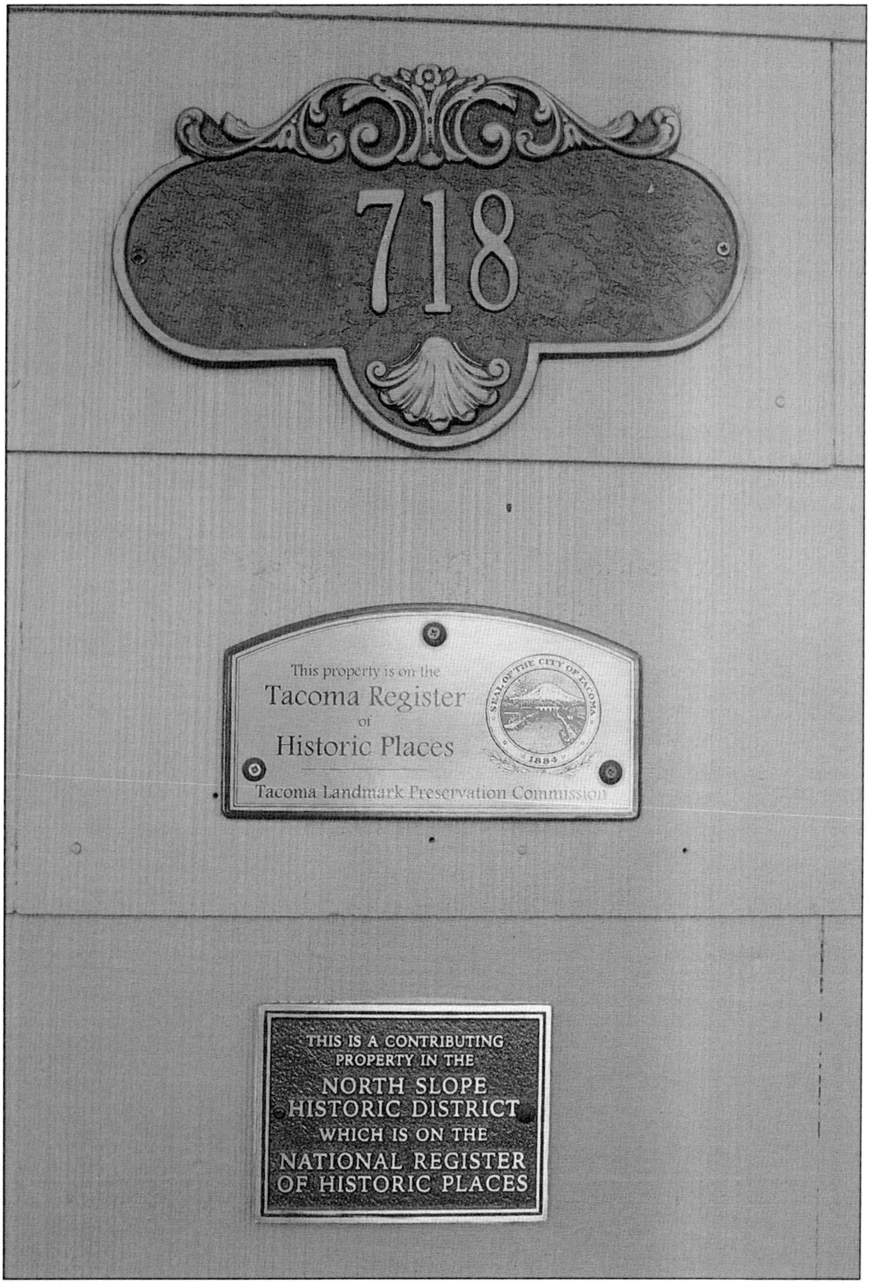

This is an example of the bronze plaques on some of the houses in the North Slope Historic District. In the photograph, the plaque at the top is the house number on that street. It blends well with the other plaques on the front of the home. The one in the middle is from the Tacoma Register of Historic Places, presented to local places of major historical significance. It is bronze with an emblem on the right. The bottom plaque has bronze raised letters on a black background and may be purchased by any residents of the North Slope. It reads as follows: "This is a contributing property in the North Slope Historic District which is on the National Register of Historic Places." The plaques are one way for homeowners to share their pride in the historical significance of their dwellings. (Gyda May photograph.)

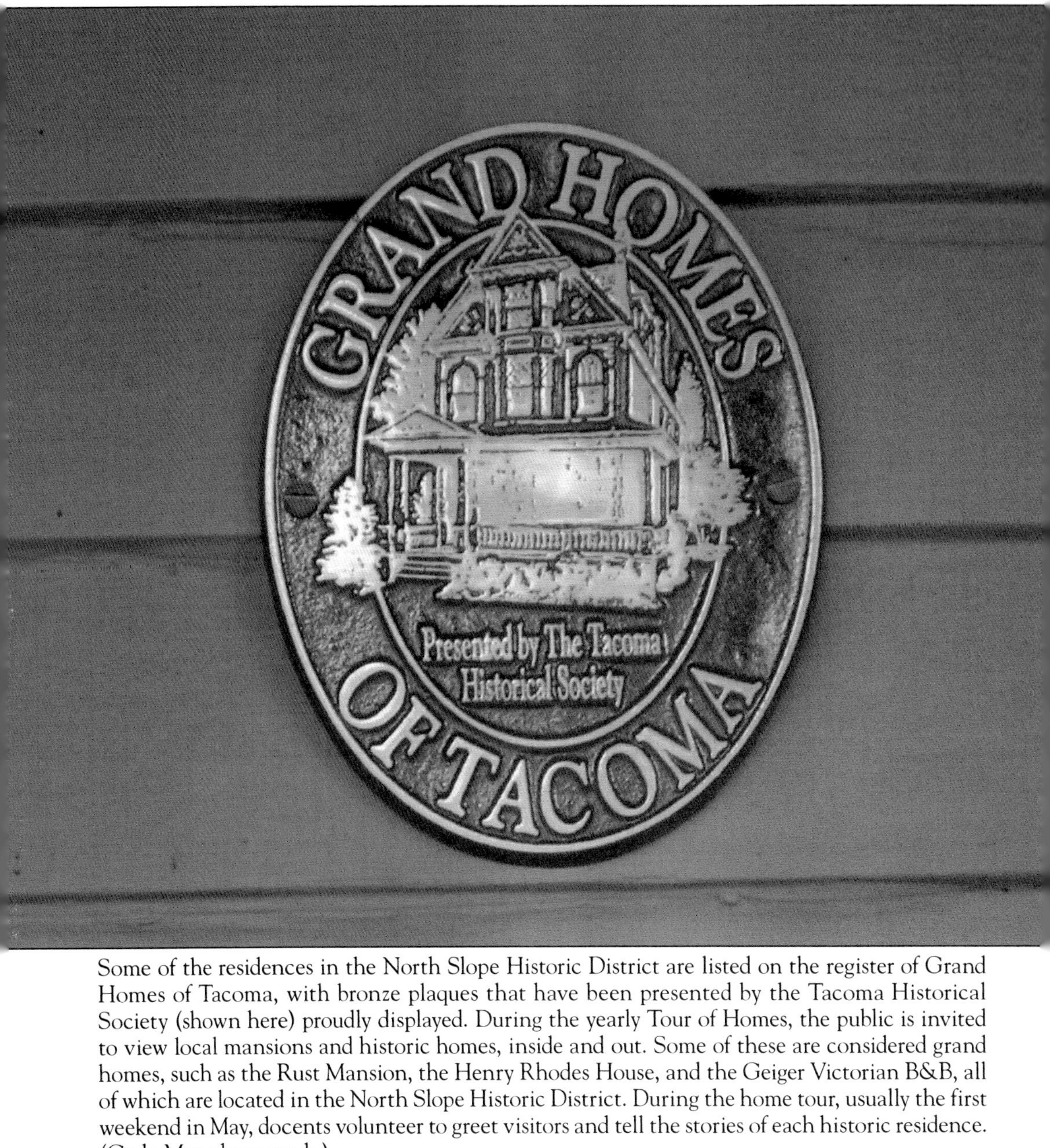

Some of the residences in the North Slope Historic District are listed on the register of Grand Homes of Tacoma, with bronze plaques that have been presented by the Tacoma Historical Society (shown here) proudly displayed. During the yearly Tour of Homes, the public is invited to view local mansions and historic homes, inside and out. Some of these are considered grand homes, such as the Rust Mansion, the Henry Rhodes House, and the Geiger Victorian B&B, all of which are located in the North Slope Historic District. During the home tour, usually the first weekend in May, docents volunteer to greet visitors and tell the stories of each historic residence. (Gyda May photograph.)

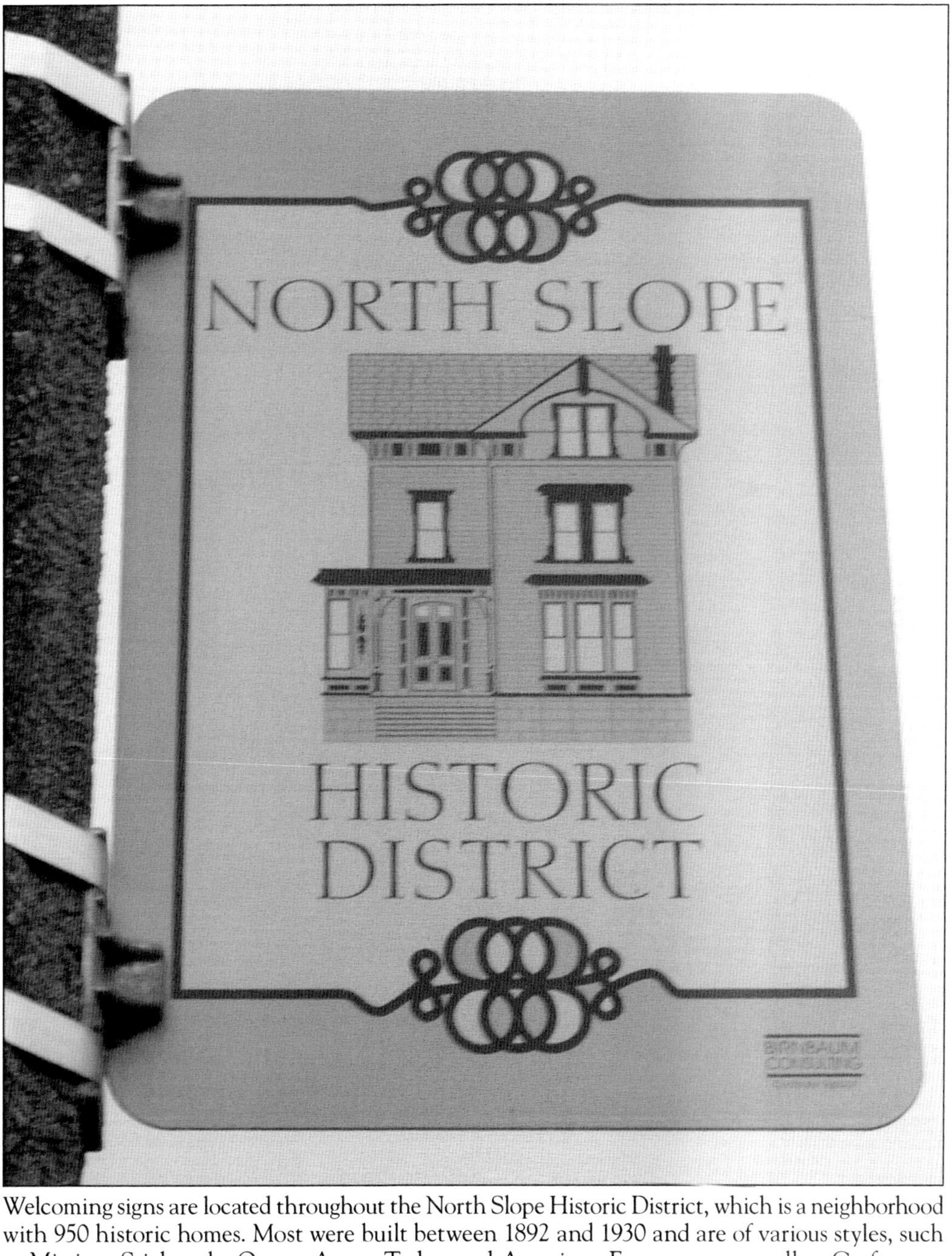

Welcoming signs are located throughout the North Slope Historic District, which is a neighborhood with 950 historic homes. Most were built between 1892 and 1930 and are of various styles, such as Mission, Stick style, Queen Anne, Tudor, and American Foursquare, as well as Craftsman. In August 1995, NSHD became the first historic residential district in Tacoma. There are signs on the lampposts proudly denoting the designation. Official Historic Home Tours have been conducted in the past. The North Slope Historic District sponsors neighborhood activities, both educational and social. The borders of the NSHD are I Street to the north, Grant Avenue to the south, Steele Street to the west, and Division Avenue to the east. The district has a website which informs the community about the history of the neighborhood, upcoming projects, and events. There is also a newsletter called the *Trolley Times*. (Gyda May photograph.)

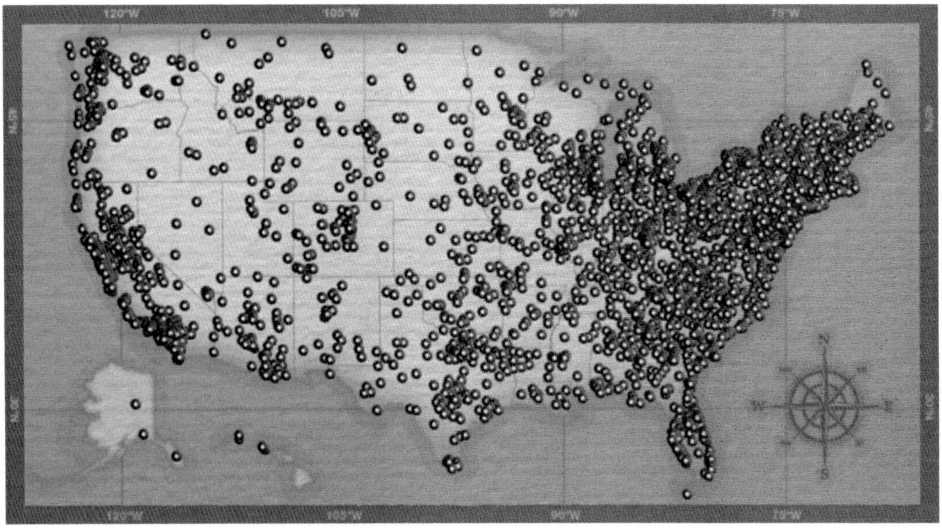